KENTUCKY PENSION ROLL OF 1835

REPORT

FROM THE

SECRETARY OF WAR,

IN OBEDIENCE TO

Resolutions of the Senate of the 5th and 30th of June, 1834, *and the 3d of March,* 1835.

IN RELATION TO THE

PENSION ESTABLISHMENT OF THE UNITED STATES.

CLEARFIELD

Originally published
Washington, D.C., 1835

Reprinted for
Clearfield Company, Inc. by
Genealogical Publishing Co., Inc.
Baltimore, Maryland
1994, 2000

International Standard Book Number: 0-8063-4502-0

Made in the United States of America

KENTUCKY PENSION ROLL.

INDEX TO COUNTIES

Statement showing the names, rank, &c. of Invalid Pensioners residing in the State of Kentucky.

NAMES AND COUNTIES.	Rank.	Annual allowance.	Sums received.	Description of service.	When placed on the pension roll.	Commencement of pension.	Laws under which inscribed, increased, and reduced; and remarks.
ADAIR.							
Thompson C. Lloyd -	Sergeant	32 00	565 89	1st U. S. rifle reg't	July 6, 1820	May 20, 1814	Acts military establishment. February 16, 1832.
Do	do	48 00	100 53	do	do	Jan. 31, 1832	
ALLEN.							
Joseph Sears -	Private	53 16	841 85	1st Virginia drag'ns	Nov. 14, 1826	Apr. 24, 1826	April 24, 1816. From Virginia. Died November 27, 1832.
Do	do	96 00	72 53	-	-	Jan. 24, 1832	February 25, 1832.
ANDERSON.							
William Cummins -	do	96 00	123 52	Kentucky dragoons	Mar. 30, 1833	Nov. 20, 1832	Acts military establishment.
Samuel Sylver -	do	96 00	206 50	Kentucky militia	Jan. 14, 1832	Jan. 12, 1832	April 24, 1816.
BARREN.							
Jeremiah Harbour -	do	72 00	627 90	Dudley's Ky. mil.	Mar. 24, 1817	June 13, 1815	Acts military establishment. March 3, 1819.
Do	do	48 00	155 59	do	-	Mar. 4, 1824	June 26, 1827.
Do	do	72 00	487 24	do	-	May 29, 1827	
BATH.							
William Boyd -	do	90 00	1488 00	7th U. S. infantry	Sep. 4, 1818	Sep. 4, 1818	Acts military establishment. From Pennsylvania.
Isaac Gray -	Lieut.	79 92	126 54	Kentucky militia	Jan. 9, 1816	Sept. 22, 1814	March 3, 1815.
Do	Captain	90 66¾	803 28	do	-	April 24, 1816	April 24, 1816.
Do	do	240 00	1614 72	do	-	Sep. 22, 1814	February 3, 1817. Increased by Secretary of War.
Do	do	160 00	1440 00	do	-	Mar. 4, 1825	March 3, 1819.
BOONE.							
Isaac Barker -	Sergeant	96 00	1573 72	U. S. artillery	Oct. 14, 1817	Oct. 14, 1817	Acts military establishment. From Ohio, from September 4, 1825.

Name	Rank			Service			Remarks
Andrew Boyle	Private	48 00	38 13	Smith's vol. drag'ns	June 21, 1833	May 20, 1833	February 6, 1812.
Willis Calvert	do	48 00	-	Kentucky militia	June 18, 1834	May 17, 1834	April 24, 1816.
John Grant	do	72 00	161 82	do	Dec. 5, 1831	Dec. 5, 1831	April 24, 1816.
Leroy Jones	do	63 84	1106 39	do	Mar. 21, 1817	Nov. 5, 1816	March 3, 1817.
James Kay	do	96 00	720 00	8th Virginia reg't	Oct. 3, 1825	Sep. 4, 1825	May 16, 1826.
Isaac D. Sanders	Sergeant	48 00	12 76	1st rifle regiment	Dec. 17, 1833	Nov. 28, 1833	Acts military establishment.
Mills Wilks	Private	48 00	26 13	Kentucky militia	Feb. 21, 1834	Aug. 20, 1833	April 24, 1816.
BOURBON.							
John Brest	do	48 00	467 60	Vol. l't dragoons	Dec. 18, 1822	Oct. 18, 1822	April 24, 1816.
Do	do	72 00	117 90	do	-	July 13, 1832	
William Campbell	Sergeant	30 00	900 08	Revolutionary army	Mar. 4, 1789	Sep. 27, 1789	March 4, 1789. From Pennsylvania from September 4, 1820.
Do	do	76 80	307 20	do	-	Mar. 4, 1819	Acts military establishment.
Clement Estes	Corporal	72 00	1154 12	Butler's Penn. reg't	Jan. 5, 1818	Feb. 21, 1813	April 24, 1816. Died July 30, 1829:
John Hinchson	Private	48 00	838 00	Kentucky militia	Mar. 21, 1817	Sep. 20, 1816	March 3, 1817.
William Israel	do	96 00	724 00	Ohio militia	Sep. 5, 1826	Aug. 21, 1896	April 24, 1816.
John M'Kinney	do	96 00	780 94	Kentucky militia	Jan. 27, 1817	Jan. 17, 1817	Acts military establishment. Died September 27, 1825.
Benjamin Kindrick	do	40 00	1307 19	Revolutionary army	Jan. 1, 1786	June 1, 1786	April 25, 1808. Died June 12, 1830.
Do	do	64 00	597 84	do	Feb. 21, 1822	Mar. 4, 1820	May 1, 1820.
Do	do	96 00	57 30	do	-	July 7, 1829	
William Scott	do	64 00	539 17	Kentucky vol. mil.	June 23, 1821	Jan. 13, 1820	April 24, 1816 and May 15, 1820.
Do	do	96 00	548 68	do	-	June 16, 1828	
Henry Towles	do	48 00	52 50	Garrard's dragoons	Mar. 1, 1833	Jan. 30, 1833	February 6, 1832.
Quinton Moore	do	20 00	120 50	U. S. army	-	Aug. 26, 1809	April 27, 1810.
Do	do	32 00	-		-	Ap'l 24, 1816	April 24, 1816.
BRACKEN.							
James Dougherty	do	48 00	862 67	Dudley's Ky. mil.	Mar. 25, 1817	May 29, 1814	Acts military establishment.
Do	do	96 00	68 42	do	-	May 18, 1832	June 9, 1832.
John King	do	76 80	1979 28	2d reg. U.S. drag'ns	Apl. 21, 1820	Oct. 18, 1806	March 3, 1807.
Do	do	96 00	154 34	do	-	July 26, 1832	
Philip King	1st Lieut.	204 00	835 35	17th reg. U.S. inf.	Feb. 4, 1830	Jan. 30, 1830	Acts military establishment.
Francis Lee	Corporal	96 00	1782 24	19th reg. U.S. inf.	Oct. 21, 1816	Aug. 11, 1815	Acts military establishment.
Jacob Rasor	Private	64 00	439 09	St. Clair's army	Jan. 29, 1823	April 24, 1816	April 24, 1816.
BULLITT.							
John Jourdon	do	60 00	288 16	Kentucky militia	Aug. 2, 1813	July 5, 1811	August 2, 1813.
Do	do	96 00	562 60	do	-	April 24, 1816	April 24, 1816.

Statement, &c. of Invalid Pensioners—Continued.

Names and countries.	Rank.	Annual allowance.	Sums received.	Description of service.	When placed on the pension roll.	Commencement of pension.	Laws under which inscribed, increased, and reduced; and remarks.
CALDWELL.							
Joseph M'Connell	Farrier	48 00	200 93	Kentucky vol. mil.	June 23, 1821	Dec. 28, 1819	April 24, 1816, and May 15, 1820.
Do	do	32 00	113 90	do	do	Mar. 4, 1824	
Do	do	48 00	309 06	do	do	Sep. 26, 1827	
Moses Archer	Private	72 00	375 55	7th reg. U. S. inf.	July 1, 1834	Dec. 16, 1828	June 3, 1834.
CAMPBELL.							
Joseph Frost	do	64 00	369 62	5th reg. U. S. inf.	Jan. 28, 1815	May 29, 1816	Acts military establishment.
Lewis Mangum	do	48 00	59 60	7th reg. U. S. inf.	Mar. 26, 1825	Oct. 8, 1824	do
Do	do	96 00	735 74	do	do	Jan. 5, 1826	do
John M'Glasson	do	48 00	127 60	Revolutionary army	Jan. 11, 1830	Jan. 8, 1830	May 24, 1828.
Joseph Paxton	do	48 00	981 46	7th reg. U.S. inf.	Jan. 24, 1818	Sep. 29, 1813	April 24, 1816.
Thomas Stevens	do	48 00	29 06	Kentucky militia	Mar. 5, 1823	Jan. 27, 1823	April 24, 1816, and February 4, 1822.
Do	do	32 00	123 83	do	do	Sep. 4, 1823	March 3, 1819.
Do	do	48 00	318 40	do	do	July 30, 1827.	
Joseph Redman	do	72 00	659 65	1st rifle regiment	Mar. 14, 1820	Jan. 6, 1820	Acts military establishment, and May 18, 1820.
Roger Cooper	do	48 00	357 46	1st U. S. rifle reg't	Aug. 3, 1816	Sep. 24, 1815	Acts military establishment.
Caleb Crichet	do	30 00	72 50	4th reg't U.S. inf.	Jan. 29, 1816	Nov. 24, 1813	do
Do	do	48 00	391 20	do	do	Ap'l 24, 1816	April 24, 1816. Died June 18, 1824.
CLARKE.							
James Brasfield	do	48 00	54 66	Kentucky militia	Dec. 13, 1831	Dec. 12, 1831	April 24, 1816.
Do	do	96 00	105 04	do	do	Feb. 1, 1833	do
Abraham Estes	do	45 00	90 87	do	Ap'l 17, 1814	Ap'l 17, 1814	March 3, 1815.
Do	do	72 00	566 96	do	do	Ap'l 24, 1816	April 24, 1816.
Do	do	48 00	48 00	do	do	Mar. 4, 1824	March 3, 1819.
Thomas Estin	do	64 00	1314 55	Garrard's co. vol.	Feb. 22, 1819	Aug. 21, 1813	April 24, 1816.
John Guynn	do	96 00	184 53	3d infantry	May 9, 1832	April 2, 1832	Acts military establishment.
Wesley Shepherd	do	32 00	480 16	44th reg't U.S. inf.	July 20, 1816	Apl. 21, 1815	Acts military establishment. From West Tennessee from March 4, 1821.

Name	Rank			Regiment or corps			Remarks
Do	do	48 00	185 47	Kentucky militia	Oct. 23, 1813	Ap.l 23, 1830	Acts military establishment.
Jesse P. Green	do	96 00	1739 38	Kentucky vol.	June 10, 1834	Jan. 23, 1816	April 24, 1816.
Samuel Kelly	Musician	96 00	-	Kentucky militia	June 18, 1834	May 23, 1834	do
James P. Bullock	Private	96 00	-	-	-	May 19, 1834	
CHRISTIAN. William Brown	do	64 00	302 23	3d reg. U.S. inf.	June 27, 1820	June 16, 1819	Acts military establishment.
Do	do	48 00	312 00	do	do	Mar. 4, 1824	April 24, 1816.
Larkin N. Apers	do	72 00	422 84	Lewis co. Ky. mil.	May 9, 1828	Ap'l 19, 1828	
CUMBERLAND. Mathew Amicks	do	48 00	737 33	Lynch's Va. reg.		April 24, 1816	April 24, 1816. From Virginia September 4, 1831.
ESTILL. Sinsfield Bicknall	do	48 00	710 53	Kentucky militia	July 28, 1820	May 17, 1819	April 24, 1816, and May 13, 1820.
Charles Lenox	do	96 00	1042 86	Marshall's reg't U. S. army	Jan. 5, 1821	Ap'l 24, 1816	April 24, 1816. From Pennsylvania from September 4, 1820.
FAYETTE. Charles Bradford	Corporal	48 00	26 53	Kentucky militia	Dec. 29, 1820	Aug. 17, 1820	April 24, 1816, and May 13, 1820.
John Baker	Private	96 00	373 46	17th inf.	Ap'l 14, 1830	Ap'l 14, 1830	Died September 1, 1822.
William Cook	do	30 00	50 48	Kentucky militia	Jan. 9, 1816	Aug. 18, 1814	Acts military establishment.
Do	do	48 00	620 84	do	do	Ap'l 24, 1816	March 3, 1815.
Do	do	72 00	664 61	do	do	Dec. 9, 1824	April 24, 1816.
Thomas Clark	Sergeant	96 00	1948 68	1st reg. U.S. rifle.	Nov. 17, 1813	Nov. 17, 1813	Acts military establishment.
Thomas Chamberlain	do	48 00	49 60	Kentucky vol.	June 4, 1833	Feb. 21, 1833	April 24, 1816.
Michael Fishell	Lieutenant	204 00	1110 04	Kentucky cavalry	June 3, 1830	Jan. 1, 1828	May 20, 1830. Died June 10, 1833.
Elkana Hendley	Private	32 00	667 00	Virginia militia	Mar. 27, 1817	Oct. 31, 1812	April 24, 1816.
Samuel Morehead	do	30 00	13 62	17th reg't U.S. inf.	Apr. 13, 1816	Nov. 10, 1815	Acts military establishment.
Do	do	48 00	329 33	do	do	Ap'l 24, 1816	April 24, 1816.
John Shaw	do	96 00	-	19th reg. U.S. inf.	Oct. 21, 1816	Aug. 2, 1816	Acts military establishment.
Willis Tandy	do	15 00	30 28	Kentucky militia	Jan. 9, 1816	Ap'l 17, 1814	March 3, 1815.
Do	do	24 00	259 66	-	-	Ap'l 24, 1816	April 24, 1816.
Do	do	48 00	337 82	-	-	Feb. 19, 1827	
Do	do	96 00		-	-	Mar. 6, 1834	
Thomas M'Barney	do	36 00	1026 80	1st rg·Price's levies	-	Mar. 4, 1789	June 7, 1785. From Pennsylvania from September 4, 1817.

Statement, &c. of Invalid Pensioners—Continued.

NAMES AND COUNTIES.	Rank.	Annual allowance.	Sums received.	Description of service.	When placed on the pension roll.	Commencement of pension.	Laws under which inscribed, increased and reduced; and remarks.
Thomas M'Barney	Private	96 00	434 86	1st reg. Price's levies	Ap'l 19, 1818	Sep. 12, 1817	March 3, 1819. Died March 23, 1822.
George M'Manning	do	72 00	535 94	28th reg. U.S. inf.	April 5, 1824	Sep. 24, 1823	Acts military establishment.
Reuben Plunkett	do	48 00	397 73	3d U. S. dragoons	-	Ap'l 24, 1816	April 24, 1816. From Virginia March 4, 1819. Died July 27, 1829.
Do	do	64 00	316 91	do			July 30, 1824. Died July 27, 1829.
Spencer Darnell	do	60 00	-	do	Jan. 9, 1816	Feb. 14, 1814	March 3, 1815.
Do	do	96 00		13th reg. Ky. mil.		Ap'l 24, 1816	April 24, 1816.
John Beatty	do	96 00	496 27	Tennessee vol.	Ap'l 12, 1820	July 3, 1818	do
William Wilson	do	48 00	435 06	Kentucky militia	Mar. 24, 1817	Nov. 5, 1816	March 3, 1817. Died April 16, 1826.
Do	do	96 00	36 68	do		Nov. 28, 1825	
Paul Cassino	do	48 00	367 73	5th reg't U. S. inf.	Ap'l 28, 1817	July 8, 1815	
Peter Murphey FLEMING.	do	72 00	260 46	17th reg't U. S. inf.	Jan. 5, 1818	July 22, 1814	Acts military establishment. From New York from September 4, 1820.
Dennis Belt	do	45 00	86 87	28th regt. infantry	Jan. 12, 1816	May 26, 1814	Acts military establishment. Dead.
Do	do	72 00	565 90	do		Ap'l 24, 1816	Acts military establishment.
Do	do	48 00	100 40	do		Mar. 4, 1824	April 24, 1816.
Do	do	96 00	663 52	do		Ap'l 7, 1826	March 3, 1819.
Joshua Davidson	Dragoon	64 00	736 00	Lee's corps of horse	Sep. 28, 1820	Sep. 4, 1822	April 21, 1826.
Zaccheus Cord	1st Lieut.	240 00	4167 80	10th reg't Ky. mil.	Aug. 3, 1816	Sep. 30, 1813	From Virginia from Mar. 4, 1822.
Thomas Jones	Private	64 00	758 18	Kentucky militia	June 17, 1823	Ap'l 30, 1822	Acts military establishment.
Patrick M'Cann	do	24 00	145 46	Gibson's Ky. militia	Mar. 31, 1825	Aug. 3, 1824	April 24, 1816, and Feb. 4, 1822.
Do	do	72 00	253 17	do		Aug. 25, 1830	February 4, 1822.
John Reams	do	64 00	858 65	28th reg't U. S. inf.	Oct. 14, 1822	Sep. 19, 1820	Acts military establishment.
Henry Shaw	do	30 00	195 56	11th reg't U. S. inf.	-	Oct. 17, 1809	April 27, 1810.
Do	do	48 00	65 33	do	-	Ap'l 24, 1816	April 24, 1816.
James Moore	Corporal	30 00	634 25	Revolutionary army	-	Mar. 4, 1795	
Do	do	48 00	449 43	do	-	Ap'l 24, 1816	April 24, 1816.
William Stocker	Private	36 00	479 40	do	-	Jan. 1, 1803	
Do	do	57 60	107 36	do	-	Ap'l 24, 1816	A;,ril 24, 1816.

Name	Rank			Service			Remarks
FLOYD.							
Samuel Brown	do	96 00	22 70	Croghan's Ky.	Jan. 21, 1834	Dec. 6, 1833	Acts military establishment.
Samuel Regem	do	48 00	704 34	24th reg't U. S. inf.	Nov. 20, 1820	June 7, 1815	Acts military establishment.
Do	do	72 00	291 90	do	-	Feb. 10, 1830	
FRANKLIN.							
William Gunter	do	96 00	-	1st reg't U. S. inf.	Feb. 15, 1819	Mar. 1, 1816	Acts military establishment.
James Hunter	Lieut.	132 00	-	Kentucky riflemen	Ap'l 14, 1834	Mar. 19, 1834	April 10, 1812.
Thomas Hickman	Private	24 00	87 52	United States army	-	Jan. 12, 1812	July 5, 1812.
Do	do	38 40	-	do	-	Ap'l 24, 1816	April 24, 1816.
Francis L. Slaughter	do	36 00	339 90	Yancey's 1st reg drg.	Sep. 7, 1807	Nov. 15, 1806	Acts military establishment. From Pa. from March 4, 1816. Died January 9, 1832.
Do	do	57 60	904 80	do	-	Ap'l 24, 1816	April 24, 1816.
Richard Taylor	Captain	300 00	2697 50	Virginia State navy	Mar. 26, 1817	Sep. 3, 1816	Mar. 1, 1817. Died Aug. 30, 1825.
Richard Taylor	do	240 00	240 00	United States army	-	Mar. 4, 1821	From Penn, from March 4, 1821.
Do	do	120 00	720 00	do	-	Mar. 4, 1828	March 3, 1819.
Do	do	240 00	480 00	do	-		
Joseph Taylor	Ser. major	48 00	63 60	Kentucky militia	Dec. 1, 1832	Nov. 8, 1832	Acts military establishment.
Ambrose White	Private	96 00	381 98	Revolutionary army	Mar. 15, 1830	Mar. 13, 1830	May 24, 1828.
GALLATIN.							
Andrew Green	do	20 04	50 61	Harmour's camp'n	Jan. 18, 1823	Oct. 10, 1813	April 18, 1814.
Do	do	32 00	207 92	do	-	Ap'l 24, 1816	April 24, 1816.
Do	do	96 00	889 12	do	-	Oct. 23, 1822	January 18, 1823.
Robert M'Mickle	do	64 00	196 42	Kentucky militia	June 23, 1821	Feb. 6, 1821	April 24, 1816, and May 15, 1820.
Do	do	48 00	467 20	do	-	Mar. 4, 1824	
Do	do	64 00	17 06	do	-	Nov. 28, 1833	
John Payne, Jr	Cadet	96 00	1528 78	Military academy	Ap'l 25, 1820	Mar. 1, 1818	Acts military establishment:
GARRARD.							
Christian Perkins	Private	96 00	354 08	Army of the rev.	Jan. 13, 1830	Dec. 28, 1829	May 24, 1828.
Merideth Tongate	do	96 00	400 78	3d infantry	May 28, 1830	Jan. 1, 1830	Acts military establishment.
GRANT.							
William Arnold	Lieut.	48 00	69 20	Kentucky militia	Mar. 21, 1817	Oct. 23, 1816	March 3, 1817.
Do	do	90 00	429 11	do	Ap'l 24, 1819	Ap'l 1, 1818	March 3, 1819.
Do	do	180 00	2094 50	do	-	July 16, 1822	February 1, 1823.
Frederick McLinn	do	48 00	482 93	17th reg't U. S. inf.	June 30, 1819	Feb. 10, 1814	Acts military establishment.
Do	do	32 00	256 00	do	-	Mar. 4, 1824	
Bartlett Collins	do	48 00	46 13	Kentucky volun'rs	Mar. 12, 1830	Mar. 10, 1830	Ap'l 24, 1816, Died Feb. 26, 1831.

Statement, &c. of Invalid Pensioners—Continued.

NAMES AND COUNTIES.	Rank.	Annual allowance.	Sums received.	Description of service.	When placed on the pension roll.	Commencement of pension.	Laws under which inscribed, increased and reduced; and remarks.
GREEN. Adam Funk	Private	48 00	118 00	Kentucky militia	Sep. 15, 1831	Sep. 10, 1831	April 24, 1816.
GREENUP. James Applegate	Sergeant	72 00	431 29	1st reg't U. S. levies	Nov. 11, 1826	Sep. 8, 1826	April 25, 1808. From Virginia Sep. 4, 1827.
HARDEN. William Bush	Private	96 00	4005 98	Kentucky militia	Mar. 18, 1800	Dec. 13, 1791	
HENDERSON. Lewis Rouse	do	48 00	838 53	Mulensburg's reg't	Feb. 28, 1827	Feb. 13, 1827	April 25, 1818.
HARRISON. Aaron Adams	do	48 00	170 93	Adams' Ky. militia	Jan. 31, 1821	Aug. 14, 1820	April 25, 1808.
Do	do	32 00	61 83	do	-	Mar. 4, 1824	March 3, 1819. Reduced to this rate.
Do	do	48 00	235 20	do	-	Feb. 8, 1826	Raised to this rate on account of increased disability.
Do	do	72 00	228 18	do	-	Jan. 3, 1831	Raised to this rate on account of increased disability.
Irvine Brown	do	96 00	30 24	Kentucky rifles	Dec. 8, 1825	Nov. 15, 1825	April 24, 1816. Died March 8, 1826.
John Bruce	do	64 00	60 16	Kentucky militia	May 21, 1833	Mar. 27, 1833	April 24, 1816.
Henry Dougherty	Corporal	48 00	835 86	do	Mar. 21, 1817	Oct. 7, 1816	March 3, 1817.
William English	Private	96 00	718 50	Butler's Pa. reg't	do	Sep. 9, 1816	March 21, 1817. Died May 2, 1827
Do	do	72 00	216 00	do	-	Mar. 4, 1824	March 3, 1819.
Daniel Holley	do	48 00	544 00	Kentucky militia	Feb. 3, 1817	May 1, 1813	Acts military establishment.
Do	do	32 00	160 00	do	-	Sep. 4, 1824	March 3, 1819.
George Hendrick	do	48 00	115 68	do	Mar. 21, 1817	Oct. 7, 1816	March 3, 1817.
Benoni Jamieson	do	48 00	89 46	do	Apl 27, 1832	Apl 24, 1832	April 24, 1816.
Bathazor Kramar	-	96 00	76 68	Bradford's U.S. rifl'n	-	Nov. 28, 1822	March 2, 1827. Died Sep. 15, 1822.

Name	Rank	Pay	Amount	Service	Date	Date	Remarks
John M'Clure	do	48 00	503 33	Kentucky militia	Mar. 21, 1817	Sep. 10, 1816	March 3, 1817.
Esaw Ritchey	do	96 00	292 78	do	July 14, 1830	Jan. 1, 1828	May 20, 1830.
Armistead Whitehead	3d lieut.	69 00	59 02	5th U. S. infantry	-	June 16, 1815	Acts military establishment.
Do	do	84 00	163 33	do	-	Ap'l 24, 1816	April 24, 1816.
2 Jesse Wolf	do	168 00	1848 00	do	-	Mar. 4, 1818	Increased by the Secretary of War.
	Private	48 00	143 20	Kentucky volun'rs	Sep. 23, 1829	Sep. 11, 1829	April 24, 1816.
David Kenedy	do	48 00	-	Kentucky militia	May 10, 1834	Ap'l 25, 1834	April 24, 1816.
William Adams	do	48 00	-	do	Ap'l 1, 1834	Mar. 4, 1834	April 24, 1816.
Spencer Shoemate	do	72 00	326 40	Allen's Ky. militia	Jan. 5, 1818	Feb. 21, 1813	April 24, 1816. Died Nov. 11, 1819.
Andrew Ward	do	48 00	183 87	17th infantry	May 5, 1830	May 5, 1830	Acts military establishment,
HENRY.							
Thomas Bell	do	64 00	505 41	Kentucky volun'rs	Dec. 9, 1825	Oct. 12, 1825	April 24, 1816.
Thomas James	do	20 00	512 21	do	May 19, 1795	July 25, 1793	From Penn. from March 4, 1819.
Do	do	32 00	277 60	do	-	Mar. 4, 1819	
Do	do	64 00	127 30	do	-	Nov. 7, 1827	December 8, 1827.
Do	do	96 00	432 26	do	-	Nov. 3, 1829	November 14, 1829.
Thomas Robertson	do	60 00	120 33	2d reg't dragoons	Nov. 24, 1814	Ap'l 16, 1814	Acts military establishment:
Do	do	96 00	1714 60	do	-	Ap'l 24, 1816	April 24, 1816.
Dan'l Welsch or Welch	do	96 00	1728 78	1st reg't U. S. inf.	Dec. 11, 1816	Mar. 1, 1816	April 24, 1816. From Mississippi from March 4, 1826.
Joseph Reeves	do	72 00	-	Kentucky militia	Ap'l 3, 1834	Mar. 6, 1834	April 24, 1816.
HICKMAN.							
Thomas Vincent	Captain	120 00	246 67	United States army	Feb. 28, 1832	Feb. 13, 1832	May 24, 1828.
HOPKINS.							
James Curtis	Private	30 00	32 16	7th reg't U. S. inf.	Jan. 24, 1816	Mar. 28, 1815	Acts military establishment.
Do	do	48 00	425 33	do	-	Ap'l 24, 1816	April 24, 1816.
Do	do	30 00	270 00	do	-	Mar. 3, 1819	March 4, 1825.
Lemuel Hewlit	do	48 00	971 20	Kentucky militia	Ap'l 16, 1823	Jan. 12, 1816	April 30, 1816.
John Montgomery	do	48 00	164 80	Wayne's army	Sep. 30, 1830	Sep. 29, 1830	April 25, 1808.
John Buskill	do	36 00	869 00	do	Mar. 4, 1781	July 7, 1785	
Do	do	57 60	1028 96	do	-	Ap'l 24, 1816	April 24, 1816.
JEFFERSON.							
Henry Asbury	do	48 00	537 20	3d reg't Ky. militia	Feb. 16, 1819	Dec. 26, 1812	Acts military establishment.
Do	do	32 00	240 00	do	-	Mar. 4, 1824	April 24, 1816.
Henry Hawkins	do	30 00	40 73	Kentucky volun'rs	Jan. 2, 1816	Dec. 15, 1814	Acts military establishment.

Statement, &c. of Invalid Pensioners—Continued.

NAMES AND COUNTIES.	Rank.	Annual allowance.	Sums received.	Description of service.	When placed on the pension roll.	Commencement of pension.	Laws under which inscribed, increased, and reduced; and remarks.
Henry Hawkins	Private	48 00	89 33	Kentucky volun'rs	-	Ap'l 24, 1816	April 24, 1816.
Do	do	24 00	-	do	-	Mar. 4, 1824	
James Stewart	do	48 00	855 20	Kentucky militia	Jan. 7, 1818	May 11, 1815	April 24, 1816.
John Fury	do	60 00	124 84	1st reg't U. S. inf.	Jan. 28, 1815	Mar. 25, 1814	Acts military establishment.
Do	do	96 00	178 60	do	-	Ap'l 24, 1816	April 24, 1816.
Joseph Shaw	do	24 00	102 72	United States army	June 18, 1818	Jan. 13, 1812	July 5, 1812.
Do	do	38 00	685 86	do	do	Ap'l 24, 1816	April 24, 1816.
Joseph Leitner	do	48 00	123 33	5th reg't U. S. inf.	Sep. 5, 1822	Aug. 12, 1821	Act's military establishment.
Do	do	32 00	32 00	do	do	Mar. 4, 1824	
Thomas Pearson	Lieut.	120 00	429 33	Col Buford's rv. ar'y	-	Jan. 1, 1803	Acts military establishment,
Do	do	160 00	1558 98	do	-	July 28, 1806	March 31, 1807. Died July 10, 1826.
Do	do	181 33	1852 02	do	-	Ap'l 24, 1816	April 24, 1816.
JESSAMINE COUNTY.							
John Sharp	Private	96 00	495 74	3d U. S. infantry	Oct. 21, 1818	July 5, 1818	Acts military establishment.
Do	do	48 00	306 40	do	-	Sept. 4, 1823	March 3, 1819.
Do	do	96 00	394 60	do	-	Jan. 22, 1830	March 6, 1830.
LAWRENCE COUNTY.							
Elzaphen Rucker	Sergeant	96 00	397 20	4th rifles	Jan. 16, 1830	Jan. 16, 1830	Acts military establishment.
LEWIS COUNTY.							
Aquilla Smith	Private	72 00	458 30	7th Md. reg. rev.	Sept. 3, 1823	Aug. 6, 1823	April 10, 1806 and February 22.
Do	do	96 00	404 16	do	-	Dec. 19, 1829	
LINCOLN COUNTY.							
James Durnham	do	26 66⅔	800 00	1st Virginia reg't	Oct. 25, 1786	Jan. 1, 1786	June 7, 1785.
Do	do	42 65	372 70	do	Ap'l 24, 1816	Apr. 24, 1815	April 24, 1816. From Virginia.
James Collier	do	60 00	1,478 50	Revolutionary army	-	Sep. 4, 1791	September 4, 1791. Died March 31, 1826.

Name	Rank			Service			Remarks
Do	do	96 00	953 86	do	-	Ap'l 24, 1816	April 24, 1816.
LIVINGSTON COUNTY.							
Robert Elder	do	40 00	190 52	Kentucky militia	July 19, 1811	July 19, 1811	July 5, 1912. From South Carolina from September 4, 1816.
Do	do	64 00	279 03	do	-	Apr. 24, 1816	April 24, 1816.
William Little	do	60 00	385 33	3d reg't U. S. inf.	-	Nov. 22, 1809	April 27, 1810. From Penn'a. Dead.
Do	do	96 00	642 34	do	-	Apl. 24, 1816	April 24, 1816. Died Jan. 3, 1823.
M'CRACKEN COUNTY.							
William Jones	do	96 00	1,585 86	Kentucky militia	-	Feb. 25, 1817	Acts military establishment.
MADISON COUNTY.							
Squire Boone	do	36 00	238 50	do	April 27, 1810	Sep. 9, 1809	April 27, 1810.
Do	do	57 60	49 76	do	-	April 24, 1816	April 24, 1816.
James Berry	do	20 00	132 49	do	Ap'l 27, 1810	Sep. 9, 1809	April 27, 1810. Died Feb. 12, 1822.
Do	do	32 00	185 74	do	-	Apl. 24, 1816	April 24, 1816.
William Kindred	do	48 00	992 13	2d U. S. dragoons	Apr. 6, 1816	July 3, 1813	April 24, 1816.
John Wood	do	32 00	500 50	Garrard's co. vol.	June 30, 1819	July 7, 1831	Acts military establishment,
Do	do	96 00	289 56	do	-	Feb. 28, 1831	do do
Bower Sudduth	do	96 00	42 86	5th reg't infantry	Mar. 26, 1832	Feb. 3, 1832	Acts mil. estab. Died July 14, 1832.
Samuel Steer	Sergeant	40 00	58 42	-	Jan. 11, 1816	Nov. 8, 1814	Acts military establishment.
Do	do	64 00	1,111 06	-	Apl. 24, 1816	do	April 24,1816.
MASON COUNTY.							
John Campbell	do	48 00	974 40	1st U. S. rifle reg't	June 14, 1817	Nov. 17, 1813	Acts military establishment.
Judah Levy	Private	96 00	1,234 86	Buford's reg't	July 6, 1820	Apl. 24, 1816	April 24, 1816. From Pennsyl'a from March 4, 1820.
William Nieves	do	30 00	154 26	7th reg't U. S. inf.	Feb. 7, 1817	Mar. 2, 1811	March 16, 1812.
Do	do	48 00	113 33	do	-	Apl. 24, 1816	April 24, 1816.
Benjamin Raynes	do	96 00	1,784 53	Kentucky militia	-	Aug. 2, 1815	Acts military establishment.
Jonathan Rees	2d lieut.	90 00	79 25	19th infantry	Ap'l 20, 1831	Apl. 18, 1831	do do
Edward Turner	Private	96 00	2,012 68	Kentucky volunt's	Oct. 1, 1819	Mar. 18, 1813	April 24, 1816.
Henry Grelick	do	96 00	308 00	6th infantry	Nov. 15, 1823	July 12, 1823	Acts mil. est. Died Sept. 27, 1826.
MEAD COUNTY.							
Zadock Hard	do	32 00	331 67	Revol'y army	Aug. 22, 1825	Ap'l 24, 1816	April 24, 1816. From N. Hampshire from September 4, 1824.

Statement, &c. of Invalid Pensioners—Continued.

Names and counties.	Rank.	Annual allowance.	Sums received.	Description of service.	When placed on the pension roll.	Commencement of pension.	Laws under which inscribed, increased, and reduced; and remarks.
MERCER COUNTY.							
John Abel	Private	96 00	1,496 53	Lt. Bell's 7th US. inf	Oct. 28, 1820	Dec. 5, 1815	Acts mil. estab. From Indiana. Died July 7, 1831.
William Simson	do	30 00	-	Morgan's rev. rifles	-	-	February 2, 1798. From N. Carolina from September 4, 1817.
Do	do	48 00	-	do	-	Apr. 24, 1816	April 24, 1816. Died middle of March, 1818.
Do	do	96 00	-	do	Ap'l 21, 1819	Sep. 5, 1817	March 3, 1819. No pay in Kentucky.
MONROE COUNTY.							
Joseph Kingeny	do	96 00	202 08	Kentucky militia	Feb. 28, 1825	July 27, 1824	April 24, 1816.
Do	do	91 00	637 00	do	-	Sep. 4, 1826	
MONTGOMERY COUNTY.							
Joseph Bay	do	72 00	995 32	Kentucky militia	Dec. 29, 1820	May 6, 1820	April 24, 1816 and May 15, 1820.
John Howard	do	96 00	291 38	Virginia militia	Feb. 10, 1831	Feb. 10, 1831	April 24, 1816.
George Huffman	do	96 00	-	Kentucky militia	Mar. 12, 1834	Feb. 4, 1834	April 24, 1816. No pay.
Daniel M'Carty	do	76 80	398 48	Buford's regiment United States artil.			
Do	do	72 00	1,286 00	do	-	Feb. 16, 1811	July 5, 1812. From Virginia from September 4, 1823.
Edward Stivers	Musician	96 00	1,159 28	3d United States infantry	-	Ap'l 24, 1816	April 24, 1816.
NICHOLAS COUNTY.							
Joseph Wilkinson	Corporal	96 00	987 38	United States frigate Boston	Mar. 3, 1817	Nov. 13, 1815	Acts military establishment. From North Carolina. Died December 10, 1827.
William Fleet	Ensign	78 00	208 34	Kentucky militia	Mar. 23, 1817 Jan. 26, 1822	Dec. 23, 1816 Jan. 1, 1822	March 3, 1817. Died April 4, 1827. April 24, 1816 and May 15, 1820.

Name	Rank			Service			Remarks
OLDHAM COUNTY.							
Benjamin Coons	Lieutenant	153 00	575 45	Tennessee militia	June 1, 1830	May 31, 1830	April 24, 1816.
OWEN COUNTY.							
James McHatton	Corporal	64 00	37 00	Kentucky militia	Aug. 24, 1833	Aug. 6, 1833	April 24, 1816.
Stephen Richey	Private	48 00	42 66	Wayne's army	June 14, 1833	Apl. 15, 1833	April 25, 1808.
Thomas Ward	do	24 00	418 67	Kentucky militia	Dec. 2, 1814	Mar. 26, 1815	April 24, 1816.
William Dahoney	do	60 00	–	do	July 19, 1821	June 4, 1821	April 24, 1816, and May 15, 1820.
PENDLETON COUNTY.							
Albert Ammerman	do	48 00	662 66	1st regt. Ky. militia	Nov. 30, 1820	May 16, 1820	April 24, 1816, and May 15, 1820.
John H. Fugate	do	48 00	171 73	Kentucky militia	Sep. 6, 1820	Aug 7, 1820	April 24, 1816, and May 15, 1820.
Do	do	24 00	240 00	–	–	Mar. 4, 1824	
Leonard Highfield	do	24 00	112 80	do	Sep. 6, 1820	Aug. 9, 1820	April 24, 1816, and May 15, 1820.
Do	do	48 00	401 73	do	–	Apr. 21, 1825	
Ebenezer Jayne	do	96 00	1,807 74	23d regiment United States infantry	July 20, 1815	May 5, 1815	Acts military establishment. From New York from September 4, 1825.
Michael Glaves	Captain	120 00	276 67	Kentucky militia	Nov. 30, 1820	May 16, 1820	April 24, 1816, and May 15, 1820.
PULASKI COUNTY.							
Samuel Newell	Lieutenant	96 00	493 72	Campbell's regiment revolutionary army	Jan. 6, 1817	Mar. 2, 1811	July 5, 1812. From West Tennessee from September 4, 1816.
Do	do	108 00	1,888 88	do	–	Apr. 24, 1816	April 24, 1816.
ROCKCASTLE COUNTY.							
James Dysart]	Captain	120 00	1,346 00	Revolutionary army	Dec. 18, 1806	Dec. 18, 1806	March 3, 1807.
SCOTT COUNTY.							
William Armstrong	Private	72 00	745 24	1st regt. Ky. rifle	Oct. 10, 1821	June 9, 1821	April 24, 1816, and May 15, 1820. Died October 16, 1831.
William Berry	do	60 00	124 00	Johnson's regiment	Dec. 11, 1815	Mar. 31, 1814	March 3, 1815.
Do	do	96 00	1,714 90	–	–	Apr. 24, 1816	April 24, 1816.
Major Breedlove	do	96 00	132 16	Kentucky militia	Jan. 22, 1833	Oct. 20, 1832	April 24, 1816.
William Carter	do	64 00	474 08	Scott's Kentucky militia	–	Oct. 7, 1816	March 3, 1817.
Do	do	48 00	96 00	do	Nov. 17, 1833	Mar. 4, 1824	March 3, 1819.
Thomas H. Graves	do	48 00	59 87	Kentucky militia	Jan. 22, 1833	Dec. 5, 1832	April 24, 1816.

Statement, &c. of Invalid Pensioners—Continued.

NAMES AND COUNTIES.	Rank.	Annual allowance.	Sums received.	Description of service.	When placed on the pension roll.	Commencement of pension.	Laws under which inscribed, increased and reduced; and remarks.
SCOTT CO.—continued.							
Michael Kendrick -	Private	72 00	97 70	Kentucky militia	Jan. 22, 1833	Oct. 26 1832	April 24, 1816.
John J. Mahanna -	do	96 00	1,883 64	4th regiment United States infantry	May 6, 1816	July 22, 1814	Acts military establishment. From Ohio from March 4, 1818.
Nathaniel Mothershead	do	96 00	395 38	Revolutionary army	Jan. 23, 1830	Jan. 23, 1830	May 24, 1828.
Robert Nunally	do	48 00	491 20	Kentucky militia	Dec. 13, 1823	Dec. 12, 1823	April 24, 1816.
Samuel Sharon	do	30 00	50 62	do	Aug. 17, 1814	Aug. 17, 1814	March 3, 1815.
Do	do	48 00	465 63	do	-	Apr. 24, 1816	April 24, 1816.
Do	do	72 00	579 90	do		Jan. 13, 1826	March 14, 1826.
Henry Spoon -	do	48 00	203 60	17th infantry	Dec. 12, 1829	Dec. 7, 1829	Acts military establishment.
George Manvearing -	Musician	60 00	71 16	United States artil.	Dec. 11, 1815	Feb. 17, 1815	Acts military establishment. From New York.
Do	do	96 00	466 60	do	do	Apr. 24, 1816	April 24, 1816.
Richard M. Johnson -	Colonel	360 00	6,333 00	Kentucky mounted volunteers	Dec. 12, 1822	Aug. 1, 1816	April 24, 1816.
SHELBY COUNTY.							
Bland W. Ballard -	Captain	120 00	1,640 33	1st rifle regiment	May 22, 1821	July 3, 1820	April 24, 1816, and May 15, 1820.
Thomas Knowles -	Private	30 00	68 38	2d U.S. dragoons	Apr. 6, 1816	Jan. 13, 1814	Acts mil. est.
Do	do	48 00	184 53	do	do	Apr. 24, 1816	April 24, 1816
Do	do	64 00	896 68	do	Mar. 18, 1820	Feb. 28, 1820	March 18, 1820
Andrew Salisbury	do	45 00	87 25	do	Jan. 13, 1815	May 16, 1814	Acts mil. est.
Do	do	72 00	1,249 79	do		Apr. 24, 1816	April 24, 1816
Samuel W. White -	do	30 00	113 86	Ky. volunteers	Nov. 24, 1814	July 7, 1812	April 10, 1812
Do	do	48 00	857 33	do	-	Ap'l 24, 1816	April 24, 1816
James Devouriex -	do	96 00	351 28	7th U. S. inf'y	June 18, 1816	July 8, 1815	April 30, 1816
John Kincaid -	do	60 00	1,508 46	Revolutionary army	-	Mar. 4, 1791	
Do	do	96 00	2,352 00	do	-	Ap'l 24, 1816	April 24, 1816

	Rank			Corps			Remarks
TODD COUNTY.							
Buckner Haygood	do	24 00	430 76	Tenn. cavalry	Jan. 14, 1819	May 27, 1814	April 24, 1816. From W. Tennessee
Do	do	48 00	87 60	do	-	May 8, 1852	
UNION COUNTY.							
Daniel V. Bealmear	Corporal	48 00	831 38	7th reg. U.S. inf'y	Dec. 23, 1816	Apr. 9, 1815	Acts mil. est.
WASHINGTON CO.							
James Dowling	Dragoon	40 00	847 00	Smallwood's Md. r.	Mar. 14, 1820	Jan. 1, 1803	Mar. 3, 1803. From Penn. from Mar. 4, 1824. Died May 8, 1831
Do	do	64 00	444 60	do	-	Mar. 4, 1824	
Do	do	96 00	21 46	do	-	Feb. 15, 1831	
Jeremiah Searcy	Private	60 00	68 50	Moultrie's S. S. reg	May 7, 1815	Mar. 3, 1815	March 3, 1815. From S. Carolina.— Died April 30, 1833
Do	do	96 00	1,633 60	6th U. S. inf'y	Aug. 30, 1816	Apr. 24, 1816	April 24, 1816
Levi Tarr	do	48 00	899 60	do	-	June 7, 1815	Acts mil. est. From Maryland. From March 4, 1822
WARREN COUNTY.							
John Grider	Lieutenant	102 00	472 91	1st Ky. militia	Mar. 21, 1821	July 17, 1820	April 24, 1816, and May 15, 1820
WAYNE COUNTY.							
James S. Davis	Private	60 00	58 00	17th reg. U.S. inf'y	Dec. 29, 1815	May 3, 1815	Acts mil. est.
Do	do	96 00	754 60	do	do	Apr. 24, 1816	April 24, 1816
Do	do	48 00	120 00	do	-	Mar. 4, 1824	March 3, 1819
Do	do	72 00	540 00	do	-	Sep. 20, 1826	August 18, 1828
Do	do	20 00	28 53	do	Mar. 13, 1816	Nov. 20, 1814	March 5, 1815
Do	do	32 00	427 53	do	-	Apr. 24, 1816	April 24, 1816
WHITELY COUNTY.							
Michael Stevens	do	48 00	911 74	24th U. S. inf'y	Dec. 11, 1815	Mar. 6, 1815	Acts mil. est. From Ohio
WOODFORD COUNTY.							
John Brown	Sergeant	30 00	161 84	23d reg. U.S. inf'y	-	Dec 1, 1810	March 3, 1811
Do	do	48 00	281 46	do	-	Ap'l 24, 1816	April 24, 1816
Enoch Ducker	Private	60 00	133 63	Col. Dudley's reg't	Sep. 26, 1820	Feb. 2, 1814	April 18, 1814
Do	do	96 00	1,714 60	do	do	Apr. 24, 1816	April 24, 1816
John Kersiner	do	40 00	85 86	U. States' army	-	Mar. 1, 1814	April 18, 1814
Do	do	64 00	215 03	do	-	Apr. 24, 1816	April 24, 1816
Do	do	96 00	854 24	do	-	Apr. 11, 1825	April 25, 1825
Archibald Morrison	Captain	120 00	1,008 00	10th reg. Ky. mil'a	Jan. 14, 1821	Aug. 8, 1820	April 24, 1816, and May 15, 1820.— Died July 1, 1829
Bird Smith	Private	96 00	-	Ky. volunteers	Apr. 7, 1834	Mar. 1, 1834	April 24, 1816

Statement of the Names, &c., of the Heirs of non-commissioned Officers, Privates, &c., who died in the United States' service; who obtained five years' half-pay in lieu of bounty land, under the second section of the act of April 16, 1816, and who resided in the State of Kentucky.

Names of the original claimants.	Rank.	Description of service.	Time of decease.	Names of the heirs.	Annual allowance.	Sums received.	When placed on the roll.	Commencement of pension.	Ending of pension.
BATH COUNTY.									
James Guines, *alias* Goans	Private	28th reg't inf.	Nov. 24, 1814	Sophia, James, Patrick, Blair, and Mary Goans	48 00	240 00	Mar. 7, 1817	Feb. 17, 1815	Feb. 17, 1820
CHRISTIAN COUNTY.									
Geo. K. Campbell	Sergeant	7th	Dec. 3, 1814	Amelia A, and Louisa S. Campbell	66 00	330 00	Feb. 9, 1819	do	do
CLARKE COUNTY.									
David Scott	Private	17th	Nov. 8, 1814	Henry, Joseph, William, John, Anne, Carolina, Devy, Buby and Sally Scott	48 00	240 00	Sep. 29, 1817	do	do
FAYETTE COUNTY.									
Beverly A. Blake	do	do	Jan. 22, 1813	Cordelia, Jane and Lucy Blake	48 00	240 00	Sep. 8, 1817	do	do
John Gardner	do	do	Jan. 22, 1813	William, Thomas, James, John and Elizabeth Gardner	48 00	240 00	Apl. 25, 1818	do	do
S'l Koyle, or Kyle	do	1st reg't riflem.	January 1814	Joseph, Polly, Sherill, Patsey, Alexander and Elizabeth Kyle					
Nath'l Robinson	do	28th reg't inf.	Oct. 22, 1814	George, James, John, Carrick and Benjamin Robinson	48 00	240 00	Mar. 4, 1820	Dec. 4, 1819	Dec. 4, 1824
Terence Smith	do	17th	July 21, 1813	William Smith	48 00	240 00	Jan. 8, 1818	Feb. 17, 1815	Feb. 17, 1820
					48 00	240 00	Oct. 12, 1821	do	do
FRANKLIN COUNTY.									
Benjamin Towson	do	do	Dec. 13, 1814	Mary and Susanna Towson	48 00	240 00	July 21, 1821	June 19, 1821	June 19, 1826

Name	Rank	Regiment	Date	Heirs / Beneficiaries					
Matthew McCrab	do	7th	Feb. 14, 1815	**HOPKINS COUNTY.** John Washington McCrab	48 00	240 00	Nov. 28, 1820	Sep. 11, 1820	Sep. 11, 1825
Braxton Blake	do	17th	Jan. 22, 1813	**JESSAMINE COUNTY.** Elvira Blake	48 00	240 00	Jan. 9, 1818	Feb. 17, 1815	Feb. 17, 1820
Thomas Gaines	do	2d reg't riflem.	Feb. 2, 1815	William and Madison Gaines	48 00	240 00	Nov. 23, 1817	do	do
Ludwell Lee	do	17th reg't inf.	July 22, 1813	Elizabeth and James Lee	48 00	240 00	June 4, 1818	do	do
Robert Read	do	do	Jan. 22, 1813	Robert Reed	48 00	240 00	Sep. 8, 1813	do	do
Hugh Scott	do	2d reg't art'y	October, 1813	Eliza Green, Anderson Hughes, Merit Cowthers, and Edmond Waller Scott	48 00	240 00	Aug. 28, 1817	do	do
William Gilbert	do	17th reg't inf.	Sep. 4, 1814	**LOGAN COUNTY.** Samuel, Benedict, Peter, and Richard M. Gilbert	48 00	240 00	Sep. 23, 1819	do	do
James Fitzpatrick	do	do	Nov. 10, 1813	**LOYD COUNTY.** Jacob, Peggy, Samuel and Sally Fitzpatrick	48 00	240 00	Dec. 18, 1820	Nov. 13, 1820	Nov. 13, 1825
Thos. K. Wells	do	do	Jan. 22, 1813	**MADISON COUNTY.** Sally Wells	48 00	240 00	Dec. 24, 1821	Nov. 8, 1821	Nov. 8, 1826
Richard Tible	do	1st reg't inf.	Jan. 2, 1814	**MASON COUNTY.** Mary, Jane, Hannah, Matilda, Elizabeth, Sarah and Margaret Tible	48 00	240 00	Mar. 12, 1817	Feb. 17, 1815	Feb. 17, 1820
Peter Tevis	Corporal	17th reg't inf.	Jan. 10, 1815	Eliza, Catharine, George and Andrew Tevis	60 00	300 00	Ap'l 16, 1818	do	do
Alex'r McCord	do	28th	April 16, 1814	**MONTGOMERY COUNTY.** Eleanor McCord	60 00	300 00	Feb. 24, 1821	Jan. 1, 1821	Jan. 1, 1826
William Redding	Private	17th	Jan. 22, 1813	**SCOTT COUNTY.** Anne Redding	48 00	240 00	Aug. 22, 1817	Feb. 17, 1815	Feb. 17, 1820
Henry Brown	do	do	Jan. 11, 1815	**WAYNE COUNTY.** Betsey, John, Polly, Harmon, and Henry Brown	48 00	240 00	Mar. 5, 1817	do	do

Statement showing the names, rank, &c. of persons residing in Adair county, in the State of Kentucky, who have been inscribed on the pension list under the act passed the 18th of March, 1818.

NAMES:	Rank.	Annual allowance.	Sums received.	Description of service.	When placed on the pension roll.	Commencement of pension.	Ages.	Laws under which they were formerly inscribed on the pension roll; and remarks.
William Caldwell, 2d.	Private	96 00	523 87	Virginia line	July 20, 1819	Jan. 22, 1819	66	Died July 5, 1825
Leighton Cooper -	do	96 00	58 32	do	July 29, 1831	July 27, 1831	77	
Charles Jones -	do	96 00	295 03	do	Feb. 14, 1831	Feb. 8, 1831	71	
Augustin alias Austin Lawless -	do	96 00	661 44	do	Dec. 15, 1825	Oct. 15, 1825	88	
William Mosby -		96 00	1487 43	do	Feb. 1, 1819	Sep. 7, 1818	80	
John Miller -	Sergeant	96 00	519 99	do	April 9, 1821	Oct. 5, 1818	79	
John Ross -	Private	96 00	471 16	do	May 25, 1829	April 8, 1829	77	
William Tucker -	Lieut.	240 00	2971 69	do	Dec. 9, 1830	June 1, 1818	77	Died May 23, 1829.
John Townsend -	Private	96 00	615 73	do	Dec. 22, 1827	Oct. 6, 1827	73	
Joseph Weir -	do	96 00	1383 99	Pennsylvania line	Feb. 1, 1819	Oct. 5, 1818	75	
William Warmack -	do	96 00	957 64	Maryland line	Mar. 19, 1824	Mar. 18, 1824	72	

Statement, &c. of Allen county, Kentucky.

NAMES.	Rank.	Annual allowance.	Sums received.	Description of service.	When placed on the pension roll.	Commencement of pension.	Ages.	Laws under which they were formerly inscribed on the pension roll; and remarks.
Robert Johnson -	Private	96 00	162 36	Virginia line	Feb. 26, 1819	June 26, 1818	60	Suspended under act of May 1, 1820.
Hugh Morrison -	do	96 00	345 54	do	Sep. 15, 1820	May 18, 1820	69	Died December 23, 1823.
John Richey -	do	96 00	588 41	Maryland line	April 4, 1826	July 19, 1825	80	Transferred from West Tennessee from September 4, 1825. Died April 1, 1826.
Walter Tiffany -	do	96 00	55 46	Connecticut line	Oct. 2, 1819	Aug. 3, 1819	65	
John Weaver -	do	96 00	1,492 64	Virginia line	May 1, 1820	Aug. 18, 1818	78	

Statement, &c. of Anderson county, Kentucky.

NAMES.	Rank.	Sums received.	Annual allowance.	Description of service.	When placed on the pension roll.	Commencement of pension.	Ages.	Laws under which they were formerly inscribed on the pension roll; and remarks.
Edward Atkins -	Private	1,487 20	96 00	Virginia line	July 15, 1819	Sep. 7, 1818	77	

Statement, &c. of Barren county, Kentucky.

NAMES.	Rank.	Sums received.	Annual allowance.	Description of service.	When placed on the pension roll.	Commencement of pension.	Ages.	Laws under which they were formerly inscribed on the pension roll; and remarks.
John Brownlee -	Private	1,513 80	96 00	Virginia line	Sep. 6, 1819	May 29, 1818	75	
Elisha Boon -	do	912 00	96 00	North Carolina line	Oct. 4, 1821	Feb. 3, 1821	80	Transferred from North Carolina from September 4, 1824.
Samuel Downing -	do	1,373 29	96 00	Maryland line	May 8, 1820	Nov. 15 1819.	81	
John Forrester -	do	501 06	96 00	Virginia line	Jan. 10, 1821	June 16, 1818	79	
John Foster -	do	867 03	96 00	do	May 6, 1825	Feb. 22, 1825		
John Kelly -	do	421 41	96 00	do	Ap'l 10, 1822	Aug. 11, 1818	-	
Samuel Luckett -	Sergeant	986 83	96 00	Maryland line	June 4, 1819	May 12, 1818.	71	Died December 31, 1822.
Francis Scott -	Private	1,501 15	96 00	Virginia line	July 11, 1821	July 15, 1818	76	Died August 22, 1828.

Statement, &c. of Bath county, Kentucky.

Names.	Rank.	Annual allowance.	Sums received.	Description of service.	When placed on the pension roll.	Commencement of pension.	Ages.	Laws under which they were formerly inscribed on the pension roll; and remarks.
Thomas Ashley	Private	96 00	788 80	Virginia line	Sep. 10, 1819	June 17, 1818	81	
John Birch	do	96 00	1517 29	Penn. line	Aug. 1, 1821	June 15, 1818	81	
Daniel Desking	do	96 00	1220 76	Virginia line	Apr. 10, 1819	June 17, 1818	74	
John Fosbrook	do	96 00	1516 76	Pennsylvania line	Nov. 26, 1819	do	104	
John Gorrell	do	96 00	1420 64	do	Mar. 10, 1819	do	70	
Gordon Griffin	do	96 00	1508 76	do	Nov. 15, 1820	do	80	
James Hines	do	96 00	1110 81	Virginia line	Feb. 13, 1819	July 10, 1818	80	Died Feb. 4, 1830.
John Hasty	do	96 00	724 69	do	Feb. 12, 1819	July 15, 1818	73	Died February 2, 1826.
Mark Love	do	96 00	1194 40	South Carolina line	Sep. 15, 1819	June 22, 1819	68	Died November 30, 1831.
John Mulberry	do	96 00	1429 03	Virginia line	Ap'l 9, 1819	June 17, 1818	79	
Michael Moore	do	96 00	1524 76	do	Ap'l 7, 1819	do	74	
William Purvis	do	96 00	889 66	do	Ap'l 9, 1819	do	77	Dropped under act May 1, 1820. Restored commencing August 17, 1826.
Matthew Petit	do	96 00	1420 76	Penn. line	Apr. 6, 1819	do	74	
Elisha Sorrell	do	96 00	678 05	Virginia line	Ap'l 9, 1819	do	71	Died July 9, 1825.

Statement, &c. of Boone county, Kentucky.

NAMES.	Rank.	Annual allowance.	Sums received.	Description of service.	When placed on the pension roll.	Commencement of pension.	Ages.	Laws under which they were formerly inscribed on the pension roll; and remarks.
Isham Allen	Private	96 00	426 40	Virginia line	Oct. 21, 1823	Sep. 24, 1823	70	Transferred from Virginia from April 7, 1828, from Mar. 4, 1828.
James Burns	do	96 00	1461 32	Pennsylvania line	May 13, 1819	June 15, 1818	80	
Asa Beech	do	96 00	919 73	Connecticut line	Ap'l 15, 1819	Aug. 6, 1818	84	
Richard Butler	do	96 00	511 74	New Jersey line	Jan. 4, 1823	Oct. 2, 1830	70	Died January 31, 1826.
Jacob Bruner	do	96 00	989 41	do	Jan. 22, 1824	Nov. 15, 1823	75	
William Brady	do	96 00	788 38	S. Carolina line	Ap'l 6, 1826	Dec. 19, 1825	76	
Joseph Barlow	do	96 00	593 03	Virginia line	Sep. 6, 1830	Jan. 1, 1828	74	
Jeremiah Haden	do	96 00	1520 23	do	July 7, 1819	May 5, 1818	72	
Alexander McPherson	do	96 00	416 66	Pennsylvania line	Ap'l 21, 1819	Sep. 26, 1818	82	Dropped May 22,1829. Restored from December 26, 1829. Died November 18, 1832.
Zachariah Reed	do	96 00	105 03	Georgia line	June 8, 1820	Feb. 1, 1819	57	Suspended under act of May 1, 1820.
Samuel Stribling	do	96 00	1423 99	Virginia line	July 7, 1819	May 5, 1818	92	
John Taylor	do	96 00	96 00	Maryland line	May 21, 1819	Ap'l 22, 1818	84	Transferred from Virginia from March 4, 1833.
Thomas Vance	do	96 00	1496 25	New Jersey line	Nov. 23, 1818	Aug. 4, 1818	73	

Statement, &c. of Bourbon county, Kentucky.

NAMES.	Rank.	Annual allowance.	Sums received.	Description of service.	When placed on the pension roll.	Commencement of pension	Ages	Laws under which they were formerly inscribed on the pension roll; and remarks.
Samuel Butterton	Private	96 00	1,328 61	Virginia line	May 7, 1819	Aug. 11, 1818	76	Died June 12, 1833.
Elijah Barbey	do	96 00	1,411 04	do	Ap'l 15, 1819	Aug. 14, 1818	76	Died April 24, 1833.
Thomas Bates	do	96 00	1,420 38	do	Aug. 11, 1819	Aug. 19, 1818	79	
James Busby	do	96 00	1,514 64	do	Jan. 6, 1819	May 25, 1818	78	
Peter Cockerel	do	96 00	771 64	do	Ap'l 16, 1819	Aug. 22, 1818	75	
William Dawson	do	96 00	304 30	Pennsylvania line	Mar. 29, 1819	July 2, 1818	96	
John Drebuler	do	96 00	1,494 44	Maryland line	June 7, 1819	Aug. 11, 1818	83	
Joseph Humphreys	do	96 00	1,514 83	Pennsylvania line	Sep. 21, 1819	May 25, 1819	66	
John Jameison	do	96 00	483 25	Virginia line	July 1, 1820	Dec. 8, 1819	82	
Benson Kendrick	do	96 00	937 80	do	June 23, 1819	May 29, 1818	76	
Thomas Kelly	do	96 00	325 67	Pennsylvania line	Oct. 2, 1819	May 10, 1818	84	Died December 30, 1822.
John Miller	do	96 00	689 66	South Carolina line	Feb. 15, 1819	June 17, 1818	73	Died August 23, 1825.
James Pritchett	do	96 00	157 15	Virginia line	Feb. 13, 1819	July 16, 1818	58	Dropped under act May 1, 1820.
Robert Pater	do	96 00	750 45	Pennsylvania line	Ap'l 15, 1818	Ap'l 1, 1818	76	Died January 25, 1826.
Nathaniel Raine	do	96 00	547 43	Virginia line	June 5, 1820	Nov. 22, 1819	77	
Edward Stoker	do	96 00	501 25	do	Ap'l 14, 1819	June 17, 1818	77	Suspended under act May 1, 1820. Restored, commencing September 3, 1830.
John Terrill	do	96 00	385 83	Pennsylvania line	July 2, 1819	Aug. 29, 1818	81	
Isham Talbot	do	96 00	941 93	Virginia line	July 18, 1823	May 13, 1823	75	
John Whittington	do	96 00	350 78	Delaware line	Sep. 6, 1819	Jan. 15, 1819	86	Died September 9, 1822.
Benjamin Williams	do	96 00	1,494 19	Maryland line	do	Aug. 12, 1818	72	

Statement, &c. of Bracken county, Kentucky.

NAMES.	Rank.	Annual allowance.	Sums received.	Description of service.	When placed on the pension roll.	Commencement of pension.	Ages.	Laws under which they were formerly inscribed, on the pension roll ; and remarks.
Michael Dean	Private	96 00	1,232 79	Virginia line	Mar. 18, 1819	Nov. 2, 1818	94	
Andrew Dilman	do	96 00	135 99	Pennsylvania line	Nov. 15, 1820	Oct. 5, 1818	67	Dropped under act of May 1, 1820
Joseph Franklin	do	96 00	1117 15	Virginia line	Mar. 18, 1819	May 11, 1818	73	Died Dec. 30, 1829.
William Jaco	do	96 00	829 93	do	Aug. 2, 1821	July 13, 1818	98	
Nathaniel G. Morris	Captain	240 00	1,280 64	do	Mar. 18, 1819	May 4, 1818	76	Died Sept. 15, 1824.
Thomas Moore	Private	96 00	653 37	do	Mar. 18, 1819	May 2, 1818	84	Died August 18, 1825.
George Maines	do	96 00	478 40	do	Dec. 16, 1828	Nov. 16, 1828	84	Died November 9, 1833.
John T. Thomas	do	06 00	1,187 08	Lee's legion	Mar. 18, 1819	May 4, 1828	74	Suspended under act of May 1, 1820. Restr'd from Aug.23,1825.

Statement, &c. of Breckenridge county, Kentucky.

NAMES.	Rank.	Annual allowance.	Sums received.	Description of service.	When placed on the pension roll.	Commencement of pension.	Ages.	Laws under which they were formerly inscribed on the pension roll ; and remarks.
Obadiah Bassham	Private	96 00	1,159 62	Virginia line	Apr. 14, 1819	July 25, 1818	74	Suspended. Restored from Sept. 17, 1823.
Edward Dehaven	do	96 00	1,530 57	Pennsylvania line	Oct. 26, 1822	Mar 19, 1818	82	Suspended under act of May 1, 1820.
Samuel Fate	do	96 00	162 00	do	Oct. 3, 1818	June 27, 1818	64	
John Goatley	do	96 00	154 83	Virginia line	Sept. 9, 1819	July 25, 1818		Suspended under act of May 1, 1820.
George Pullim	do	96 00	1,498 83	do	Sept. 9, 1819	July 25, 1818	75	Restored, commencing May 2, 1828.
Jacob Weatherhall	do	96 00	692 12	do	Feb. 15, 1820	Oct. 23, 1818	75	
James Wells	do	96 00	1,497 27	do	Jan. 16, 1922	Apr. 20, 1819	74	

Statement, &c. of Bullitt county, Kentucky.

NAMES.	Rank.	Annual allowance.	Sums received.	Description of service.	When placed on the pension roll.	Commencement of pension.	Ages.	Laws under which they were formerly inscribed on the pension roll; and remarks.
John Buzan -	Private	96 00	1259 89	Virginia line	Sep. 17, 1819	July 21, 1819	79	Dropped July 19, 1820. Reinstated May 26, 1821.
William Cornwell -	do	96 00	1259 38	New York line	Oct. 2, 1819	July 23, 1819	73	
John Edens -	do	96 00	512 59	S. Carolina line	Feb. 10, 1819	Sep. 21, 1818	77	Died Jan 23, 1826.
Henry Field -	do	96 00	484 12	Virginia line	do	May 12, 1818	74	Died May 27, 1823.
John Goldsmith -	do	96 00	30 96	do	July 30, 1825	July 4, 1825	68	Died October 30, 1825.
Eppa Hubbard -	Sergeant	96 00	1100 49	do	Mar. 14, 1820	Mar. 27, 1819	73	Died September 12, 1830.
Isaac Johnson -	Private	96 00	1493 41	do	Aug. 28, 1819	June 1, 1818	85	Died October 21, 1833.
Henry Isbell -	do	96 00	559 16	do	Aug. 13, 1818	June 8, 1818	75	
Charles Langsdon -	do	96 00	1098 89	do	May 6, 1820	Sep. 24, 1819	72	
Joseph Lloyd -	do	96 00	832 25	do	July 30, 1825	July 4, 1825	73	
Charles McMannis -	do	96 00	821 93	do	Sept. 9, 1819	July 9, 1819	69	Died January 31, 1828.

Statement, &c. of Butler county, Kentucky.

NAMES.	Rank.	Annual allowance.	Sums received.	Description of service.	When placed on the pension roll.	Commencement of pension.	Ages.	Laws under which they were formerly inscribed on the pension roll; and remarks.
Peter Brown -	do	96 00	1016 32	do	Mar. 5, 1819	Apr'l 12, 1818	69	Died September 20, 1833.
Abraham Lindsay -	do	96 00	634 06	do	Dec. 10, 1827	July 28, 1827		

Statement, &c. of Caldwell county, Kentucky.

NAMES.	Rank.	Annual allowance.	Sums received.	Description of service.	When placed on the pension roll.	Commencement of pension.	Ages.	Laws under which they were formerly inscribed on the pension roll; and remarks.
Justinian Cartwright -	Sergeant	96 00	1,377 86	Virginia line	June 5, 1819	Apl. 27, 1819	73	Died September 27, 1832.
William Farmer -	Private	96 00	51 09	N. Carolina line	Sept. 28, 1818	Aug. 24, 1818	•	Suspended under act of May 1, 1820.
Aaron Freeman -	do	96 00	224 47	do	Oct. 29, 1819	July 26, 1819	77	Died November 26, 1821.
William Gholson -	Sergeant	96 00	1,514 83	Virginia line	Sep. 18, 1819	May 25, 1818	76	
James Jennings -	Private	96 00	1,370 89	S. Carolina line	May 23, 1819	Nov. 24, 1818	79	
Matthew Lyon -	Lieutenant	240 00	965 82	N. Hampshire line	Apl. 20, 1819	Aug. 24, 1818	85	Died August 1, 1822.
William Porter -	do	240 00	1,848 53	Virginia line	Aug. 2, 1820	Aug. 24, 1820	71	Died January 6, 1828.
Henry Thomas -	Private	96 00	624 00	do	Nov. 24, 1818	May 26, 1819	77	Transferred from West Tennessee, commencing September 4, 1827.
Elijah Veach -	do	96 00	1,514 83	do	June 30, 1818	May 25, 1818	79	
Thomas Williams -	do	96 00	645 06	Delaware line	June 28, 1819	Sep. 29, 1818	84	
Peter Waterfield -	do	96 00	596 90	Virginia line	Jan. 10, 1828	Dec. 17, 1827	73	Died June 17, 1825.

Statement, &c. of Callaway county, Kentucky.

NAMES.	Rank.	Annual allowance.	Sums received.	Description of services.	When placed on the pension roll.	Commencement of pension.	Ages.	Laws under which they were formerly inscribed on the pension roll; and remarks.
Benjamin Bridges -	Private	96 00	661 86	N. Carolina line	June 30, 1818	May 25, 1818	80	Died December 17, 1824.

4

Statement, &c. of Campbell county, Kentucky.

NAMES.	Rank.	Annual allowance.	Sums received.	Description of service.	When placed on the pension roll.	Commencement of pension.	Ages.	Laws under which they were formerly inscribed on the pension roll; and remarks.
Ransom Allphin	Private	96 00	185 86	Virginia line	July 30, 1831	July 30, 1831	84	Dead
Samuel Davis	do	96 00	530 12	do	Sep. 16, 1819	Apr. 27, 1818	98	
John Keen	do	96 00	994 32	do	Dec. 19, 1823	Oct. 27, 1823	74	
Benjamin Maren	do	96 00	165 29	do	Mar. 14, 1820	June 15, 1818	74	Dropped July 16, 1821.
James Marston	do	96 00	932 12	N. Hampshire line	Sep. 16, 1819	May 1, 1818	83	Died January 16, 1828.
John Massey, or Mercy	do	96 00	721 06	Armand's legion	May 16, 1823	Mar. 1, 1823	73	
Jacob Mefford	do	96 00	918 96	Maryland line	Mar. 26, 1825	Aug. 9, 1824	70	
James Perkings	do	96 00	743 43	New York line	June 19, 1826	June 7, 1826	75	
James White	do	96 00	238 73	Virginia line	Mar. 12, 1830	Mar. 10, 1830	89	

Statement, &c. of Casey county, Kentucky.

NAMES.	Rank.	Annual allowance.	Sums received.	Description of service.	When placed on the pension roll.	Commencement of pension.	Ages.	Laws under which they were formerly inscribed on the pension roll; and remarks.
James Clark	Private	96 00	242 77	Virginia line	July 21, 1819	Feb. 23, 1819	73	Died July 12, 1832.
Jacob Coffman	do	96 00	1,178 36	Maryland line	Jan. 11, 1822	Nov. 26, 1821	73	
Jacob Havely	do	96 00	1,474 57	do	Jan. 13, 1823	Aug. 11, 1818	70	Dead.
Andrew Hogue	do	96 00	291 88	North Carolina line	Mar. 2, 1831	Feb. 19, 1831	83	
William Jones	do	96 00	743 43	Virginia line	July 7, 1825	June 7, 1825	84	
Thomas Morrow	do	96 00	1,151 74	Pennsylvania line	Ap'l 5, 1820	Sep. 1, 1818	79	Died August 30, 1830.
Jonathan M'Connell	Lieutenant	240 00	2,608 45	N. Hampshire line	Dec. 14, 1819	Nov. 28, 1818	81	Died May 10, 1829.
Jacob Minor	Private	96 00	395 35	Virginia line	Jan. 23, 1830	Jan. 23, 1830	75	
John Skéen	do	96 00	1,153 31	North Carolina line	Ap'l 15, 1820	Aug. 31, 1818	76	

Statement, &c. of Christian county, Kentucky.

NAMES.	Rank.	Annual allowance.	Sums received.	Description of service.	When placed on the pension roll.	Commencement of pension.	Ages.	Laws under which they were formerly inscribed on the pension roll; and remarks.
Henry Brewer -	Private	96 00	1,082 82	N. Carolina line	Mar. 31, 1820	July 5, 1819	74	Suspended under act May 1, 1820. Restored from July 25, 1823.
John Carter .	do	96 00	482 86	Pennsylvania line	May 18, 1819	Aug. 25, 1818	70	
John Conner .	do	96 00	465 31	Col. Armand's corps	Dec. 4, 1818	Oct. 31, 1818	81	
Absalom Nixon .	do	96 00	110 70	S. Carolina line	Jan. 26, 1833	Jan. 10, 1833	82	
Thomas Woolsey .	do	96 00	1,414 96	Virginia line	May 18, 1820	July 9, 1819		
Robert Warner -	do	96 00	763 35	do	Feb. 16, 1822	Sep. 1, 1819	68	Died August 13, 1827.

Statement, &c. of Clarke county, Kentucky.

NAMES.	Rank.	Annual allowance.	Sums received.	Description of service.	When placed on the pension roll.	Commencement of pension.	Ages.	Laws under which they were formerly inscribed on the pension roll; and remarks.
Seth Botts	Private	96 00	889 86	Virginia line	Jan. 26, 1819	June 27, 1818	81	Died September 3, 1827.
John Dunn	do	96 00	640 51	do	Ap'l 3, 1819	July 3, 1818	85	
Elisha Eastis	do	96 00	1530 36	do	July 21, 1819	June 26, 1818	82	
John Fletcher	do	96 00	1515 43	do	Ap'l 3, 1819	June 22, 1818	85	
William Foster	do	96 00	171 43	do	Feb. 11, 1819	do	73	Dropped under act of May 1, 1820.
John Hathpenny, alias Halfpenny	do	96 00	465 56	Connecticut line	Ap'l 1, 1819	Ap'l 29, 1818	82	
Martin Johnston	do	96 00	179 96	Virginia line	Mar. 31, 1819	June 20, 1818	63	Dead.
Price Key	Corporal	96 00	1069 93	Pennsylvania line	Nov. 25, 1819	May 23, 1818	75	Died July 14, 1829.
Benjamin Lockett	Private	96 00	1523 09	Virginia line	July 22, 1819	June 23, 1818	71	
John Martin	do	96 00	1480 25	do	June 19, 1820	Oct. 4, 1818	74	
William Martin	do	96 00	137 83	do	June 4, 1819	Sep. 28, 1818	77	
Tho:nas Melton, or Milton	do	96 00	1505 29	do	Oct. 10, 1820	June 30, 1818	84	
John Pool	do	96 00	726 38	New Jersey line	June 3, 1819	Aug. 5, 1818	76	Died February 20, 1826.
John Sidebottom	do	96 00	79 22	Virginia line	July 8, 1819	May 8, 1819	70	Dropped under act of May 1, 1820.
Drury Scott	do	96 00	995 35	do	Oct. 26, 1820	Oct. 23, 1819	74	
James Wilson	do	96 00	970 57	Maryland line	June 9, 1824	Jan. 26, 1824	71	

Statement, &c. of Clay county, Kentucky.

NAMES.	Rank.	Annual allowance.	Sums received.	Description of service.	When placed on the pension roll.	Commencement of pension.	Ages.	Laws under which they were formerly inscribed on the pension roll; and remarks.
William Jacobs	Private	96 00	1476 38	Virginia line	May 31, 1819	Oct. 19, 1818	79	
Jacob Seaborn	do	96 00	1484 76	do	May 12, 1819	Sep. 17, 1818	71	
Samuel Wood	do	96 00	293 66	Maryland line	Sep. 14, 1819	July 5, 1819	75	Died December 13, 1825.

Statement, &c. of Cumberland county, Kentucky.

NAMES.	Rank.	Annual allowance.	Sums received.	Description of service.	When placed on the pension roll.	Commencement of pension.	Ages.	Laws under which they were formerly inscribed on the pension roll; and remarks.
Lawrence Conner -	Private	96 00	720 91	Virginia line	July 7, 1820	Sep. 14, 1818	73	Died March 17, 1826.
John Monroe -	do	96 00	1,518 63	do	Oct. 22, 1819	June 9, 1818	79	
James Maccoun -	do	96 00	191 19	do	Jan. 24, 1824	Sept. 8, 1823	9?	
William Rowe -	do	96 00	645 28	do	Dec. 27, 1820	June 9, 1818	78	Died February 26, 1825.

Statement, &c. of Estill county, Kentucky.

NAMES.	Rank.	Annual allowance.	Sums received.	Description of service.	When placed on the pension roll.	Commencement of pension.	Ages.	Laws under which they were formerly inscribed on the pension roll; and remarks.
James Best	Private	96 00	1,538 74	Virginia line	Feb. 12, 1819	Feb. 23, 1818	73	
Tandy Hartman	do	96 00	1,483 43	do	May 12, 1819	Sep. 22, 1818	84	Died Aug. 10, 1823.
Thomas Harris	do	96 00	1,336 02	do	May 19, 1819	Oct. 5, 1818	63	
Israel Meadows	do	96 00	859 46	do	May 12, 1819	Sep. 22, 1818	78	
James McChristy	do	96 00	321 80	do	Jan. 2, 1828	Oct. 29, 1827	74	
Zachariah Phillips	do	96 00	361 83	N. Carolina line	May 29, 1830	May 29, 1830	71	
William Styvers	do	96 00	1,479 73	Virginia line	Feb. 12, 1819	Oct. 6, 1818	78	
Lawrence Ward	do	96 00	1,038 07	do	July 10, 1819	April 20, 1819	84	Died February 11, 1830.

Statement, &c. of Fayette county, Kentucky.

Names.	Rank,	Annual allowance.	Sums received.	Description of service:	When placed on the pension roll.	Commencement of pension.	Age.	Laws under which they were formerly inscribed on the pension roll; and remarks.
David Allen	Private	96 00	569 03	N. Hampshire line	Apr. 18, 1818	Apl. 1, 1818	79	Dropped under act May 1, 1820. Restored commencing from August 4, 1833.
William Adams, 2d	Fifer	96 00	590 66	New York line	Mar. 29, 1819	July 10, 1818	66	
William Barker	Private	96 00	146 83	Maryland line	Dec. 23, 1818	Aug. 25, 1818	61	Dropped under act May 1, 1820.
James Ball	do	96 00	1137 03	Virginia line	Sep. 19, 1818	May 1, 1818	83	
Frederick Coons	do	96 00	1177 83	do	Ap'l 26, 1819	May 29, 1818		
Robert Craige	Lieut.	240 00	3683 91	Penn. line	Sep. 19, 1818	Ap'l 29, 1818	78	
Obadiah Carter	Private	96 00	173 03	Virginia line	July 7, 1819	June 16, 1818	65	
Charles Cullin	do	96 00	485 82	do	Oct. 10, 1818	May 27, 1818	87	Suspended under act May 1, 1820.
William Christian	do	96 00	101 44	do	July 7, 1819	Aug. 15, 1818	62	Died June 17, 1823.
Adrian Davenport	do	96 00	1503 73	Maryland line	May 21, 1819	July 6, 1818	76	Suspended under act May 1, 1820.
James Fletcher	do	96 00	1291 69	Virginia line	June 5, 1820	Sep. 21, 1819	69	Died June 18, 1833.
Isaac Farrell	do	96 00	1400 48	do	Feb. 9, 1828	Feb. 3, 1828	70	
William Hicks	do	96 00	425 59	do	Mar. 5, 1819	June 15, 1818	82	Died November 20, 1822.
Jonathan Howell	do	96 00	866 06	New Jersey line	Nov. 17, 1818	May 11, 1818	70	Died May 18, 1827.
Daniel Hickey	do	96 00	1490 83	Penn. line	Oct. 22, 1819	Aug. 25, 1818	84	
Fielding Jeter	do	96 00	1515 96	Virginia line	June 9, 1820	June 20, 1818	72	
Littleton Jeter	do	96 00	502 70	do	Dec. 11, 1828	Dec. 10, 1828	80	
Christopher McGraw	Drummer	96 00	941 93	Maryland line	Oct. 18, 1819	May 13, 1818	74	
Hiram Mitchell	Private	96 00	170 89	U. States Navy	Dec. 7, 1818	June 24, 1818	63	Dropped February 14, 1822.
Daniel M'Vay	do	96 00	1202 06	Virginia line	Dec. 23, 1818	Aug. 28, 1818	86	
William Miles	do	96 00	170 36	do	Feb. 13, 1819	June 26, 1818	71	Suspended under act May 1, 1820.
James Murray	do	96 00	1387 96	New Jersey line	Oct. 26, 1822	Sep. 20, 1819	73	
John Nelson	Ensign	240 00	2363 24	Virginia line	Nov. 4, 1818	Ap'l 30, 1818	71	Off under act May 15, 1828.
Isaac Nailor	Private	96 00	170 06	do	July 12, 1819	May 28, 1818	70	Dead.
Charles Norwood	do	96 00	63 51	do	Jan. 7, 1831	Jan. 7, 1831	78	Dead.
Byrd Prewitt	do	96 00	113 54	do	Jan. 11, 1832	Dec. 30, 1831	80	
Christopher Reilly	do	96 00	1027 35	Penn. line	Sep. 19, 1818	May 1, 1818	74	
Hugh Rankin	do	96 00	67 43	do	Feb. 11, 1819	June 22, 1818	66	Died January 13, 1829.

NAMES.	Rank.	Annual allowance.	Sums received.	Description of service.	When placed on the pension roll.	Commencement of pension.	Ages.	Laws under which they were formerly inscribed on the pension roll; and remarks.
George Shindlebowe	do	96 00	139 43	Virginia line	May 6, 1819	Sep. 22, 1818	63	Suspended under act May 1, 1820.
William Sharp, 2d	do	96 00	1397 41	do	April 15, 1819	Aug. 15, 1819	73	Died September 20, 1833.
John Stephens	do	96 00	147 09	do	do	Aug. 24, 1818	62	Dropped under act May 1, 1820.
Reuben Stiver	Musician	96 00	906 39	Penn. line	Feb. 13, 1819	June 17, 1818	76	Died November 25, 1827.
Arthur Shannon	Private	96 00	739 09	Virginia line	Oct. 21, 1818	May 18, 1818	71	Died January 29, 1826.
James Vaughan	do	96 00	1513 03	do	May 24, 1819	July 1, 1818	89	
Nathan White	do	96 00	1509 29	do	July 7, 1819	June 15, 1818	82	
John Wingate	do	96 00	712 15	do	Mar. 16, 1826	Feb. 14, 1826	73	
John York	do	96 00	1496 51	do	Sep. 23, 1818	Aug. 3, 1818	82	
John Yount	do	96 00	339 06	Penn. line	Nov. 10, 1821	Feb. 22, 1819	-	Dead.

Statement, &c. of Fleming county, Kentucky.

NAMES.	Rank.	Annual allowance.	Sums received.	Description of service.	When placed on the pension roll.	Commencement of pension.	Ages.	Laws under which they were formerly inscribed on the pension roll; and remarks.
Edward Bavor	Sergeant	96 00	814 18	New York line	May 13, 1819	July 20, 1818	65	Died January 12, 1826.
William Boyd	Private	96 00	989 87	Washington life guards	Oct. 13, 1821	Sep. 8, 1818	74	Died December 30, 1828.
William Combes	Sergeant	96 00	1,508 76	Virginia line	June 29, 1819	June 17, 1818	77	Died January 21, 1828.
John Collins	Private	96 00	903 99	do	Ap'l 16, 1819	Aug. 22, 1818	70	Susp'd under act of May 1, 1820.
William Davis	do	96 00	143 16	do	May 17, 1819	Sep. 8, 1818	60	
William Estell	do	96 00	1,513 03	Pennsylvania line	May 22, 1820	June 1, 1818	72	
John Finley	Briga. maj.	240 00	360 00	do	Jan. 13, 1820	Oct. 7, 1819	80	Transferred from ——, Penn.; commencing from June 13, 1826.
Benjamin Hennis	Private	96 00	1,498 83	Maryland line	Sept. 18, 1819	July 25, 1818	74	
Philip Helphinstine	do	96 00	1,251 35	Virginia line	July 24, 1821	Oct. 2, 1819	77	Died October 14, 1831.
Peter Kendall	do	96 00	625 96	do	May 17, 1819	Sep. 12, 1818	58	Dropped July 16, 1821. Reinstated February 23, 1822. Died March 19, 1825.
Thomas McAtinney	do	96 00	305 27	Pennsylvania line	June 5, 1820	Dec. 6, 1819	72	Died February 9, 1823.
Guion McKee	do	96 00	910 58	do	Sep. 18, 1819	June 15, 1818	77	Died December 9, 1827.
William McCullough	do	96 00	1,102 36	Maryland line	June 5, 1820	Sep. 11, 1818	78	
George Muse	do	96 00	878 16	Virginia line	Oct. 6, 1820	June 4, 1818	73	Died July 27, 1827.
Alexander McCoy	do	96 00	310 96	Pennsylvania line	Jan. 6, 1826	Dec. 9, 1825	82	
William Stoker	do	96 00	1,073 59	Virginia line	Sept. 18, 1819	June 29, 1818	79	
Samuel Strahan	do	96 00	646 93	Pennsylvania line	June 20, 1822	Sep. 7, 1818	73	Died June 2, 1825.
Andrew Wilson	do	96 00	563 12	do	May 23, 1820	Oct. 23, 1818	74	

Statement, &c. of Floyd county, Kentucky.

NAMES.	Rank.	Annual allowance.	Sums received.	Description of service.	When placed on the pension roll.	Commencement of pension.	Ages.	Laws under which they were inscribed on the pension roll; and remarks.
Joseph Bouney	Private	96 00	674 63	Virginia line	July 3, 1820	Ap'l 24, 1819	74	Died May 3, 1826.
Richard Caines	do	96 00	123 96	do	June 22, 1819	Nov. 20, 1818	66	Suspended under act May 1, 1820.
Pleasant Childres	do	96 00	887 48	N. Carolina line	Feb. 10, 1825	Dec. 7, 1824	71	Suspended. Restored from Aug.
William Furguson	do	96 00	1,090 30	Pennsylvania line	May 23, 1820	May 20, 1818	79	11, 1824.
Garner Hopkins	do	96 00	964 41	New York line	Sep. 22, 1819	July 12, 1819	82	Suspended. Restored from Jan. 12, 1824. Died June 4, 1832.
William Haney	do	96 00	650 83	Virginia line	July 21, 1826	May 25, 1826	76	Died February 19, 1825.
Gabriel Jones	do	96 00	1,332 67	N. Carolina line	Sep. 28, 1819	Oct. 18, 1818	108	Died June 12, 1833.
Roby Jacobs	do	96 00	608 77	Virginia line	Sep. 6, 1820	Oct. 19, 1818	72	Suspended. Restored from April 26, 1824.
Ambrose Jones	do	96 00	730 93	do	Dec. 12, 1825	Nov. 2, 1825	73	
Thomas Murray	do	96 00	1,118 48	Pennsylvania line	May 23, 1820	May 20, 1818	80	
John Mullens	do	96 00	1,034 57	Virginia line	Sep. 10, 1823	May 26, 1823	76	Suspended. Restored Novem. 4, 1824. Died August 6, 1832.
Nathan Preston	do	96 00	915 32	do	May 31, 1819	May 20, 1818	71	
Moses Preston	do	96 00	722 59	do	May 29, 1820	June 16, 1818	72	Suspended. Restored from June 14, 1828.
Cudbeth Stone	do	96 00	1,078 22	Maryland line	June 10, 1819	Oct. 21, 1818	62	Dropped under act May 1, 1820. Restored April 26, 1824.
John Smith 3d	do	96 00	666 83	Virginia line	June 10, 1824	Mar. 25, 1823	88	Died November 1, 1829.
Peter Sullivan	do	96 00	841 03	do	June 20, 1825	June 1, 1825	82	
Alexander Young	do	96 00	155 86	S. Carolina line	Nov. 27, 1819	July 21, 1818	75	Dropped under act May 1, 1820.

Statement, &c. of Franklin county, Kentucky.

NAMES.	Rank.	Annual allowance.	Sums received.	Description of service.	When placed on the pension roll.	Commencement of pension.	Ages.	Laws under which they were formerly inscribed on the pension roll; and remarks.
William Bond	Private	96 00	98 57	Virginia line	May 6, 1826	Mar. 13, 1826	94	Died March 22, 1827.
John Casey	do	96 00	1,499 86	do	April 14, 1819	July 21, 1818	71	
Joseph Cavender	do	96 00	763 60	do	May 12, 1819	Aug. 31, 1818	67	Died August 13, 1826.
Matthew Cummings	do	96 00	1,020 19	do	Feb. 3, 1819	Nov. 13, 1818	84	Dropped March 10, 1821. Rest'd from November 11, 1823.
Bernard Clemons	do	96 00	1,317 29	do	Aug. 2, 1819	June 15, 1819	79	
John Curtcher	do	96 00	650 89	do	Nov. 30, 1827	May 24, 1827	70	
John Hollis	do	96 00	331 60	Pennsylvania line	Dec. 31, 1823	July 14, 1823	90	Died December 27, 1826.
John Long	do	96 00	52 58	Virginia line	Sept. 6, 1819	July 22, 1819	69	Died Feb. 7, 1820.
Mechack Pearson	do	96 00	361 03	do	July 19, 1819	Mar. 1, 1819	80	Suspended under act May 1, 1820. Restored from June 4, 1831.
Virgil Poe	do	30 00	201 00	do	July 16, 1812	Sep. 23, 1811	-	Invalid Pensioner. Relin. for the benefit of the act Mar. 18, 1818. July 5, 1812.
Do	do	96 00	1,518 96	do	July 10, 1820	May 9, 1818	76	Suspen'd under act May 1, 1820. Restored from June 25, 1824.
George Richards	do	96 00	301 47	do	Feb. 10, 1819	July 10, 1818	84	Died Aug. 15, 1827.
Henry Roberts	do	96 00	303 22	do	Jan. 8, 1831	Jan. 8, 1831	76	Dropped April 21, 1821.
John Roberts	Surgeon	240 00	374 19	do	June 21, 1819	Aug. 14, 1818	74	Died March 7, 1829.
John S. Satterwhite	Private	96 00	1,012 38	do	May 12, 1819	Aug. 22, 1818	79	Dropped under act May 1, 1820. Restored from Jan. 12, 1823.
Medley Shelton	do	96 00	1,085 02	do	Nov. 25, 1819	Oct. 25, 1819	74	
John Story (R.)	do	96 00	1,507 43	do	June 5, 1820	June 22, 1818	72	
Charles Tyler	do	96 00	1,067 81	do	Aug. 9, 1819	July 20, 1818	76	Suspen'd under act May 1, 1820. Restored from Sep. 6, 1824.

5

Statement, &c. of Gallatin county, Kentucky.

NAMES.	Rank.	Annual allowance.	Sums received.	Description of service.	When placed on the pension roll.	Commencement of pension.	Ages.	Laws under which they were formerly inscribed on the pension roll; and remarks.
Henry Carter	Private	96 00	1487 96	Virginia line	Dec. 26, 1818	Nov. 5, 1818	83	Suspended under act of May 1, 1820. Restored from Nov. 20, 1823.
James Coghill	do	96 00	1110 93	- do	May 25, 1820	Nov. 16, 1819	76	
David Driskell	do	96 00	1037 79	N. Carolina line	July 3, 1820	do	71	Suspended under act of May 1, 1820. Restored from September 2, 1823.
Henry Eaton	Sergeant	96 00	168 82	Pennsylvania line	Sept.20, 1827	Sep. 4, 1827	95	Died June 7, 1829.
Job Garvey	Private	96 00	130 57	Virginia line	Sept. 17, 1819	Oct. 26, 1818	60	Suspended under act of May 1, 1820.
Thomas Hardin	do	96 00	1250 60	do	Apl. 10, 1821	Aug. 26, 1819	74	
Thomas Lester	do	96 00	794 09	do	Jan. 2, 1827	Nov. 27, 1826	77	
Darby McGannon	Corporal	96 00	146 32	Pennsylvania line	Dec. 13, 1819	Aug. 27, 1818	69	Suspended under act of May 1, 1820.
Alexander McDowell	Sergeant	96 00	1395 09	do	Feb. 12, 1819	Aug. 24, 1818	79	
William McIntire	Private	96 00	489 08	Virginia line	Dec. 24, 1818	do	79	Suspended under act of May 1, 1820. Restored from August 9, 1826.
David Severn	do	96 00	381 05	Washington's li'e gua	May 28, 1819	Ap'l 23, 1818	74	Died April 11, 1823.
John Short	do	96 00	599 22	Virginia line	Jan. 7, 1828	Dec. 8, 1827	74	
Cyrus Tubbs	do	96 00	1190 19	Conn. line	Dec. 11, 1821	Oct. 12, 1821	74	

Statement, &c. of Garrard county, Kentucky.

NAMES.	Rank.	Annual allowance.	Sums received.	Description of service.	When placed on the pension roll.	Commencement of pension.	Ages.	Laws under which they were formerly inscribed on the pension roll; and remarks.
John Bryant	Sergeant	96 00	1490 57	Virginia line	Aug. 11, 1819	Aug. 26, 1818	83	Died Sept. 18, 1898.
John Brady	Private	96 00	938 66	do	Mar. 5, 1819	Nov. 21, 1818	-	
John Bryant	do	96 00	981 41	do	Jan. 13, 1824	Dec. 15, 1823	72	
John Clark	do	96 00	1057 03	do	July 7, 1823	Mar. 1, 1823	78	
Thomas Diddleston	do	96 00	923 92	do	April 21, 1820	Sept. 25, 1818	84	Died May 9, 1828.
Mark Goolsbury	do	96 00	1400 77	do	Dec. 7, 1820	Aug. 2, 1819	83	
William Hicks	Corporal	96 00	429 16	do	Feb. 6, 1819	June 30, 1818	78	Died Dec. 19, 1822.
Samuel Hackney	Private	96 00	988 76	do	Jan. 1, 1824	Nov. 17, 1823	74	Died Feb. 19, 1831.
George Jackson	do	96 00	1120 88	do	Feb. 6, 1819	June 18, 1818	72	Died Jan. 25, 1827.
John Johnson, 4th	do	96 00	678 70	do	May 6, 1820	Dec. 31, 1819	79	Commenced June 17, 1823.
Daniel McCoy	do	96 00	1214 59	do	Oct. 17, 1818	Apr. 28, 1818	71	Suspended & restored June 17,1823.
Richard Powell	do	96 00	562 41	do	April 21, 1820	Sep 20, 1819	67	Died July 29, 1825.
Thomas Ramsay	do	96 00	843 09	do	Feb. 6, 1819	June 30, 1818	77	Dropped under act of May 1, 1820. Restored from Jan. 29, 1827.
George Small	do	96 00	1172 74	New York line	Mar. 5, 1819	Nov. 25, 1818	75	Died Feb. 11, 1831.
William Sims	do	96 00	810 88	Virginia line	do	do	71	Dropped under act of May 1, 1820. Restored May 19, 1823. Died July 19, 1830.
John Somerville	do	96 00	1244 64	Pennsylvania line	Feb. 5, 1819	May 18, 1818	77	Died May 4, 1831.
Thadeus H. Warmouth	do	96 00	631 27	Virginia line	do	Sep. 21, 1818	74	Dropped under act of May 1, 1820. Restored from Jan. 22, 1829.
John Webb	do	96 00	485 31	Maryland line	Mar. 3, 1828	Feb. 14, 1828	70	

Statement, &c. of Grant county, Kentucky.

NAMES.		Rank.	Annual allowance.	Sums received.	Description of service.	When placed on the pension roll.	Commencement of pension.	Ages.	Laws under which they were formerly inscribed on the pension roll ; and remarks.
Stephen Barker	-	Private	96 00	1502 89	New York line	May 17, 1819	Sep. 9, 1818	75	
Joseph Spencer	-	Captain	240 00	2699 99	Virginia line	Feb. 13, 1819	May 28, 1818	84	Died August 27, 1829.

Statement, &c. of Graves county, Kentucky.

NAMES.		Rank.	Annual allowance.	Sums received.	Description of service.	When placed on the pension list.	Commencement of pension.	Ages.	Laws under which they were formerly inscribed on the pension roll ; and remarks.
James Ross	-	Private	96 00	197 99	N. Carolina line	July 1, 1829	Feb. 7, 1829	78	Died February 27, 1831.

Statement, &c. of Grayson county, Kentucky.

NAMES.	Rank.	Annual allowance.	Sums received.	Description of service.	When placed on the pension roll.	Commencement of pension.	Ages.	Laws under which they were formerly inscribed on the pension roll ; and remarks.
Joseph Beatty -	Sergeant	96 00	380 38	Pennsylvania line	Dec. 13, 1823	Sep. 22, 1823	81	Died September 8, 1827.
Jonathan Bozworth -	Private	96 00	670 03	do	do	do	80	Died September 14, 1830.
Joseph Minns or Minzes	do	96 00	338 06	N. Carolina line	Aug. 28, 1830	Aug. 28, 1830		

Statement, &c. of Greene county, Kentucky.

NAMES.	Rank.	Annual allowance.	Sums received.	Description of service.	When placed on the pension roll.	Commencement of pension.	Ages.	Laws under which they were formerly inscribed on the pension roll; and remarks
Thomas Berry	Private	96 00	1159 24	Pennsylvania line	Oct. 1, 1819	Ap'l 28, 1818	82	Suspended. Restored from Dec. 15, 1823.
John Emerson	Lieut.	240 00	1169 75	Virginia line	July 21, 1819	do	82	Dropped under act of May 1, 1820. Restored from October 21, 1823, and dropped under act of May 15, 1828.
John Miles, 2d	Private	96 00	848 77	Maryland line	Sep. 22, 1819	May 2, 1818	94	Died March 17, 1827.
Larkin Minor	do	96 00	170 06	Virginia line	May 14, 1819	May 28, 1818	54	Dropped under act of May 1, 1820.
Jesse Puryear	do	96 00	1040 72	do	July 10, 1819	Ap'l 28, 1818	80	Suspended. Restored from Dec. 21, 1824.
Joshua Phipps	do	96 00	1514 83	do	June 25, 1819	May 25, 1818	89	Dropped—not continental.
John Reily, 2d	do	96 00	128 80	do	July 21, 1819	May 2, 1818	65	
Joshua Short	do	96 00	1514 06	do	May 14, 1819	May 28, 1818	82	
John S. Taylor	do	96 00	1185 86	do	July 21, 1819	Ap'l 28, 1818	76	
Joseph Timberlake	do	96 00	988 49	do	Dec. 12, 1822	Nov. 18, 1822	82	
Thomas Wright	do	96 00	938 83	do	Oct. 2, 1819	May 28, 1818	80	Suspended. Restored from March 2, 1826.

Statement, &c. of Greenup county, Kentucky.

NAMES.	Rank.	Annual allowance.	Sums received.	Description of service.	When placed on the pension roll.	Commencement of pension.	Ages.	Laws under which they were formerly inscribed on the pension roll; and remarks
Jeremiah Burns	Private	96 00	596 00	Virginia line	Dec. 9, 1818	July 28, 1818	72	Died October 13, 1824.
John Johnson, 2d	do	96 00	584 51	Conn. line	July 21, 1819	July 29, 1818	80	Died August 30, 1824.
Elisha Mayhew	do	96 00	121 30	Congress reg't	Oct. 13, 1818	do	-	Died November 2, 1816.
Godfrey Smith	do	96 00	34 32	Virginia line	May 11, 1820	Oct. 24, 1819	59	Suspended under act of May 1, 1820.
Andrew Zornes	do	96 00	1186 92	Pennsylvania line	Jan. 15, 1823	Ap'l 24, 1820	77	

Statement, &c. of Hamilton county, Kentucky.

NAMES.	Rank.	Annual allowance.	Sums received.	Description of service.	When placed on the pension roll.	Commencement of pension.	Ages.	Laws under which they were formerly inscribed on the pension roll; and remarks.
Patrick Leonard	Private	96 00	395 89	Pennsylvania line	June 23, 1819	June 27, 1818	82	Transferred from Ohio, from March 4, 1820. Died August 11, 1822.

Statement, &c. of Hardin county, Kentucky.

NAMES.	Rank.	Annual allowance.	Sums received.	Description of service.	When placed on the pension roll.	Commencement of pension.	Ages.	Laws under which they were formerly inscribed on the pension roll; and remarks.
Jonas Belknap	Private	96 60	387 79	Massachusetts line	June 25, 1819	May 27, 1818	76	Transferred from New York Mar. 4, 1820. Died February 16, 1824.
John Carson	do	96 00	575 46	South Carolina line	May 14, 1819	Sep. 7, 1818	87	
Jacob Flanders	do	96 00	1513 28	N. Hampshire line	Ap'l 28, 1820	June 30, 1818	74	
John How	Sergeant	96 00	749 51	Maryland line	May 18, 1819	Sep. 19, 1818	80	Dropped January 10, 1821. Restored March 1, 1824.
Samuel Haycraft, sen.	Private	96 00	307 99	Virginia line	Ap'l 30, 1822	June 20, 1820	80	
John McCandless	do	96 00	825 63	Pennsylvania line	June 3, 1820	June 27, 1818	72	Died February 2, 1827.
Charles Melton	do	96 00	843 86	Virginia line	Jan. 29, 1819	Nov. 20, 1818	78	Died February 9, 1830.
John Newton	do	96 00	1061 92	Maryland line	June 30, 1819	Jan. 19, 1819	74	
James State	do	96 00	1486 89	Virginia line	May 14, 1819	Sep. 9, 1818	77	
Solomon Turner	do	96 00	143 43	Maryland line	June 4, 1819	Sep. 7, 1818	60	Suspended under act of May 1, 1820
Isaac Vertrees	do	96 00	447 43	Pennsylvania line	Sep. 24, 1819	do	72	
Thomas Wilkins	do	96 00	1487 43	Virginia line	May 14, 1819	do	77	

Statement, &c. of Harrison county, Kentucky.

NAMES.	Rank.	Annual allowance.	Sums received.	Description of service.	When placed on the pension roll.	Commencement of pension	Ages.	Laws under which they were formerly inscribed on the pension roll; and remarks.
Elijah Abbot	Private	96 00	807 74	Virginia line	Oct. 17, 1825	Oct. 3, 1825	73	
John Barnes	do	96 00	1,406 44	do	May 28, 1819	July 11, 1818	78	
Moore Beggs	do	96 00	669 59	Pennsylvania line	Dec. 23, 1818	Sep. 14, 1818	92	Died April 22, 1825.
Archibald Casey	do	96 00	652 56	Delaware line	Nov. 27, 1820	July 6, 1818	75	Died August 10, 1823.
Jacob Henry	do	96 00	462 96	Pennsylvania line	May 28, 1819	Oct. 15, 1818	71	Died July 17, 1830.
William Jenkins	do	96 00	1,088 50	Virginia line	July 21, 1819	Mar. 16, 1818	64	Suspended under act May 1, 1820.
Jesse Rose	do	96 00	157 93	do	May 28, 1819	July 13, 1818	70	Suspended under act May 1, 1820.
Thomas Ravenscraft	do	96 00	150 19	do	Dec. 24, 1818	Aug. 12, 1818	68	Dropped under act May 1, 1820.
Zachariah Robertson	do	96 00	1,045 40	Maryland line	May 21, 1819	June 15, 1818	74	Restored Jan. 6, 1825.
John Scott	do	96 00	805 41	Pennsylvania line	Feb. 11, 1819	Oct. 14, 1818	76	Died March 3, 1827.
Samuel Sellers	do	96 00	628 44	do	Sep. 15, 1823	July 17, 1823	82	Died February 2, 1830.
John Tinney	do	96 00	1,485 56	Virginia line	Ap'l 21, 1819	Sep. 14, 1818	87	
John Taylor	do	96 00	141 29	Maryland line	May 21, 1819	Sep. 15, 1818	68	Dropped under act May 1, 1820.
William Whaley	Sergeant	96 00	568 94	Virginia line	May 17, 1819	Sep. 11, 1818	70	Died August 14, 1824.

Statement, &c. of Hart county, Kentucky.

NAMES.	Rank.	Annual allowance.	Sums received.	Description of service.	When placed on the pension roll.	Commencement of pension.	Ages.	Laws under which they were formerly inscribed on the pension roll; and remarks.
John Defever	Private	96 00	640 51	Virginia line	July 22, 1826	July 3, 1826	81	
John Humphrey	do	96 00	811 43	do	Dec. 21, 1820	Sep. 21, 1818	79	

Statement, &c. of Henderson county, Kentucky.

NAMES.	Rank.	Annual allowance.	Sums received.	Description of service.	When placed on the pension roll.	Commencement of pension.	Ages.	Laws under which they were formerly inscribed on the pension roll; and remarks
Joel Gibson	Private	96 00	530 66	North Carolina line	May 19, 1825	Ap'l 25, 1825	87	
John Hughes	Sergeant	96 51	1,169 59	do	Ap'l 23, 1819	June 29, 1818	87	Died December 23, 1830.

Statement, &c. of Henry county, Kentucky.

NAMES.	Rank.	Annual allowance.	Sums received.	Description of service.	When placed on the pension roll.	Commencement of pension.	Ages.	Laws under which they were formerly inscribed on the pension roll; and remarks,
John Adams	Private	96 00	111 49	Pennsylvania line	Aug. 12, 1818	Jan. 6, 1819	65	Dropped under act May 1, 1820.
Barich Bryan	do	96 00	1,007 96	Virginia line	May 29, 1824	Sep. 5, 1823	83	
Thomas Downey	do	96 00	50 93	Pennsylvania line	Nov. 12, 1818	May 16, 1818	70	Transferred from Ohio. Died September 15, 1823.
William Guthery	do	96 00	439 74	do	Sep. 29, 1819	Aug. 12, 1818	87	Died March 10, 1823.
Leonard Grimes	do	96 00	791 19	do	Jan. 30, 1826	June 8, 1824	75	
John Johnson, 3d	do	96 00	881 62	New Jersey line	Sep. 17, 1819	June 21, 1819	88	Died August 27, 1828.
Joseph Johnston	do	96 00	81 28	Virginia line	Nov. 27, 1819	May 13, 1819	-	Died March 17, 1820.
John Mead	do	96 00	463 72	do	Dec. 24, 1818	Nov. 6, 1818	80	
Thomas McCarty	Sergeant	96 00	492 93	do	Dec. 1, 1818	July 17, 1818	97	
John Miles	Private	96 00	127 96	do	Dec. 26, 1818	Nov. 5, 1818	61	Suspended under act May 1, 1820.
John Read	do	96 00	-	do	Mar. 14, 1820	Nov. 12, 1818	65	do　do　do
David Smith, sen.	do	96 00	477 92	do	Dec. 24, 1818	Aug. 10, 1818	74	Died August 1, 1823.
Thomas Swift	do	96 00	1,157 18	do	Dec. 23, 1818	Aug. 15, 1818	74	
George Spillman	do	96 00	1,398 70	do	do	Aug. 10, 1818	76	Suspend'd under act May 1, 1820, and
Joseph Sidebottom	do	96 00	1,196 38	do	do	Aug. 17, 1818	79	rest'd commencing July 7, 1823.

colored

NAMES.	Rank.	Annual allowance.	Sums received.	Description of service.	When placed on the pension roll.	Commencement of pension.	Ages.	Laws under which they were formerly inscribed on the pension roll; and remarks.
John Waldren	do	96 00	-	Lee's legion	Sep. 29, 1819	May 20, 1818	60	Suspended under act May 1, 1820.
John Williams	do	96 00	573 26	Maryland line	July 11, 1825	June 18, 1825	86	Suspended and restored February 21, 1826, from January 23, 1826, and transferred from New York from the last date. Died June 7, 1831.
John Williams	do	96 00	-	N. Carolina line	May 30, 1832	May 28, 1832	78	

Statement, &c. of Hickman county, Kentucky.

NAMES.	Rank.	Annual allowance.	Sums received.	Description of service.	When placed on the pension roll.	Commencement of pension.	Ages.	Laws under which they were formerly inscribed on the pension roll; and remarks.
Jeremiah Simpson	Private	96 00	356 49	Virginia line	Dec. 14, 1827	June 18, 1827	78	

Statement, &c., of Hopkins county, Kentucky.

NAMES.	Rank.	Annual allowance.	Sums received.	Description of service.	When placed on the pension roll.	Commencement of pension.	Ages.	Laws under which they were formerly inscribed on the pension roll; and remarks.
Charles Brown	Private	96 00	487 54	Virginia line	Jan. 27, 1820	Sep. 9, 1819	81	Suspended. Restored from March 4, 1830.
Robert Brown	do	96 00	237 44	Massachusetts line	April 5, 1824	Feb. 28, 1824	-	Died August 20, 1826.
John Davis	do	96 00	79 22	Virginia line	Nov. 1, 1828	Oct. 17, 1828	82	Died August 13, 1829.
Samuel Gray	do	96 00	1,220 01	do	May 13, 1819	Sep. 14, 1818	72	Died May 29, 1832.
John Littlepage	do	96 00	163 60	do	Feb. 15, 1820	July 8, 1818	-	Died March 23, 1820.

Statement, &c. of Jefferson county, Kentucky.

NAMES.	Rank.	Annual allowance.	Sums received.	Description of service.	When placed on the pension roll.	Commencement of pension.	Ages.	Laws under which they were formerly inscribed on the pension roll; and remarks.
Henry Brock	Private	96 00	139 79	Virginia line	Jan. 30, 1822	Nov. 10, 1821	75	Died March 24, 1822.
John Bartlett	do	96 00	861 32	do	Jan. 8, 1824	Sep. 15, 1823	84	
Thomas Bateman	do	96 00	752 77	Maryland line	May 18, 1826	May 2, 1826	79	
Leven Cooper	do	96 00	1374 22	Virginia line	June 8, 1819	June 8, 1818	79	Died December 27, 1832.
George Gray	Captain	240 00	323 32	Penn. line	Feb. 10, 1819	May 12, 1818	-	Suspended under act May 1, 1820.
Reuben Griffin	Private	96 00	1131 99	Virginia line	May 6, 1820	Ap. 30, 1818	73	
William Griffin	do	96 00	1134 70	do	Feb. 1, 1821	Nov. 20, 1819	79	Dead.
William Huson	do	96 00	301 56	do	Feb. 10, 1819	Oct. 12, 1820	78	
James Horseley	do	96 00	330 06	do	Nov. 27, 1821	July 13, 1821	63	Died January 1, 1824.
Thomas Kelly, 2d	do	96 00	576 00	do	May 23, 1822	July 24, 1821	73	Died February 14, 1826.
Michael Leatherman	do	96 00	65 83	Pennsylvania line	June 29, 1830	Feb. 15, 1821	80	Died July 6, 1831.
Archelaus Merritt	do	96 00	276 64	Virginia liue	Nov. 27, 1821	June 28, 1830	64	Died March 30, 1824.
Thomas McKinney	do	96 00	70 96	do	Sept. 25, 1823	July 13, 1821	62	Died December 30, 1823.
Benjamin Penn	do	96 00	113 54	Maryland line	April 3, 1820	Mar. 15, 1823	81	Transferred from Indiana, from March 4, 1826. Died May 10, 1827.
Robert Pike	do	96 00	1305 54	Virginia line	Sep. 7, 1819	July 30, 1819	88	
Nathaniel Ross	do	96 00	217 44	New York line	Feb. 10, 1819	July 14, 1818	75	
Jacob Rooksbury	do	96 00	167 16	Georgia line	Feb. 11, 1820	June 8, 1818	60	Dropped under act May 1, 1820. Died September 18, 1820.
James Stevenson	do	96 00	314 12	Penn. line	June 8, 1819	June 9, 1818	78	Suspended under act May 1, 1820. Died September 16, 1821.
William Taylor	Major	240 00	1470 49	Virginia line	Nov. 6, 1818	May 1, 1818	81	Dropped under act May 1, 1820. Restored, commencing November 23, 1824; and relinquished for the benefit of act May 15, 1828.
Benjamin Wilkenson	do	95 00	1517 15	do	May 23, 1822	May 16, 1818	80	
Robert Wilson	Captain	240 00	1897 41	Penn. line	June 8, 1819	May 9, 1818		

Statement, &c. of Jessamine county, Kentucky.

NAMES.	Rank.	Annual allow-ance.	Sums re-ceived.	Description of ser-vice.	When placed on the pen-sion roll.	Commencement of pension.	Ages.	Laws under which they were for-merly inscribed on the pension roll; and remarks.
Benjamin Adams	Private	96 00	1,512 00	Virginia line	Sep. 12, 1820	June 4, 1818	85	Died August 7, 1824.
John Biswell	do	96 00	597 41	do	Feb. 13, 1819	May 18, 1818	64	
John Cox	do	96 00	1,156 17	N. Carolina line	June 14, 1822	Feb. 18, 1822	71	Died June 6, 1819.
John Ficklin	do	96 00	93 33	Virginia line	Apr. 22, 1820	June 17, 1818	64	Died May 17, 1831.
Robert Green	do	96 00	306 83	do	Apr. 21, 1818	April 6, 1818	70	
Michael Grindstaff	Corporal	96 00	1,386 89	N. Carolina line	June 5, 1820	Sep. 24, 1819	80	
John Gilloch	Private	96 00	251 38	Virginia line	Feb. 1, 1830	Jan. 23, 1830	81	
James Irvin	do	96 00	1,514 83	do	Jan. 6, 1819	May 25, 1818	84	
Jeremiah King	Corporal	96 00	981 15	Maryland line	Dec. 13, 1824	Dec. 16, 1823	75	
William Lloyd	Private	96 00	1,529 03	Virginia line	Apr. 21, 1818	April 1, 1818	85	
David Moore	do	96 00	1,491 09	do	June 2, 1820	Aug. 24, 1818	82	
James Richards	do	96 00	1,077 06	Pennsylvania line	Mar. 5, 1819	June 16, 1818	78	
Daniel Ross	do	96 00	1,511 16	Massachusetts line	June 20, 1818	June 8, 1818	79	Died February 23, 1822.
William Sharp	do	96 00	332 97	Virginia line	Feb. 11, 1819	Sept. 7, 1818	70	Died July 1, 1821.
Samuel Wise	do	96 00	357 03	do	Mar. 5, 1819	June 16, 1818	78	

Statement, &c. of Knox county, Kentucky.

NAMES.	Rank.	Annual allow-ance.	Sums re-ceived.	Description of ser-vice.	When placed on the pen-sion roll.	Commencement of pension.	Ages.	Laws under which they were for-merly inscribed on the pension roll; and remarks.
Brown Edwards	Private	96 00	1405 67	North Carolina line	Sept. 29, 1819	July 14, 1819	82	
John Garland	do	96 00	899 35	do	Dec. 24, 1824	Oct. 23, 1824	77	
Christopher Horn	do	96 00	983 22	Virginia line	Jan. 13, 1824	Dec. 8, 1823	82	
William Henson	do	96 00	350 73	North Carolina line	Ap'l 29, 1828	Jan. 10, 1828	89	
William Patterson	do	96 00	492 64	Virginia line	Jan. 23, 1829	Jan. 18, 1829	84	

Statement, &c. of Lawrence county, Kentucky.

NAMES.	Rank.	Annual allowance.	Sums received.	Description of service.	When placed on the pension roll.	Commencement of pension.	Ages.	Laws under which they were formerly inscribed on the pension roll; and remarks.
David Atkinson	Private	96 00	826 93	Virginia line	May 8, 1826	July 21, 1825	80	
William Bates	do	96 00	1503 20	do	Feb. 18, 1819	July 7, 1818	69	
Edward Burges	do	96 00	1609 29	do	Oct. 31, 1822	June 15, 1818		
Silas P. Wooton	do	96 00	781 15	do	Mar. 1, 1826	Jan. 16, 1826	75	

Statement, &c. of Lewis county, Kentucky.

NAMES.	Rank.	Annual allowance.	Sums received.	Description of service.	When placed on the pension roll.	Commencement of pension.	Ages.	Laws under which they were formerly inscribed on the pension roll; and remarks.
John Campbell	Private	96 00	1038 96	Virginia line	May 31, 1819	Oct. 19, 1818	80	Died August 14, 1829.
Samuel Criswell	do	96 00	1525 03	do	Ap'l 16, 1819	Ap'l 16, 1818	73	
William Dorch	do	96 00	1499 61	Maryland line	June 5, 1819	July 22, 1818	74	
Joseph Finch	do	96 00	922 83	do	June 7, 1819	July 25, 1818	94	
James M. Hulet	do	96 00	621 03	Virginia line	June 11, 1824	Sept. 16, 1823	70	
Ichabod Whedon	do	96 00	1066 81	Massachusetts line	Oct. 5, 1819	June 4, 1818	70	Died July 14, 1829.

Statement, &c. of Lincoln county, Kentucky.

NAMES.	Rank.	Annual allowance.	Sums received.	Description of service.	When placed on the pension roll.	Commencement of pension.	Ages.	Laws under which they were formerly inscribed on the pension roll; and remarks.
Peter Curtis	Private	96 00	304 51	North Carolina line	Jan. 3, 1831	Jan. 3, 1831	73	
James Durham	do	96 00	77 93	Virginia line	Ap'l 5, 1820	May 13, 1819	75	Dropped October 8, 1821. Restored March 14.
John Dinwiddie	do	96 00	1254 24	do	do	Sept. 25, 1818	72	Died October 18, 1831.
John Fleece	do	96 00	150 19	Va. line & Lee's leg'n	Feb. 3, 1819	Aug. 12, 1818	62	Suspended under act May 1, 1820.
Bartlee Greenwood	du	96 00	204 38	Virginia line	Jan. 19, 1833	Jan. 19, 1832	80	
Mark M'Pherson	Lieut.	240 00	823 36	Maryland line	May 1, 1819	Aug. 11, 1818	80	Dropped under act May 1, 1820. Restored act March 4, 1823. Dropped under act May 15, 1828.
Dennis M'Kinney	Private	96 00	859 19	Virginia line	Ap'l 4, 1820	Sept. 23, 1818	70	
Jesse Peak	do	96 00	1440 00	do	Dec. 10, 1822	Sep. 4, 1819	70	
Dun Salyas	do	96 00	1494 44	North Carolina line	Feb. 5, 1820	Aug. 11, 1818	76	Died January 10, 1828.

Statement, &c. of Livingston county, Kentucky.

NAMES.	Rank.	Annual allowance.	Sums received.	Description of service.	When placed on the pension roll.	Commencement of pension.	Ages.	Laws under which they were formerly inscribed on the pension roll; and remarks.
Robert Kirk	Lieut.	240 00	271 61	Virginia line	May 25, 1820	Jan. 18, 1819	65	Dropped under act May 1, 1820.

Statement, &c. of Logan county, Kentucky.

NAMES.	Rank.	Annual allowance.	Sums received.	Description of service.	When placed on the pension roll.	Commencement of pension.	Ages.	Laws under which they were formerly inscribed on the pension roll; and remarks.
George Berry	Captain	240 00	1323 36	Virginia line	Nov. 24, 1818	Ap'l 24, 1818	72	Died October 29, 1823.
John Curd	Private	96 00	865 11	do	Ap'l 7, 1820	Ap'l 20, 1818	77	Dropped April 3, 1826. Restored commencing January 16, 1827.
John Clarke	Sergeant	96 00	1294 36	Maryland line	July 1, 1822	Sep. 11, 1820	91	
William Dunnington	Private	96 00	1499 09	do	May 21, 1819	July 24, 1818	84	
John Grinter	do	96 00	263 99	Virginia line	Aug. 28, 1829	Aug. 15, 1889	77	Died May 27, 1831.
James Johnson	do	96 00	156 12	Georgia line	Feb. 11, 1819	July 20, 1818	-	Suspended under act May 1, 1820. Restored November 30, 1824. No payments since restoration.
James Jones	do	96 00	1259 38	Virginia line	Mar. 5, 1819	July 23, 1818	90	
James Karr	Lieut.	240 00	1163 21	North Carolina line	June 16, 1819	May 9, 1818	-	Dropped July 16, 1821. Reinstated April 30, 1822. Died March 13, 1823.
James M'Cowan	Private	96 00	156 12	Virginia line	Feb. 17, 1819	July 21, 1818	-	Suspended under act May 1, 1820.
Alexander M'Lardy	Sergeant	96 00	172 64	do	Mar. 5, 1819	May 18, 1818	-	Dropped under act May 1, 1820.
Archibald Rutherford	Private	96 00	1475 09	do	July 3, 1821	Oct. 24, 1818	79	

Statement, &c. of Madison county, Kentucky.

Names.	Rank.	Annual allowance.	Sums received.	Description of service.	When placed on the pension roll.	Commencement of pension.	Ages.	Laws under which they were formerly inscribed on the pension roll; and remarks.
Peter Allembaugh	Private	96 00	290 13	Virginia line	Jan. 16, 1824	Sep. 12, 1823	94	
Henry Duke	do	96 00	1341 32	do	May 11, 1819	Sep. 15, 1818	76	
Jacob Dooley	do	96 00	1508 23	do	Ap'l 14, 1819	June 19, 1818	78	Suspended under act of May 1, 1820.
Samuel Gupison	do	96 00	No pay't	do	Mar. 5, 1819	June 8, 1818	67	Died August 29, 1822.
Joseph Goine	do	96 00	380 81	do	May 4, 1819	Sep. 11, 1818	64	
John Galloway	Lieut.	240 00	1908 66	do	Jan. 13, 1821	Sep. 22, 1818	85	
Joseph Kinnard	Private	96 00	1485 15	Pennsylvania line	June 19, 1820	Sep. 15, 1818	70	
John Land	do	96 00	1438 19	Virginia line	Oct. 25, 1819	Mar. 12, 1819	78	Suspended under act of May 1, 1820.
Joshua McQueen	do	96 00	172 38	do	Oct. 2, 1819	May 19, 1819	64	Suspended under act of May 1, 1820.
William Parish	do	96 00	143 43	do	May 19, 1819	Sep. 7, 1818	70	Suspended under act of May 1, 1820.
Enoch Rawson	do	96 00	495 22	do	Jan. 19, 1829	Jan. 8, 1829	71	Dropped under act of May 1, 1820. Restored from January 29, 1827.
Jacob Stevens	do	96 00	864 50	do	Nov. 6, 1819	June 19, 1818	75	
John Shanks	do	96 00	551 99	do	Ap'l 28, 1824	Sep. 6, 1823	76	Died April 5, 1829.
John Timberlake	do	96 00	660 26	do	June 3, 1819	June 3, 1818	72	Died April 18, 1825.
John Tutwiler	do	96 00	1137 19	do	do	do	78	
Solomon Tracy	do	96 00	1234 35	do	Nov. 25, 1819	Oct. 27, 1819	75	

Statement, &c. of Marion county, Kentucky.

NAMES.	Rank.	Annual allowance.	Sums received.	Description of service.	When placed on the pension roll.	Commencement of pension.	Ages.	Laws under which they were formerly inscribed on the pension roll, and remarks.
John Cockerell	Private	96 00	1513 03	Virginia line	Sep. 23, 1819	June 1, 1818	83	

Statement, &c. of Mason county, Kentucky.

NAMES.	Rank	Annual allowance.	Sums received.	Description of service.	When placed on the pension roll.	Commencement of pension.	Ages.	Laws under which they were formerly inscribed on the pension roll, and remarks.
Barnabas Allen	Marine	96 00	174 20	U. S. Navy	Mar. 18, 1819	May 11, 1818	-	Suspended under the act of May 1, 1820.
Leonard Bean	Private	96 00	1,519 96	Maryland line	April 16, 1819	May 5, 1818	76	
John Breeze	do	96 00	887 74	Pennsylvania line	Sep. 18, 1819	May 28, 1818	79	Died August 27, 1827.
Richard Boucher	do	96 00	291 98	Virginia line	May 13, 1822	May 31, 1819	70	Died June 14, 1822.
Benjamin Cole	do	96 00	1,333 29	German regiment	July 21, 1819	Ap'l 15, 1818	82	Died July 12, 1832.
William Deaver	do	96 00	1,130 57	Maryland line	May 14, 1819	May 26, 1818	78	Transferred from Ohio August 14, 1822.
Samuel Dehart	do	96 00	550 18	Pennsylvania line	Feb. 2, 1819	Aug. 29, 1818	80	
Benjamin Fitzgerald	do	96 00	1,509 93	Maryland line	June 8, 1819	June 12, 1818	81	Died May 21, 1824.
John Howard	do	96 00	1,515 61	do	June 4, 1819	May 22, 1818	74	
Daniel Hukins	do	96 00	1,405 93	do	July 21, 1819	July 13, 1818	73	Died June 6, 1833.
Abiah Hukill or Hucans	do	96 00	560 49	Lee's legion	Mar. 18, 1819	May 4, 1818	75	
Hugh Johnson	do	96 00	290 09	Pennsylvania line	Oct. 6, 1820	Mar. 28, 1820	74	Died April 4, 1823.
Charles Pelham	Major	96 00	1,604 25	Virginia line	Ap'l 1, 1819	Ap'l 13, 1818	80	Relinquished for the benefits of the act of May 15, 1828.
Nathan Thomas	Private	96 00	401 80	Maryland line	Sep. 7, 1819	May 18, 1818	61	Died July 24, 1822.
Joshua York	do	96 00	513 29	Pennsylvania line	Sep. 23, 1819	Ap'l 30, 1818	78	Dropped under act of May 1, 1820. Restored commencing February 4, 1829.

Statement, &c. of Mead county, Kentucky.

NAMES.	Rank.	Annual allowance.	Sums received.	Description of service.	When placed on the pension roll.	Commencement of pension.	Ages.	Laws under which they were formerly inscribed on the pension roll; and remarks.
John Shanks, 2d	Private	96 00	204 50	Maryland line	May 29, 1827	Feb. 6, 1827	75	Died March 23, 1829.

Statement, &c. of Mercer county, Kentucky.

NAMES.	Rank.	Annual allowance.	Sums received.	Description of service.	When placed on the pension roll.	Commencement of pension.	Ages.	Laws under which they were formerly inscribed on the pension roll; and remarks.
William Alexander	Private	96 00	232 51	Virginia line	Feb. 3, 1819	Nov. 2, 1818	81	Suspended. Restored from Aug. 4, 1823.
Larner Bradshaw	do	96 00	576 28	do	June 19, 1820	Oct. 4, 1819	77	
Charles Brown, 2d.	do	96 00	401 03	do	June 5, 1830	Jan. 1, 1830	80	
Samuel Brittain	do	96 00	325 15	do	Oct. 16, 1830	Oct. 16, 1830	65	Suspended under act of May 1, 1820.
Isaac Coovert	Fifer	96 00	136 25	New Jersey line	Jan. 27, 1820	Oct. 4, 1819		
Samuel Decker	Private	96 00	794 32	Virginia line	Mar. 5, 1819	May 1, 1818	75	Died August 9, 1826.
Benjamin Dean	do	96 00	1512 25	New Jersey line	Feb. 16, 1819	June 3, 1818	79	Died March 2, 1824.
Daniel Ellis	do	96 00	541 92	do	Feb. 16, 1819	July 11, 1818	79	
Robert Jones	do	96 00	1486 89	Pennsylvania line	Feb. 3, 1819	Sep. 9, 1818	66	Suspended under act of May 1, 1820.
Peter Jordan	do	96 00	38 44	Virginia line	Nov. 1, 1819	Oct. 11, 1819	70	
John Lafferty	do	96 00	399 76	New York line	Feb. 15, 1819	July 6, 1818	82	
William Leonard	do	96 00	798 36	New Jersey line	Dec. 20, 1825	Nov. 11, 1825	83	
Mark McGohan	do	96 00	1503 73	Pennsylvania line	Feb. 15, 1819	July 6, 1818	84	Off October 12, 1321. Reinstated December 26, 1822.

Statement, &c. of Mercer county—Continued.

NAMES.	Rank.	Sums received.	Annual allowance.	Description of service.	When placed on the pension roll.	Commencement of pension.	Ages.	Laws under which they were formerly inscribed on the pension roll; and remarks.
George McCormick	Captain	382 57	240 00	Virginia line	Feb. 6, 1819	June 17, 1818	-	Died January 30, 1890.
Jacob Phillips (R.)	Private	1071 74	96 00	do	Jan. 27, 1820	Aug. 2, 1819	-	Died September 30, 1830.
James Rains	do	308 90	96 00	do	Dec. 17, 1830	Dec. 17, 1830	76	
James Sandifer	do	538 66	96 00	do	Feb. 3, 1819	Nov. 13, 1818	74	Died June 22, 1824.
George Speak	do	927 95	96 00	Maryland line	Oct. 25, 1819	May 3, 1818	76	Died February 26, 1828.
John Snead	do	532 90	96 00	Virginia line	Jan. 27, 1820	Sep. 30, 1819	79	Dropped under act of May 1, 1820. Restored from Jan. 22, 1829.
William Servants	do	1154 60	96 00	do	Jan. 27, 1820	Aug. 26, 1619	82	
Samuel Woods	Lieutenant	513 10	240 00	do	Jan. 7, 1824	Dec. 15, 1823	88	Died February 3, 1826.

Statement, &c. of Monroe county, Kentucky.

NAMES.	Rank.	Sums received.	Annual allowance.	Description of service.	When placed on the pension roll.	Commencement of pension.	Ages.	Laws under which they were formerly inscribed on the pension roll; and remarks.
Thomas Brown	Musician	1223 16	96 00	Virginia line	July 3, 1820	June 8, 1918	80	
Luke Metheany	Private	720 00	96 00	do	May 6, 1819	Sep. 14, 1818	81	Transferred from Tennessee Feb. 22, 1826, from Mar. 4, 1826.
John Rasner	do	1387 96	96 00	do	Dec. 20, 1820	Sep. 20, 1819	84	
Samuel Shipley	do	231 99	96 00	Maryland line	Oct. 10, 1831	Oct. 5, 1831	96	

Statement, &c. of Montgomery county, Kentucky.

NAMES.	Rank.	Annual allowance.	Sums received.	Description of service.	When placed on the pension roll.	Commencement of pension.	Ages.	Laws under which they were formerly inscribed on the pension roll; and remarks.
John Adams, 2d	Private	96 00	—	Virginia line	Feb. 12, 1819	Dec. 3, 1818	67	Dead.
John Brown	do	96 00	683 35	Delaware line	Feb. 13, 1819	July 7, 1818	70	Died August 20, 1825.
Henry Benningfield	do	96 00	158 66	Virginia line	Jan. 26, 1819	do	79	Dropped: not continental.
Reuben Caffen	Corporal	95 00	1,464 51	do	Feb. 12, 1819	Dec. 3, 1819	71	Suspended under act May 1, 1820.
Robert Downs	Private	96 00	157 93	Delaware line	do	July 13, 1818	64	
James Dunlap	do	96 00	1,503 22	Pennsylvania line	do	July 8, 1818	94	
John Gaff	do	96 00	407 73	Virginia line	do	Dec. 3, 1818	80	Died March 1, 1823.
James Howard	do	96 00	1,465 51	do	Feb. 11, 1819	do	80	
Philip Hammon	do	96 00	29 83	do	April 1, 1820	Nov. 13, 1819	69	Suspended under act May 1, 1820.
James Johnson, 2d	do	96 00	1,503 48	do	June 15, 1819	July 7, 1818	80	
Nicholas Moore	do	96 00	241 48	do	Feb. 12, 1819	Dec. 3, 1818	85	Died June 15, 1821.
James M'Cullough	do	96 00	42 83	do	Feb. 10, 1819	July 7, 1818	62	Died December 17, 1818.
James M'Culley	do	96 00	—	do	Feb. 12, 1819	Dec. 3, 1818	–	Suspended under act May 1, 1820.
William Piles	do	96 00	39 48	do	Feb. 13, 1819	do	66	Died prior to December 17, 1818.
Edward Roberts	do	96 00	—	Pennsylvania line	Nov. 6, 1819	Oct. 7, 1819	62	Suspended under act May 1, 1880.
John Smith	do	96 00	1,503 22	do	Feb. 12, 1819	July 8, 1818	68	Suspended under act May 1, 1820.
Edward Steen	do	96 00	1,513 56	Virginia line	Feb. 13, 1819	do	74	
John Sinns	do	96 00	539 09	do	Sep. 9, 1819	Oct. 9, 1819	69	
Eli Tolen	do	96 00			Feb. 12, 1819	Dec. 3, 1818		
Aquila White	Captain	240 00	998 14	Pennsylvania line	Jan. 27, 1819	July 8, 1818	89	Montgomery. Died July 14, 1824.

Statement, &c. of Morgan county, Kentucky.

NAMES.	Rank.	Annual allowance.	Sums received.	Description of service.	When placed on the pension roll.	Commencement of pension.	Ages.	Laws under which they were formerly inscribed on the pension roll ; and remarks.
Alexander Montgomery	Private	96 00	294 74	Virginia line	April 5, 1828	Feb. 9, 1828	84	
Benjamin Wages -	do	96 00	1,475 35	do	do	do	93	

Statement, &c. of Muhlenberg county, Kentucky.

NAMES.	Rank.	Annual allowance.	Sums received.	Description of service.	When placed on the pension roll.	Commencement of pension.	Ages.	Laws under which they were formerly inscribed on the pension roll ; and remarks.
Hardy Hines -	Private	96 00	358 73	N. Carolina line	Mar. 31, 1820	Dec. 8, 1818	62	Suspended under act May 1, 1820.
John Harper. -	do	96 00	1,512 51	Pennsylvania line	Oct. 24, 1821	June 2, 1818	79	Suspended under act May 1, 1820.
John McMahan -	do	96 00	176 76	S. Carolina line	Ap'l 24, 1820	do	70	

Statement, &c. of Nelson county, Kentucky.

NAMES.	Rank.	Annual allowance.	Sums received.	Description of service.	When placed on the pension roll.	Commencement of pension.	Ages.	Laws under which they were formerly inscribed on the pension roll; and remarks.
Joshua Bird	Private	96 00	1,378 32	Virginia line	Ap'l 25, 1820	Oct. 4, 1819	90	Dropped under act May 1, 1820.
James Brooks	do	96 00	285 89	do	Nov. 6, 1819	Aug. 10, 1819	91	Restored from Nov. 14, 1825. Died April 10, 1827.
Barnabas Carter	do	96 00	505 03	do	Dec. 16, 1828	Dec. 1, 1828	77	Died December 30, 1829.
James Hagan	do	96 00	1,402 83	Maryland line	Mar. 22, 1819	Mar. 20, 1818	80	Dropped July 16, 1821. Reinstated April 30, 1822. Died May 15, 1825.
John J. S. Keech	do	96 00	647 22	do	June 10, 1819	Aug. 19, 1818	-	
George Lamb	do	96 00	700 67	Massachusetts line	Jan. 22, 1819	May 18, 1818	106	
George Moxley	do	96 00	152 51	Virginia line	Jan. 29, 1819	Aug. 3, 1818	61	Suspended under act May 1, 1820.
James Murphy	Drummer	96 00	788 41	Pennsylvania line	June 9, 1819	May 19, 1818	72	
Gabriel Murphy	Private	96 00	1,057 03	Virginia line	July 30, 1823	Mar. 1, 1823	75	
Gabriel Murphy	do	96 00	193 55	do	Nov. 27, 1819	Sept. 3, 1819	62	Dropped under act May 1, 1820.
Thomas O'Conner	do	96 00	709 41	Maryland line	June 5, 1819	Oct. 5, 1818	83	
George Tennell	do	96 00	1,497 80	Virginia line	Ap'l 21, 1819	July 29, 1818	78	
Samuel Townsend	do	96 00	212 38	New York line	Jan. 29, 1819	Aug. 4, 1818	67	Died October 20, 1820.
Raphael Winsett	do	96 00	640 77	Maryland line	Mar. 22, 1819	May 27, 1818	75	Restored from July 1, 1823. Died May 25, 1828.
David Wilson	do	96 00	1,392 49	Virginia line	Jan. 27, 1820	Sep. 3, 1819	80	

Statement, &c. of Nicholas county, Kentucky.

NAMES.	Rank.	Annual allowance.	Sums received.	Description of service.	When placed on the pension roll.	Commencement of pension.	Age.	Laws under which they were formerly inscribed on the pension roll; and remarks.
William Ballanger	Private	96 00	136 77	Virginia line	Dec. 24, 1818	Oct. 2, 1818	–	Suspended under act May 1, 1820.
Richard Bishop	do	96 00	578 40	do	April 3, 1819	June 10, 1818	70	Died June 19, 1824.
John Burns	do	96 00	834 63	Penn. line	Ap'l 18, 1820	June 23, 1818	85	
Samuel Blackburn	do	96 00	1508 76	do	Oct. 25, 1819	June 17, 1818	79	
John Caughey	do	96 00	641 56	do	Ap'l 18, 1820	June 29, 1819	87	
Robert Caldwell	do	96 00	1507 16	do	Jan. 29, 1822	June 23, 1818	77	
James Fitzpatrick	do	96 00	1419 43	Virginia line	Apr. 13, 1820	June 22, 1818	74	
John Geoghan	Ensign	240 00	1733 63	Maryland line	Jan. 6, 1819	Dec. 2, 1818	78	Died February 20, 1826.
Richard Grovesnor	Drummer	96 00	132 26	Penn. line	April 13, 1819	June 25, 1818	–	Died November 10, 1819.
Robert Hopkins	Private	96 00	165 03	Connecticut line	Apr. 10, 1819	June 16, 1818	60	Dropped under act May 1, 1820.
John Hanna	do	96 00	1486 63	Penn. line	July 6, 1819	Sept. 10, 1818	80	
John Hargus	Ensign	240 00	3741 29	Virginia line	Nov. 12, 1822	July 30, 1818	85	
Benjamin Ishmael	Private	96 00	362 58	Penn. line	Jan. 15, 1823	Oct. 1, 1818	83	
Thomas Morris	Fifer	96 00	1515 43	Virginia line	Apr. 13, 1820	June 22, 1818	81	
Nicholas Miller	Private	96 00	586 35	Congress reg.	June 25, 1819	July 27, 1818	86	
Daniel Neves	do	96 00	953 32	Virginia line	Jan. 8, 1819	Sep. 30, 1818	81	
Stephen Robertson	do	96 00	1299 86	do	Aug. 1, 1822	July 3, 1820	92	
John Smith, 2d	do	96 00	591 76	Penn. line	May 23, 1822	July 6, 1818	–	Died July 10, 1822.
Reuben Walls	do	96 00	336·00	Virginia line	Sep. 6, 1830	Sept. 4, 1830	77	

Statement, &c. of Ohio county, Kentucky.

NAMES.	Rank.	Annual allow-ance.	Sums received.	Description of service.	When placed on the pension roll.	Commencement of pension.	Ages.	Laws under which they were formerly inscribed on the pension roll; and remarks.
Peter Brandon	Private	96 00	1395 09	Virginia line	July 6, 1822	Aug. 24, 1819	84	
William Cooper	do	96 00	1501 93	Maryland line	May 21, 1819	July 13, 1818	84	
William Campbell	do	96 00	1501 93	Lee's legion	May 6, 1819	do	81	Relinquished for act May 15, 1828.
John Howell	Captain	240 00	2296 77	New Jersey line	Ap'l 24, 1820	Aug. 20, 1818	73	
Moses Johnson	Private	96 00	1501 93	Virginia line	Feb. 15, 1820	July 13, 1818	85	
Robert Mosely	Lieut.	240 00	126 36	Pennsylvania line	Feb. 15, 1819	Nov. 11, 1818	69	Susp'd under act May 1, 1820.
Thomas Pender	Private	96 00	1261 96	Maryland line	May 21, 1819	July 13, 1818	76	Died January 14, 1833.
Peter Parks	do	96 00	873 28	N. Carolina line	Mar. 1, 1925	Jan. 31, 1825	70	

Statement, &c. of Owen county, Kentucky.

NAMES.	Rank.	Annual allow-ance.	Sums received.	Description of service.	When placed on the pension roll.	Commencement of pension.	Ages.	Laws under which they were formerly inscribed on the pension roll; and remarks.
Solomon Jennings	Private	96 00	81 54	New York line	May 3, 1820	Jan. 26, 1820	69	Died November 30, 1820.
James Mason	do	96 00	1025 20	do	Dec. 20, 1822	Nov. 11, 1822	106	Died July 15, 1833.

Statement, &c. of Pendleton county, Kentucky.

NAMES.	Rank.	Annual allowance.	Sums received.	Description of service.	When placed on the pension roll.	Commencement of pension.	Ages.	Laws under which they were formerly inscribed on the pension roll; and remarks.
Solomon Belew	Private	96 00	74 57	Virginia line	Dec. 28, 1818	May 26, 1818	-	Susp'd under act May 1, 1820.
John Lawless	do	96 00	1513 80	do	Feb. 16, 1819	May 29, 1818	84	Susp'd under act May 1, 1820.
Charles Love	do	96 00	165 29	do	Sep. 16, 1819	June 15, 1818	67	Susp'd under act May 1, 1820.
John Mountjoy	Captain	240 00	2332 90	do	Nov. 6, 1819	do	77	Susp'd under act May 1, 1820.
Alven Mountjoy	Lieut.	240 00	412 90	do	Mar. 14, 1820	do	73	Susp'd under act May 1, 1820.
Benjamin Mann	Private	96 00	165 15	do	do	do	77	Restored commencing January 7, 1826.
William Wharton	do	96 00	1545 80	Pennsylvania line	Ap'l 21, 1819	Sep. 3, 1818	87	Susp'd under act May 1, 1820.
Henry Wyatt	do	96 00	44 38	Virginia line	Nov. 25, 1819	Oct. 19, 1819	67	Susp'd under act May 1, 1820.
Bennett Williams	do	96 00	459 20	do	May 13, 1819	June 16, 1818	70	Restored commencing February 11, 1831.
John Waller	do	96 00	69 29	do	Mar. 14, 1820	June 15, 1818	67	Susp'd under act May 1, 1820.
William Yelton	do	96 00	1211 86	do	Ap'l 6, 1822	July 21, 1820	74	

Statement, &c. of Perry county, Kentucky.

NAMES.	Rank.	Annual allowance.	Sums received.	Description of service.	When placed on the pension roll.	Commencement of pension.	Ages	Laws under which they were formerly inscribed on the pension roll; and remarks.
John Combs	Private	96 00	796 23	Virginia line	Jan. 15, 1826	Nov. 19, 1825	73	
Charles Ellis	do	96 00	461 67	Massachusetts line	July 1, 1829	May 14, 1829	72	
Anthony Hall	do	96 00	796 64	Virginia line	Dec. 14, 1835	Nov. 17, 1825	82	
John Kelly	do	96 00	654 44	N. Carolina line	Sept. 10, 1827	July 11, 1827	79	
George McDaniel	do	96 00	851 33	do	Dec. 19, 1823	Oct. 23, 1823	86	
Joshua Mullens	do	96 00	108 12	Virginia line	Jan. 20, 1832	Jan. 20, 1832	76	
Edward Polly	do	96 00	582 45	do	Feb. 15, 1828	Feb. 10, 1828	76	

Statement, &c. of Preble county, Kentucky.

NAMES.	Rank.	Annual allowance.	Sums received.	Description of service.	When placed on the pension roll.	Commencement of pension.	Ages.	Laws under which they were formerly inscribed on the pension roll; and remarks.
Dennis Dailey	Private	96 00	1296 00	Virginia line	April 29, 1819	Aug. 11, 1818	73	Transferred from Ohio Sept. 1820.

Statement, &c. of Pulaski county, Kentucky.

NAMES.	Rank.	Annual allowance.	Sums received.	Description of services.	When placed on the pension roll.	Commencement of pension.	Ages.	Laws under which they were formerly inscribed on the pension roll; and remarks.
Francis Aldridge	Private	96 00	209 06	N. Carolina line	Feb. 25, 1832	Dec. 24, 1831	71	
Michael Beakman	do	96 00	1248 83	S. Carolina line	Dec. 14, 1819	Oct. 21, 1818	82	Died Sept. 9, 1831..
Ichabod Blackledge	do	96 00	1042 09	N. Jersy line	Jan. 12, 1821	Apr. 27, 1818	90	Died June 15, 1829.
John Edwards	Drummer	95 00	177 29	Pennsylvania line	Apr. 22, 1820	Apr. 30, 1818	60	Dropped under act of May 1, 1820
James Girdler	do	96 00	1521 29	do	Feb. 2, 1819	do	78	
William Hansford	do	96 00	801 54	Virginia line	Dec. 14, 1819	Oct. 30, 1818	80	
William Heath	do	96 00	612 12	N. Carolina line	Mar. 15, 1824	Mar. 1, 1823	65	Died July 16, 1829.
James Lee	do	96 00	1478 56	Virginia line	Dec. 14, 1819	Oct. 30, 1818	73	
John Perry	do	96 00	1489 28	do	April 5, 1820	Aug. 31, 1818	83	
James Raincy	do	96 00	129 80	N. Carolina line	Feb. 2, 1819	Oct. 29, 1818	68	
Michael Reagan	do	96 00	154 32	Pennsylvania line	Apr. 17, 1820	do	74	
Thomas Seaton	do	96 00	1204 43	Virginia line	Feb. 1, 1819	July 27, 1818	82	Died Feb. 11, 1831.
Robert Sayers	do	96 00	1009 03	do	Mar. 15, 1824	Sept. 1, 1823	82	
Michael Young	do	96 00	146 57	N. Carolina line	Sep. 16, 1831	Aug. 26, 1831	78	Died Aug. 24, 1833.

Statement, &c. of Rockcastle county, Kentucky.

NAMES.	Rank.	Annual allowance.	Sums received.	Description of service.	When placed on the pension roll.	Commencement of pension.	Ages.	Laws under which they were formerly inscribed on the pension roll; and remarks.
William Abney	Private	96 00	1,487 20	Virginia line	Oct. 25, 1818	Sep. 7, 1818	77	
James Chasteen	do	96 00	1,487 43	do	Oct. 25, 1819	do	73	
John Hamm	do	96 00	770 74	do	Feb. 23, 1826	Feb. 23, 1826	76	
William Moore	do	96 00	928 77	do	Dec. 22, 1823	July 2, 1823	78	
Thomas Onsley, sen.	Sergeant	96 00	666 40	do	Mar. 5, 1819	Nov. 25, 1818	74	Died November 3, 1825.
John Pruett	Private	96 00	336 00	do	Sep. 6, 1830	Sep. 4, 1830	80	Paid to March 1820. Suspended under act May 1, 1820, and restored commencing July 29, 1827.
Jacob Stevens	do	96 00	702 56	do	Nov. 6, 1819	June 17, 1819	81	

Statement, &c. of Russell county, Kentucky.

NAMES.	Rank.	Annual allowance.	Sums received.	Description of service.	When placed on the pension roll.	Commencement of pension.	Ages.	Laws under which they were formerly inscribed on the pension roll; and remarks.
John Miller	Private	96 00	666 19	Pennsylvania line	Sep. 18, 1819	Sep. 15, 1818	-	Died August 23, 1825.

Statement, &c. of Scott county, Kentucky.

NAMES.	Rank.	Annual allowance.	Sums received.	Description of service.	When placed on the pension roll.	Commencement of pension.	Ages.	Laws under which they were formerly inscribed on the pension roll; and remarks.
Alexander Atkins	Private	96 00	131 12	Virginia line	Jan. 6, 1819	Apl. 24, 1818	67	Dropped Jan, 12, 1820. Not continental.
Henry Brown	do	96 00	1,216 67	Va. cont'l line	Nov. 17, 1818	Apr. 13, 1818	83	Died December 15, 1830.
Richard Bennett	do	96 00	1,054 19	do	Nov. 27, 1819	June 1, 1818	71	Died May 24, 1829.
George Chism	do	96 00	1,215 61	U. S. army	Nov. 17, 1818	Apr. 15, 1818	74	Died December 13, 1830.
Thomas Carothers	do	96 00	144 76	N. Carolina line	Jan. 12, 1819	Sep. 2, 1818	67	Suspen'd under act May 1, 1820.
Francis Erwin	do	96 00	-	Va. cont'l line	Feb. 9, 1820	June 3, 1818	58	Suspen'd under act May 1, 1820.
Charles Ervin	do	96 00	174 44	do	Nov. 17, 1818	May 11, 1818	67	Died March 9, 1820.
William Ewing	do	96 00	180 12	Penn. line	Jan. 6, 1819	Mar. 8, 1821	80	Died January 23, 1823.
Larkin Fargeson	do	96 00	130 92	Virginia line	Jan. 6, 1821	Apr. 24, 1818	60	Dropped. Not continental.
John Garrott	Dragoon	96 00	1,400 51	do	Sep. 23, 1818	Aug. 3, 1818	78	Suspen'd under act May 1, 1820.
Charles Green	Private	96 00	79 99	do	Sep. 5, 1818	May 5, 1818	66	Died February 12, 1830.
John Green	do	96 00	1,145 35	Penn. line	Nov. 17, 1818	May 9, 1818	76	
John Guill	do	96 00	1,476 38	Virginia line	Dec. 23, 1818	Oct. 19, 1818	63	Suspen'd under act May 1, 1820.
William Hubbell	L:eutenant	240 00	325 24	New York line	May 28, 1819	Apr. 27, 1818	67	Died May 19, 1822.
Morris Haloy	Private	96 00	376 63	Penn. line	Feb. 13, 1819	June 17, 1818	68	Suspen'd under act May 1, 1820.
Joseph James	do	96 00	143 43	Virginia line	Dec. 23, 1818	Sep. 7, 1818	84	
Charles Johnson	do	96 00	274 09	Mary'land line	Jan. 6, 1819	Apr. 27, 1818	76	
John Johnson	Ensign	240 00	1,704 07	S. C. line	Feb. 13, 1819	April 6, 1818	76	Died May 27, 1825.
John Kirley	Private	96 00	1,422 96	Virginia line	July 15, 1819	May 9, 1819	75	
John, *alias* Edward D. Kenney	do	86 00	539 09	Penn. line	Aug. 26, 1828	July 24, 1828	81	Dropped. Not continental.
Thomas Laidrum	do	96 00	-	-	Jan. 27, 1819	May 1, 1818	61	
Daniel Mc Clain, *alias* Mc Lean,	do	96 00	183 73	Penn. line	Feb. 9, 1820	Sept. 8, 1819	72	Died June 6, 1821.
Hugh Mc Cormick	do	96 00	391 27	do	Feb. 13, 1819	Apr. 24, 1818	65	Died May 22, 1822.
Samuel March	do	96 00	508 67	New Jersey line	Jan. 6, 1819	May 18, 1818	96	
John Milligan	do	96 00	586 57	Virginia line	Feb. 12, 1819	July 16, 1818	86	Died August 25, 1824.
John Mc Hatton	Captain	240 00	747 90	Penn. line	Feb. 4, 1828	Jan. 12, 1828	100	Died February 21, 1831.
Charles Neal	Private	96 00	1,281 36	Virginia line	Feb. 13, 1819	Apr. 22, 1818	69	Died August 27, 1831.
John Patterson	do	96 00	172 12	N. H. line	June 2, 1819	May. 20, 1818	67	Suspen'd under act May 1, 1820.

Statement, &c. of Scott county—Continued.

NAMES.	Rank.	Annual allowance.	Sums received.	Description of service.	When placed on the pension list.	Commencement of pension.	Ages.	Laws under which they were formerly inscribed on the pension roll; and remarks.
Thomas Paslay	Private	96 00	395 60	Virginia line	Feb. 27, 1830	Feb. 27, 1830	73	Died September 3, 1831.
William Price	do	96 00	64 28	do	Jan. 4, 1831	Jan. 3, 1831	83	Dropped. Not continental.
Gerard Smith	do	96 00	65 76	Maryland line	June 6, 1818	Jan. 6, 1819	64	
John Tucker	do	96 00	1,524 76	N. C. line	Nov. 17, 1818	Apr. 17, 1818	81	
Robert Thompson	Musician	96 00	787 36	Delaware line	June 23, 1820	Apr. 25, 1818	73	Died July 9, 1826.
Joseph Vance	Private	96 00	1,110 44	Virginia line	Sep. 23, 1818	Aug. 1, 1818	79	Dropped October 31, 1820. Restored March 15, 1824.
Thomas West	do	96 00	238 19	do	June 2, 1819	July 17, 1818	65	Died January 9, 1830.
James Wright	do	96 00	130 49	do	Oct. 6, 1818	Apr. 18, 1818	-	Dropped. Not continental.
Samuel Wells	do	96 00	168 18	do	Mar. 2, 1829	Feb. 19, 1829	79	Died November 20, 1830.
Nathan Young	do	96 00	171 61	do	Feb. 13, 1819	May 22, 1818	108	Suspen'd under act May 1, 1820.

Statement, &c. of Shelby county, Kentucky.

NAMES.	Rank.	Annual allowance.	Sums received.	Description of service.	When placed on the pension roll.	Commencement of pension.	Ages.	Laws under which they were formerly inscribed on the pension roll; and remarks.
Jesse Alvis	Private	96 00	1410 13	Virginia line	Sep. 16, 1819	June 24, 1819	77	Died September 13, 1818.
Charles Ballow	Sergeant	96 00	28 26	do	Sep. 29, 1819	May 28, 1818	67	Dropped Oct. 19, 1820. Restored Feb. 22, 1826. Died Sep. 21, 1830.
John Callett	Private	96 00	579 90	do	June 2, 1819	Sep. 23, 1818	73	Died February 17, 1820.
Amos Chapman	Sergeant	96 00	167 15	Pennsylvania line	Ap'l 20, 1820	May 18, 1818	75	
John Dougherty, or Doherty	Private	96 00	1313 29	Virginia line	Sep. 6, 1820	June 30, 1820	78	Dropped under act May 1, 1820.
Thomas Fitzsimmons	do	96 00	170 06	do	Sep. 24, 1819	May 28, 1818	61	
Daniel Hartley	do	96 00	1506 83	Morgan's rifle reg.	Dec. 24, 1819	June 25, 1818	80	Suspended under act May 1, 1820. Restored, commencing, Nov. 30, 1824.
James Johnson, 1st	do	96 00	965 40	Virginia line	Jan. 6, 1819	May 20, 1818	80	
James Johnson, 2d	do	96 00	1357 93	do	Oct. 18, 1821	Jan. 13, 1820	77	Dropped under act May 1, 1820.
William Morgan	do	96 00	33 03	do	Ap'l 20, 1820	Nov. 1, 1819	63	
John Mullikin	do	96 00	1228 64	do	June 26, 1822	May 18, 1818	84	
Thomas Petit	do	06 00	1352 76	Maryland line	Nov. 29, 1821	Ap'l 17, 1920	70	
Henry Randolph	do	96 00	1385 83	Pennsylvania line	Sep. 7, 1820	Sep. 28, 1819	83	
Seth Stratton	do	96 00	163 96	Virginia line	Feb. 5, 1825	June 20, 1818	61	Suspended under act May 1, 1820.
Isaac Sampson	do	96 00	444 12	N. Carolina line	Ap'l 8, 1825	July 20, 1824	69	Died April 21, 1829.
James Sacrey	do	96 00	215 48	Virginia line	Dec. 8, 1830	Dec. 7, 1830	79	
Levi Wentworth	do	96 00	750 44	Connecticut line	Oct. 13, 1818	May 11, 1813	72	
Joshua Wayland	do	96 00	87 73	Virginia line	Dec. 3, 1819	Ap'l 5, 1619	60	Suspended under act May 1, 1820.
Samuel Yager	do	96 00	1505 03	do	Ap'l 20, 1820	July 1, 1819	82	

Statement, &c. of Simpson county, Kentucky.

NAMES.	Rank.	Annual allowance.	Sums received.	Description of service.	When placed on the pension roll.	Commencement of pension.	Ages.	Laws under which they were formerly inscribed on the pension roll; and remarks.
George Pearce	Private	96 00	1045 03	Maryland line	Nov. 29, 1823	Apr. 16, 1823	74	

Statement, &c. of Spencer county, Kentucky.

NAMES.	Rank.	Annual allowance.	Sums received.	Description of service.	When placed on the pension roll.	Commencement of pension.	Ages.	Laws under which they were formerly inscribed on the pension roll; and remarks.
William Maffitt	Private	96 00	631 55	Virginia line	Jan. 29, 1819	Aug. 14, 1818	79	
Michael McMasters	do	96 00	70 99	do	Dec. 30, 1828	Dec. 9, 1828	84	Dropped under act of May 1, 1820. Restored from February 16, 1829.

Statement, &c. of Todd county, Kentucky.

NAMES.	Rank.	Annual allowance.	Sums received.	Description of service.	When placed on the pension roll.	Commencement of pension.	Ages.	Laws under which they were formerly inscribed on the pension roll; and remarks.
Robert Acock - -	Private	96 00	1,515 46	North Carolina line	June 3, 1819	May 21, 1818	80	
John M'Allister - -	do	96 00	895 36	do	Mar. 5, 1819	July 21, 1818	71	Died November 17, 1827.

Statement, &c. of Trigg county, Kentucky.

NAMES	Rank.	Annual allowance.	Sums received.	Description of service.	When placed on the pension roll.	Commencement of pension.	Ages.	Laws under which they were formerly inscribed on the pension roll; and remarks.
William Anderson -	Private	96 00	1,353 06	Virginia line	July 11, 1821	Jan. 28, 1820	78	
Peter Bets -	do	95 00	1,455 16	Lee's legion	Sep. 5, 1820	Oct. 7, 1818	75	Died December 4, 1833.
Eleazor Gow -	do	96 00	471 12	S. Carolina line	Feb. 3, 1825	July 24, 1824	68	Died February 14, 1830.

Statement, &c. of Union county, Kentucky.

NAMES.	Rank.	Annual allowance.	Sums received.	Description of service.	When placed on the pension roll.	Commencement of pension.	Ages.	Laws under which they were formerly inscribed on the pension roll; and remarks.
Thomas Blackwell -	Captain	240 00	2,368 38	Virginia line	Feb. 16, 1820	Ap'l 22, 1818	77	
William Baylis -	Lieutenant	240 00	3,313 34	do	Mar. 29, 1819	May 5, 1818	77	Dropped under act May 15, 1828.

Statement, &c. of Versailles county, Kentucky.

NAMES.	Rank.	Annual allowance.	Sums received.	Description of service.	When placed on the pension roll.	Commencement of pension.	Ages.	Laws under which they were formerly inscribed on the pension roll; and remarks.
John Allison	Sergeant	96 00	500 26	Pennsylvania line	Ap'l 22, 1818	Ap'l 2, 1818	75	Died June 16, 1823.

Statement, &c. of Warren county, Kentucky.

NAMES.	Rank.	Annual allowance.	Sums received.	Description of service.	When placed on the pension roll.	Commencement of pension.	Ages.	Laws under which they were formerly inscribed on the pension roll; and remarks.
Charles Allen	Private	96 00	793 33	Virginia line	Oct. 11, 1819	May 30, 1818	83	
Rich'd Bettersworth	Sergeant	96 00	686 68	do	Dec. 19, 1820	Sep. 15, 1818	74	Died November 9, 1825.
William Brown	Private	96 00	759 51	do	Dec. 11, 1822	Oct. 7, 1822	79	
John Franklin	do	96 00	505 06	do	Dec. 18, 1821	June 1, 1818	-	Died March 4. 1823.
Nathan Nabois	do	96 00	944 59	do	Jan. 15, 1824	May 5, 1823	90	
John Ragland	do	96 00	583 88	Maryland line	Jan. 8, 1828	Feb. 5, 1827	78	

Statement, &c. of Washington county, Kentucky.

NAMES.	Rank.	Annual allowance.	Sums received.	Description of service.	When placed on the pension roll.	Commencement of pension.	Ages.	Laws under which they were formerly inscribed on the pension roll; and remarks.
Charles Bever	Lieutenant	240 00	1,560 00	Maryland line	June 30, 1819	Mar. 10, 1819	80	Transferred from Maryland December 11, 1825.
Jacob Corbert	Private	96 00	707 35	do	Dec. 6, 1826	Oct. 23, 1826	76	
Adam Darnell, jun.	do	96 00	486 99	Virginia line	Mar. 14, 1820	Aug. 9, 1819	94	Died October 18, 1820.
Michael Fagan	do	96 00	226 27	Pennsylvania line	Mar. 14, 1820	Aug. 9, 1819	90	Died December 5, 1825.
George Fielder	do	96 00	628 90	Virginia line	Mar. 14, 1820	May 18, 1819	73	Transferred from Indiana March 7, 1828. Commencing from March 4, 1828.
Joseph Fields	do	96 00	577 03	Maryland line	Mar. 19, 1823	Mar. 1, 1823	78	
William Hill	do	96 00	1,235 35	Virginia line	Mar. 14, 1820	Oct. 13, 1818	83	Died July 25, 1831.
Randall Hoskins	do	96 00	878 70	Maryland line	Jan. 26, 1825	Jan. 10, 1825	76	
Frederick Hill	do	96 00	307 09	Pennsylvania line	Dec. 27, 1830	Dec. 24, 1830	75	
James Lewis	do	96 00	782 00	Virginia line	Mar. 14, 1820	July 9, 1818	75	

Names	Rank	Annual allowance	Sums received	Description of service	When placed on the pension roll	Commencement of pension	Ages	Laws under which they were formerly inscribed on the pension roll; and remarks.
Andrew Rogers -	Lieutenant	240 00	667 70	do	June 10, 1819	May 16, 1818	81	Suspended under act of May 1, 1820. Rest'd from July 7, 1823. Died June 29, 1825.
Aaron Spalding -	Private	96 00	1,014 70	Maryland line	Mar. 14, 1820	Aug. 10, 1819	81	
George Spalding -	do	96 00	878 70	do	Jan. 29, 1825	Jan. 10, 1825	76	Dropped June 13, 1821. Died August 29, 1824.
William Thurman -	do	96 00	172 38	Virginia line	Mar. 14, 1820	May 19, 1818	65	
Perry Thorp -	do	96 00	-	Pennsylvania line	do	Nov. 1, 1819	84	Suspended under act May 1, 1820.
Lewis Thomas -	Lieutenant	240 00	79 99	Virginia line	do	Nov. 4, 1819	68	do do
Robert Yates -	Sergeant	96 00	462 66	Maryland lihe	Jan. 27, 1819	Nov. 10, 1818	80	do do

Statement, &c. of Wayne county, Kentucky.

Names.	Rank.	Annual allowance.	Sums received.	Description of service.	When placed on the pension roll.	Commencement of pension.	Ages.	Laws under which they were formerly inscribed on the pension roll, and remarks.
Frederick Cooper -	Private	96 00	-	North Carolina line	Mar. 31, 1820	Oct. 20, 1818	-	Suspended under act May 1, 1820
Elisha Thomas -	do	96 00	131 09	Virginia line	Jan. 28, 1819	Oct. 24, 1818	60	do do

Statement, &c. of Whitely county, Kentucky.

Names.	Rank.	Annual allowance.	Sums received.	Description of service.	When placed on the pension roll.	Commencement of pension.	Ages.	Laws under which they were formerly inscribed on the pension roll; and remarks.
Joseph Moore -	Private	96 00	468 41	New Jersey line	Jan. 28, 1819	Oct. 19, 1818	83	
James Rogers -	do	96 00	519 22	N. Carolina line	Nov. 1, 1828	Oct. 8, 1828	74	Died December 31, 1830.
William Sexton -	do	96 00	536 00	Virginia line	Oct. 21, 1826	July 16, 1826	81	
Daniel Twigg -	do	96 00	488 74	N. Carolina line	May 12, 1829	Feb. 2, 1829	-	

9

Statement, &c. of Woodford county, Kentucky.

NAMES.	Rank.	Annual allowance.	Sums received.	Description of service.	When placed on the pension roll.	Commencement of pension.	Ages.	Laws under which they were formerly inscribed on the pension roll; and remarks.
Daniel Barnet	Private	96 00	348 53	Maryland line	July 15, 1819	June 7, 1819	75	Died January 23, 1823.
Nicholas Baker	do	96 00	173 03	Virginia line	June 11, 1819	June 16, 1818	-	Suspended under act of May 1, 1820.
John Booz	do	96 00	694 70	do	Dec. 1, 1820	June 9, 1818	92	
Thomas Coleman	do	96 00	174 89	do	Apr. 19, 1820	June 9, 1818	68	Suspended under act of May 1, 1820.
William Dale	do	96 00	164 49	do	Mar. 5, 1819	June 18, 1818	64	Dropped July 16, 1821.
John Dossey	do	96 00	585 03	New York line	Feb. 7, 1828	Feb. 1, 1828	74	
Henry Goodloe	do	96 00	210 06	Virginia line	Jan. 11, 1832	Dec. 28, 1831	95	
John Malone	do	96 00	1519 73	do	May 17, 1820	May 6, 1818	80	
Leonard Mosley	do	96 00	1077 06	do	July 7, 1819	June 16, 1818	78	
William McCoy	do	96 00	374 63	Connecticut line	Apr. 19, 1819	June 10, 1818	80	Died December 9, 1829.
Enos Mix	do	96 00	504 79	Virginia line	July 15, 1819	June 2, 1818	91	
William Pullen	do	96 00	1413 29	do	Aug. 19, 1819	June 15, 1818	75	
John Pollet	do	96 00	624 00	do	Mar. 29, 1819	May 11, 1818	78	Transferred from Va. Feb. 13, 1828, from Sept. 4, 1827.
George Peyton	do	96 00	288 26	do	Sep. 21, 1819	June 17, 1818	71	Died June 17, 1831.
Presley Terril	do	96 00	1511 69	do	Feb. 17, 1819	June 6, 1818	72	
Robert Yancey	Captain	240 00	1557 13	do	June 28, 1819	May 23, 1818	84	Died November 17, 1824.

Statement showing the names, rank, &c. of persons residing in Adair county, in the State of Kentucky, who have been inscribed on the Pension List under the act passed on the 7th of June, 1832.

NAMES.	Rank.	Annual allowance.	Sums received.	Description of service.	When placed on the pension roll.	Commencement of pension.	Ages.	Laws under which they were formerly inscribed on the pension roll; and remarks.
Abraham Aarons	Private	40 00	120 00	Virginia line	Ap'l 12, 1833	Mar. 4, 1831	75	
Joshua Atkinson	do	30 00	90 00	do	June 7, 1833	do	79	
Henry Armstrong	do	30 00	90 00	do	Nov. 12, 1833	do	80	
Elisha Bailey	do	26 66	79 98	do	Sep. 23, 1833	do	70	
Robert Busby	do	80 00	240 00	do	Apl. 2, 1834	do	75	
Charles Bettsworth	Corporal	58 33	145 83	-	Aug. 22, 1833	do	76	
Jacob Cooper	Private	80 00	240 00	N. Carolina line	Nov. 6, 1832	do	100	
Thomas Cochran	do	80 00	240 00	Georgia line	Feb. 8, 1833	do	74	
Levi Conover	do	80 00	240 00	New Jersey line	Oct. 12, 1833	do	77	
Alexander Elliott	Midshipm.	144 00	432 00	Virginia navy	Oct. 11, 1833	do	71	
John Greider, sen.	Private	80 00	240 00	Virginia line	Apl 1, 1833	do	73	
Zacharias Holladay	Drummer	88 00	264 00	do	July 15, 1833	do	72	
William Hopkins	Private	80 00	240 00	do	Jan. 28, 1834	do	70	
William Hurt	do	50 00	150 00	do	Mar. 21, 1834	do	77	
Jeremiah Ingram	do	80 00	240 00	Virginia militia	Feb. 28, 1833	do	75	
William James	do	40 00	120 00	N. Carolina line	Aug. 17, 1833	do	76	
James Irvine	do	46 66	139 98	Virginia line	Oct. 12, 1833	do	78	
Joseph Miller, sen.	do	73 33	219 99	do	Dec. 28, 1833	do	81	
William McKinney	do	80 00	-	Virginia militia	Feb. 2, 1833	do	76	
Charles Moore	do	33 33	99 99	N. Carolina militia	Aug. 21, 1833	do	74	
Matthew McGlassen	do	60 00	180 00	Virginia militia	Feb. 7, 1834	do	79	
William Rogers, sen.	do	63 33	158 33	Virginia militia	May 31, 1833	do	86	
Solomon Royse	do	80 00	240 00	N. Carolina line	Aug. 21, 1833	do	70	
Isaac Staples	do	33 33	83 33	Virginia militia	Nov. 6, 1832	do	72	
Moses Smith	do	80 00	240 00	N. Car. State troops	June 17, 1833	do	72	
John Smith, 2d	do	80 00	240 00	N. Carolina line	do	do	79	
James Smith	Ser. & pri.	36 66	109 98	Maryland militia	Oct. 12, 1833	do	79	
Archibald Skaggs	Private	25 00	-	do	July 10, 1834	do	74	Dead.
Daniel Trabue	Com. & pri.	260 00	780 00	Virginia militia	Dec. 26, 1832	do		
Philip Winfrey	Private	20 00	60 00	Virginia line	Apl. 9, 1833	do	71	
Thomas White	do	21 12	63 36	do	Aug. 21, 1833	do	71	
William Young, 2d	do	80 00	200 00	N. Carolina militia	Apl. 1, 1833	do	74	

Statement, &c. of Allen county, Kentucky.

NAMES.	Rank.	Annual allowance.	Sums received.	Description of service.	When placed on the pension roll.	Commencement of pension.	Ages.	Laws under which they were formerly inscribed on the pension roll; and remarks.
James R. Alexander	Pri. & ser.	103 33	-	Maryland militia	July 25, 1834	Mar. 4, 1831	77	
John Brook	Private	40 00	120 00	Virginia line	May 29, 1833	do	79	
Peter Borders	Pr. & sgt	91 66	274 98	N. Carolina line	Sep. 25, 1833	do	78	
Stout Brunson	do	80 00	240 00	Penn. line	Ap'l 29, 1834	do	78	
John Durham	Private	20 00	60 00	Virginia militia	Jan. 28, 1834	do	73	
John Gibson	do	26 66	79 98	Virginia line	July 15, 1833	do	73	
John Gatewood	do	45 43	136 29	do	Aug. 17, 1833	do	74	
Christopher Hains	do	80 00	240 00	do	Feb. 18, 1833	do	74	
George Heeter	do	21 66	64 98	Maryland militia	do	do	82	
Michael Hatler	do	21 55	64 65	Virginia line	July 15, 1833	do	74	
Richard Harrison	do	20 00	60 00	N. Carolina mil.	Sept. 24, 1833	do	70	
Wilson Moore	do	76 66	229 98	Virginia line	July 15, 1833	do	76	
Stephen Merrit	do	30 00	90 00	N. Carolina mil.	Oct. 18, 1833	do	72	
James McElroy	do	80 00	240 00	S. Carolina mil.	do	do	75	
Daniel Pickford	do	23 22	69 66	Virginia mil.	Aug. 17, 1833	do	73	
Benjamin Poe	Pr. of inf. and cav.	47 50	142 50	N. Carolina line	Dec. 28, 1833	do	85	
William Sherry	Private	30 00	90 00	N. Carolina mil.	Nov. 10, 1832	do	86	
George Stovall	do	30 00	90 00	Virginia mil.	May 18, 1833	do	72	
Samuel Smith, 2d	do	30 00	75 00	do	do	do	71	
Jarrett Wright	Corporal	80 00	264 00	Virginia line	Nov. 12, 1833	do	76	
James Williamson	Pr. of c. & inf.	99 42	298 26	do	Mar. 3, 1834	do	81	
Elisha Warden	Private	21 12	63 36	Virginia mil.	Apl. 14, 1834	do	73	

Statement, &c. of Anderson county, Kentucky.

NAMES.	Rank.	Annual allowance.	Sums received.	Description of service.	When placed on the pension roll.	Commencement of pension.	Ages.	Laws under which they were formerly inscribed on the pension roll; and remarks.
Reuben Boston	Private	50 00	150 00	Virginia line	Feb. 1, 1833	Mar. 4, 1831		
Ralph Cowgill	do	80 00	240 00	Virg'a State troops	Feb. 5, 1833	do	72	
Stephen Franklin	do	40 00	120 00	North Carolina line	Feb. 7, 1834	do	78	
George Jordan	do	80 00	240 00	Virginia militia	Ap'l 12, 1833	do		
James McGuire	do	96 00	8 74	Virginia line	June 5, 1820	Feb. 7, 1820	–	Drop'd under act May 1820. Ins'd on roll under act June 7, 1832.
Same	do	80 00	240 00	do	Mar. 21, 1833	Mar. 4, 1831	87	March 18, 1818.
Menan Mills	do	20 00	60 00	Virginia militia	Jan. 10, 1834	do	75	
John Penny	do	80 00	240 00	Virg'a State troops	Nov. 28, 1832	do	82	
Rodham Petty	do	48 33	144 99	Virginia militia	Sep. 26, 1833	do	72	
William Pollard	do	36 66	109 98	do	Oct. 31, 1833	do	72	
John Sladyen	do	60 00	120 00	do	Dec. 1, 1832	do	75	
Richard Searcy	do	80 00	240 00	North Carolina mil.	Dec. 23, 1833	do		
Benjamin Warford	do	80 00	240 00		Feb. 1, 1833	do	74	
John Watson, 2d	do	20 00	60 00	Virginia militia	Feb. 7, 1834	do		

Statement, &c. of Barren county, Kentucky.

Names.	Rank.	Annual allowance.	Sums received.	Description of service.	When placed on the pension roll.	Commencement of pension.	Ages.	Laws under which they were formerly inscribed on the pension roll; and remarks.
David Arnett	Private	20 00	50 00	Virginia line	Jan. 28, 1833	Mar. 4, 1831	82	
John Beavers	do	60 00	180 00	Virginia militia	Nov. 6, 1832	Mar. 4, 1832	72	
John Bagley	Sergeant	120 00	360 00	Virginia line	Jan. 28, 1833	do	73	
Callow Bailey	Private	60 00	180 00	do	May 11, 1833	do	84	
William Boyd	do	80 00	240 00	N. Carolina militia	May 30, 1833	do	80	
William Bell	do	24 66	73 98	Virginia militia	June 7, 1833	do	79	
James Bibb	Pri. & ser.	73 38	220 14	do	July 15, 1833	do	80	
Richard Bailey	Private	46 66	139 98	Virginia line	do	do	70	
John Burch	do	80 00	240 00	Virginia militia	Aug. 24, 1833	do	76	
Simeon Buferd	Ens. & pri.	116 66	349 98	Virginia line	Oct. 18, 1833	do	77	
Henry Carter	Private	80 00	240 00	do	Jan. 28, 1833	Mar. 4, 1831	82	
Thomas Coleman	do	80 00	117 63	Virginia militia	Feb. 18, 1833	do	69	Died August 17, 1832.
Philip Carter	do	46 66	139 98	do	May 31, 1833	do	68	
John Cole	do	40 00	120 00	Maryland militia	Oct. 11, 1833	do	81	
William Craig	do	30 00	90 00	Virginia militia	Nov. 28, 1833	do	79	
David Denton	do	80 00	240 00	Virginia line	Jan. 28, 1833	do	73	
William Depp	do	21 33	53 33	Virginia militia	Sep. 26, 1833	do	79	
William Dishman	do	80 00	213 34	Virginia St. troops	Dec. 24, 1833	do	75	
John Ellmore	Pri. of cav.	26 22	78 66	N. Carolina militia	Nov. 6, 1832	do	75	
William Frogget	do	100 00	300 00	Virginia line	Jan. 28, 1833	do	74	Died December 4, 1833.
Richard Fulcher	Cor. & pri.	33 22	99 66	do	Aug. 17, 1833	do	78	
Lewis Goodin	Private	80 00	200 00	do	Oct. 22, 1832	do	73	
Jacob Gibson	Pri. of art.	100 00	300 00	do	Jan. 28, 1833	do	78	
John Gorin	Ser. cor. & private						71	
Thomas Green	Private	30 88	92 64	Virginia militia	July 15, 1833	do	73	
John Hiser	do	32 22	96 66	do	Aug. 17, 1833	do	74	
Ambrose Hoffman	do	50 00	150 00	Pennsylvania militia	Jan. 28, 1833	do	80	
Clem Hill	do	60 00	180 00	Virginia militia	Mar. 1, 1833	do	77	
Abner Hamilton	do	30 00	75 00	do	Apl 2, 1833	do	72	
Absalom Hughes	Pri. & ser.	63 33	189 99	do	May 30, 1833	do	79	

Name	Rank			Service	Date		Age	Remarks
William Harris	Private	36 66	109 98	do	Nov. 28, 1833	do	79	
Joseph Higdon	Cor. & pri. of caval.	110 00	330 00	do	Jan. 13, 1834	do	75	
Jonathan Hunt	Private	24 44	73 32	N. Carolina militia	Ap'l 3, 1834	do	74	
John Jameson	do	80 00	240 00	Virginia line	Oct. 11, 1833	do	71	
Richard Jones	do	26 66	79 98	Virginia militia	Oct. 18, 1833	do	89	
Israel Lynn	do	21 12	42 24	North Carolina mil.	Jan. 28, 1833	do	75	
Rodham Larrance	do	20 00	60 00	Virginia militia	July 29, 1833	do	72	
Samuel Murrell, sen.	Ensign	80 00	240 00	Virginia line	Jan. 28, 1833	do	78	
Daniel M'Guire	Private	63 33	119 99	New Jersey line	do	do	75	
Benjamin Martin	Pri. corp. & sergt.	77 00	231 00	Virginia line	May 11, 1833	do		
Andrew M'Ginnis	Drummer	84 00	252 00	do	Sep. 24, 1833	do	75	
James Nevill	Private	22 88	-	Virginia militia	June 20, 1834	do	79	
Peter Priest	do	80 00	240 00	Virginia line	Nov. 25, 1833	do	92	
William Peers	Mariner	80 00	178 84	Virginia navy	May 6, 1834	do	74	
James Robinson	Private	80 00	240 00	Virginia line	Jan. 28, 1833	do	73	
John Renfro	Drummer & pri. of inf. & cav.					do		Died May 29, 1833.
Thomas Roberts	Pri. & ser.	39 33	117 99	Virginia militia	May 30, 1833	do	74	
Nathaniel Reynolds	Private	46 25	138 75	Virginia line	July 15, 1833	do	71	
James Spillman	do	23 33	58 33	Virginia militia	Sep. 28, 1833	do	72	
Thomas Smith	do	80 00	240 00	do	Nov. 6, 1832	do	71	
Frederick Smith	Pri. & capt.	160 00	480 00	South Carolina mil.	Nov. 9, 1833	do	73	
Thomas Terry	Private	80 00	240 00	Virginia line	Nov. 3, 1832	do		
Samuel Woodson	do	33 33	99 99	do	Jan. 28, 1833	do	73	
John Watson	do	60 00	180 00	do	Nov. 6, 1832	do	73	
Obadiah Wade	do	60 00	180 00	Virginia militia	Jan. 28, 1833	do	71	

Statement, &c. of Bath county, Kentucky.

NAMES.	Rank	Annual allowance.	Sums received	Description of service.	When placed on the pension roll.	Commencement of pension.	Ages.	Laws under which they were formerly inscribed on the pension roll; and remarks.
Moses Botts	Private	40 00	120 00	Virginia line	Mar. 6, 1833	Mar. 4, 1831	84	
Jarvis Bromigin	do	20 00	60 00	Virginia militia	Dec. 21, 1833	do	72	
Joshua Collins	do	80 00	240 00	Virginia line	Sep. 2, 1833	do	77	
William Jameson	do	26 65	79 98	do	Mar. 6, 1833	do	75	
William Kernes	do	80 00	240 00	do	Dec. 2, 1833	do	77	
Moses Nelson	do	80 00	160 00	North Carolina line	Ap'l 9, 1833	do	76	
Edward Parker	Sergeant	120 00	360 00	Virginia State troops	Ap'l 9, 1833	do	80	
Holman Rice	Pri. and captain	240 00	1,876 76	Virginia line	Sept. 15, 1819	July 14, 1819	76	Increased the captain's pay from March 28, 1829. Relinquished for the benefits of the act of June 7, 1832, but paid under act of March 18, 1818, to March 4, 1833.
Do	Captain	480 00	480 00	do	Ap'l 12, 1833	Mar. 4, 1831	76	Act March 18, 1818.
Beane Smallwood	Private	80 00	240 00	do	Oct. 21, 1833	do	76	
Richard Thomas	do	80 00	240 00	North Carolina line	Mar. 21, 1833	do	76	

Statement, &c. of Boone county, Kentucky.

NAMES.	Rank.	Annual allowance.	Sums received.	Description of service.	When placed on the pension roll.	Commencement of pension.	Ages.	Laws under which they were formerly inscribed on the pension roll; and remarks.
William Aldridge	Private	20 00	50 00	Maryland militia	Jan. 10, 1823	March 4, 1831	77	
John Bridges	do	96 00	961 03	Virginia line	May 10, 1823	March 1, 1823	78	Relinquished for the benefit of act June 7, 1832.
Same	Pri. of cav.	100 00	-		June 10, 1833	March 4, 1831	78	Act March 18, 1818.
John H. Craig	Pr. & q.m.g.	123 33	369 99	do	Jan. 19, 1833	do	72	
David Clarkson	Private	40 00	107 80	do	Dec. 7, 1833	do	72	Died November 15, 1833.
William Golding	do	80 00	240 00	do	Dec. 10, 1833	do	75	
Daniel Gaff	do	80 00	240 00	do	Mar. 14, 1834	do	80	
William Hamilton	do	46 66	-	do	Dec. 5, 1833	do	94	Dead.
Cave Johnson	do	40 00	120 00	do	Dec. 5, 1833	do	73	
James Kay	do	80 00	188 34	do	June 18, 1833	do	75	
Joseph Kennedy	do	23 33	69 99	Virginia militia	Dec. 7, 1833	do	71	Died July 12, 1833.
Jacob Pratt	Adj.& cap.	351 24	1053 72	New Jersey line	Nov. 5, 1832	do	87	
Samuel Rouse	Private	20 00	40 00	Virginia militia	Dec. 4, 1832	do	84	
Jacob Rouse	do	33 33	66 66	do	Jan. 10, 1833	do	76	
Alexander Ross	do	40 00	100 00	do	Apl 25, 1833	do	72	
James Ruddeel	do	80 00	200 00	do	Oct. 2, 1833	do	76	
John Swindle	do	20 00	40 00	do	Jan. 17, 1833	do	82	
William Smither	do	30 00	75 00	do	Apl 25, 1833	do	79	
James Stephenson	do	80 00	200 00	New Jersey line	June 12, 1833	do	79	
George Vest	do	63 33	189 99	Virginia line	Jan. 19, 1833	do	81	

10

Statement, &c. of Bourbon county, Kentucky.

NAMES.	Rank.	Annual allowance.		Sums received.		Description of service.	When placed on the pension roll.	Commencement of pension.	Ages.	Laws under which they were formerly inscribed on the pension roll; and remarks,
Philip Ament	Private.	53	33	159	99	Penn. militia	July 10, 1834	Mar. 4, 1831.	79	
John Breast	do	60	00	150	00	Virginia line	Dec. 18, 1832	do	74	
William Branham	Corporal	66	00	198	00	Virginia militia	Dec. 5, 1832	do	71	
Samuel Bowels	Private	80	00	240	00	Delaware line	Mar. 16, 1833	do	84	
Lewis Corbin	Pri.& ser.	76	66	191	65	Virginia militia	June 7, 1833	do	79	
Isaac Clinkenbeard	Private	36	66	109	98	Virginia line	Mar. 4, 1834	do	75	
James Davis	do	30	00	75	00	do	May 11, 1833	do	72	
Clementius Doudon	Ser.& pri.	41	66	124	98	Penn. militia	July 23, 1833	do	72	
George Edwards	Private	20	00	60	00	N. Carolina militia	Jan. 9, 1833	do	72	
Moses Enditcott	do	40	00	120	00	do	April 14, 1834	do	74	Died April 24, 1834.
Peter Forgueran	do	30	00	75	00	Virginia militia	May 3, 1833	do	85	
Hugh Forgey	do	40	00	120	00	Penn. militia	Dec. 28, 1835	do	80	
William Harris	Pri.& ser.	51	60	154	80	Virginia militia	Oct. 26, 1832	do	89	
Robert Hill	Private	66	66	199	98	do	May 11, 1833	do	77	
Andrew House	do	21	66	64	98	Penn. militia	July 10, 1834	do	86	
Thomas Hays	do	41	66	124	98	Maryland militia	Dec. 23, 1833	do	72	
David Jameson	do	80	00	160	00	Virginia line	Oct. 19, 1832	do	78	
Joseph Jackson	do	80	00	240	00	do	Nov. 1, 1832	do	77	
Thomas Jones	Sergeant	40	00	92	92	Virginia militia	May 11, 1833	do	77	
Charles Lander	Private	120	00	293	34	Virginia line	April 1, 1833	do	79	
Samuel Lockwood	do	80	00	240	00	Delaware militia	May 7, 1833	do	78	
Robert Luckey	do	66	66	199	98	Virginia militia	April 28, 1834	do	74	
John M'Cloud	do	33	33	99	99	Virginia line	May 11, 1833	do	94	
Daniel McDowell	do	40	00	80	00	do	May 31, 1833	do	82	
William Patton	Pri. of cav.	52	50	65	00	N. Carolina line	Nov. 5, 1832	do	75	
Thomas Rogers	Private	26	66	79	98	Virginia militia	April 12, 1833	do	80	
Abner Shropshire	do	43	33	129	99	do	Jan. 26, 1833	do	73	
Thomas Shaw	do	43	33	129	99	Penn. militia	April 16, 1833	do	81	Died July 1, 1833.
Hezekiah Speaks	do	50	00	150	00	Maryland militia	Oct. 11, 1833	do	76	Died Aug. 15, 1833.
John Stipp	do	20	00	60	00	Penn. militia	Oct. 31, 1833	do	86	
Joseph L. Stevens	do	20	00	60	00	Virginia militia	Feb. 4, 1834	do	70	
Benjamin Wheley	Ser.&capt.	240	00	-		Virginia St. troops	Aug. 7, 1833	do	74	

Statement, &c. of Bracken county, Kentucky.

NAMES.	Rank.	Annual allowance.	Sums received.	Description of service.	When placed on the pension roll.	Commencement of pension.	Ages.	Laws under which they were formerly inscribed on the pension roll; and remarks.
James Arbuckle	Private	30 00	90 00	Virginia State tr.	May 12, 1834	Mar. 4, 1831	72	
Rudolph Black	do	20 00	60 00	Virginia militia	Jan. 13, 1834	do	72	
John Hamilton	do	53 33	159 99	Penn. line	Jan. 8, 1834	do	69	
Benjamin Henderson	do	23 33	69 99	N. Carolina militia	do	do	76	
John King	do	46 66	139 98	Penn. line	Aug. 21, 1833	do	73	
William King	do	20 00	60 00	Virginia militia	Oct. 31, 1833	do	71	
Aaron Kendall	do	30 00	90 00	N. C. militia	Jan. 4, 1834	do	75	
Jacob Morris	do	20 00	60 00	N. Jersey militia	May 29, 1834	do	62	
Samuel Miranda	do	20 00	53 34	Penn. militia	Feb. 12, 1834	do	–	Died Nov. 6, 1833.
William Owens	do	20 00	50 00	Virginia militia	Feb. 18, 1833	do	71	
Philip Rice	Mus. & ser.	67 00	201 00	do	Dec. 20, 1833	do	75	
William Sergeant	Private	23 33	69 99	Maryland line	June 6, 1834	do	74	
John Tucker	do	80 00	240 00	do	July 9, 1833.	do	88	
Bartholomew Taylor	do	20 00	60 00	Maryland militia	June 17, 1834	do	79	

Statement, &c. of Breckenridge county, Kentucky.

NAMES.	Rank.	Annual allow- ance.	Sums re- ceived.	Description of ser- vice.	When placed on the pen- sion roll.	Commencement of pension.	Ages.	Laws under which they were for- merly inscribed on the pension roll; and remarks.
John Allgood	Private	21 33	63 99	Virginia militia	Mar. 4, 1834	Mar. 4, 1831	76	
James Bramblett	Pri. & cor.	22 50	67 50	do	May 11, 1833	do	70	
Valentine Fantress	Private	80 00	240 00	Virginia line	Dec. 5, 1832	do	74	
Ignatius Gough	do	80 00	200 00	do	Oct. 18, 1833	do	81	
Joseph Hutchinson	do	20 00	60 00	Virginia militia	Ap'l 12, 1833	do	77	
Henry Hashfield	do	26 66	79 98	Pennsylvania militia	May 31, 1833	do	76	
Charles Hoskinson	do	26 66	79 98	Maryland militia	Aug. 21, 1833	do	75	
Thomas Kincheloe	Sergeant	35 00	105 00	Virginia militia	Dec. 2, 1833	do	72	
Barney Miller	Private	23 33	69 99	do	Aug. 21, 1833	do	69	
Joseph Mason	Pri. & ser.	36 54	109 62	do	do	do	77	
George Paul	Private	23 33	58 33	do	do	do	68	
Samuel Parks		40 00	120 00	New York militia	Dec. 23, 1833	do	75	
George Reel	do	20 00	50 00	Maryland militia	Aug. 21, 1833	do	85	
James Robertson	do	20 00	60 00	North Carolina mil.	Mar. 14, 1834	do		
Samuel Sharp, sr.	do	36 66	109 98	do	Aug. 21, 1833	do	85	
George Seaton	Ser. & pri.	78 33	234 99	Virginia militia	Oct. 21, 1833	do	79	
William Thornhill	Private	26 66	79 98	do	Mar. 5, 1834	do	77	
Francis Wilkerson	do	36 66	109 98	North Carolina mil.	Ap'l 9, 1833	do	73	

Statement, &c. of Bullit county, Kentucky.

NAMES.	Rank.	Annual allow- ance.	Sums re- ceived.	Description of ser- vice.	When placed on the pen- sion roll.	Commencement of pension.	Ages.	Laws under which they were for- merly inscribed on the pension roll; and remarks.
Lawrence Bishop	Private	20 00	60 00	Pennsylvania militia	Sept. 9, 1833	Mar. 4, 1831	71	March 18, 1818. Relinquished for benefit of act June 7, 1852.
William Cardwell	do	96 00	1,369 31	Virginia line	Oct. 2, 1819	May 31, 1818	-	
Do	Pri. of cav.	100 00	300 00	do	Mar. 15, 1834	Mar. 4, 1831	74	

Names.		Rank.	Annual allowance.	Sums received.	Description of service.	When placed on the pension roll.	Commencement of pension.	Ages.	Laws under which they were formerly inscribed on the pension roll; and remarks.
William Chappell	-	Private	50 00	150 00	Virginia militia	Oct. 18, 1833	do	74	
Jacob Hubbs	-	do	36 66	109 98	do	Mar. 2, 1833	do	72	
Samuel Hornbeck	-	do	20 00	60 00	do	Sep. 9, 1833	do	71	
Jesse Miles	-	do	30 00	75 00	do	Sep. 25, 1833	do	71	
John Miller	-	do	30 00	90 00	do	June 6, 1834	do	85	
Reuben Northern	-	do	20 00	60 00	do	Dec. 26, 1833	do	75	
Samuel Rowland	-	do	63 33	189 99	N. Jersey St. troops	Oct. 21, 1833	do	76	
Joseph Saunders	-	Lieutenant	320 00	960 00	Virginia line	Nov. 14, 1832	do	78	
John Stringer	-	Private	43 33	129 99	Virginia militia	Mar. 2, 1833	do	79	
Isaac Skinner	-	do	23 33	58 33	do	Aug. 9, 1833	do	74	
William Spencer	-	do-	80 00	240 00	do	July 1, 1834	do	73	
Augustin Webb	-	Sergeant	60 00	180 00	Virginia St. troops	Mar. 2, 1833	do		
Elijah Wright	-	Private	28 33	84 99	Penn. St. troops	Sep. 9, 1833	do	78	

Statement, &c. of Butler county, Kentucky.

Names.		Rank.	Annual allowance.	Sums received.	Description of service.	When placed on the pension roll.	Commencement of pension.	Ages.	Laws under which they were formerly inscribed on the pension roll; and remarks.
William Busby	-	Private	60 00	180 00	N. Carolina militia	June 6, 1833	Mar. 4, 1831	72	
Jacob Borah	-	do	20 00	60 00	Pennsylvania militia	Jan. 28, 1834	do	69	
James Cook	-	do	30 00	60 00	Virginia line	Jan. 15, 1833	do	72	
Thomas Carson	-	Pr. in.& cav.	80 00	240 00	Virginia st. troops	April 2, 1833	do	74	
Matthew Kaykendall	-	Sergeant	50 00	150 00	S. Carolina line	Aug. 17, 1833	do	76	
Thomas Lawrence	-	Pri. & ser.	120 00	360 00	Virginia line	Nov. 3, 1832	do	73	
John Porter	-	Private	110 00	330 00	Virginia militia	Apr. 2, 1833	do	75	
Jesse Scholfield	-	do	80 00	240 00	Connecticut line	May 29, 1833	do	77	
John Sharp, 2d	-	do	20 00	60 00	Virginia militia	Jan. 28, 1834	do	75	
Mark Whitaker	-	do	20 00	50 00	N. Carolina line	May 29, 1833	do	84	
Abner Wornack	-	do	24 44	61 10	N. Carolina militia	Aug. 17, 1833	do	70	

Statement, &c. of Caldwell county, Kentucky.

Names.	Rank.	Annual allowance.	Sums received.	Description of service.	When placed on the pension roll.	Commencement of pension.	Ages.	Laws under which they were formerly inscribed on the pension roll; and remarks.
William Asherst	Private	20 00	60 00	Virginia militia	Mar. 13, 1835	Mar. 4, 1831	72	
William Armstrong	do	43 33	129 99	N. Carolina line	Feb. 24, 1834	do	81	
William Blackburn	Sergeant	95 00	-	Virginia militia	Mar. 15, 1833	do	77	
Thomas Beck	Private	36 66	109 98	Maryland line	Dec. 2, 1833	do	70	
John Blick	do	20 00	50 00	Vir. State troops	Dec. 9, 1833	do	72	
Tacey Cooper	Midship'n	108 00	324 00	Penn. navy	Mar. 13, 1833	do	69	
Spencer Calvert	Ser. & pri.	41 66	124 98	Virginia line	Aug. 22, 1833	do	73	
James Clinton	Pri. & lieut.	183 33	549 99	do	Oct. 11, 1833	do	72	
Joseph Dunn	Pri. inf. & cavalry	93 33	279 99	N. Carolina militia	Mar. 13, 1833	do	79	
Nathaniel Davis	Private	40 00	120 00	Virginia line	Nov. 15, 1833	do	80	
William Ford	do	36 66	109 98	Maryland militia	Ap'l 12, 1833	do	71	
Solomon Freer	Pri. of cav.	100 00	300 00	S. Carolina line	Aug. 22, 1833	do	70	
Michael Freeman	Private of cavalry & infantry	95 82	287 46	N. Carolina line	do	do	70	
Joseph Guess	Pri. of cav.	32 50	97 50	N. Carolina militia	Mar. 14, 1833	do	72	
Major Groom	Private	29 30	87 90	Virginia line	Ap'l 12, 1833	do	71	
John Hart	do	40 00	120 00	N. Carolina line	May 6, 1833	do	82	
John Hamilton	do	21 56	-	Virginia militia	Sep. 2, 1835	do	79	
John Huey	do	36 66	109 98	Penn. militia	Jan. 8, 1834	do	80	
John McNabb	do	20 00	-	S. Carolina militia	Mar. 2, 1833	do	86	
Hugh McVay	do	50 00	150 00	Virginia mihia	Mar. 14, 1833	do	92	
Benjamin Ogden	do	80 00	240 00	N. Jersey line	Oct. 6, 1832	do	70	
James Scott	do	30 00	75 00	Virginia militia	Mar. 14, 1833	do	78	

Statement, &c. of Callaway county, Kentucky.

NAMES.	Rank.	Annual allowance.	Sums received.	Description of service.	When placed on the pension roll.	Commencement of pension.	Ages.	Laws under which they were formerly inscribed on the pension roll; and remarks.
John Barham	Private	32 33	—	Virginia line	Sep. 5, 1833	Mar. 4, 1831	70	
Robert Cooke	Pri. inf. & cavalry	82 50	247 50	do	Dec. 14, 1833	do	78	
Joseph Greenwood	Private	66 66	199 98	Delaware line	Jan. 26, 1833	do	80	
Joseph Glover	Pri. of inf. & cavalry	84 54	211 35	Virginia line	Aug. 17, 1833	do	74	
Jesse Henson, senr.	Private	80 00	240 00	do	Jan. 26, 1833	do	75	
John Hamlett	do	40 00	120 00	N. Carolina militia	May 11, 1833	do	77	
John Jones	Pri. ser. &c.	24 58	61 45	Virginia militia	May 13, 1833	do	74	
Thomas McGrew	Private	80 00	240 00	South Carolina line	Jan. 26, 1833	do	102	
Andrew Melone	Pt. & capt.	87 88	263 64	Maryland line	July 9, 1833	do	80	
Charles Mullins	Pri. of inf. & cavalry	63 33	189 99	N. Carolina line	Aug. 17, 1833	do	85	
George Owens	Private	20 00	60 00	Maryland line	Jan. 26, 1833	do	85	
Kimbrough Ogilvie	do	20 00	60 00	N. Carolina militia	do	do	71	
Rowland Stone	do	23 33	69 99	S. Carolina militia	Sep. 5, 1833	do	70	
Thomas Smith	do	30 00	90 00	Virginia State troops	Dec. 18, 1833	do	93	
Edmund Tayloe	do	30 00	90 00	N. Carolina militia	Oct. 21, 1833	do	78	
Leonard West	do	43 33	129 99	do	Jan. 31, 1833	do	69	

Statement, &c. of Campbell county, Kentucky.

NAMES.	Rank.	Annual allowance.	Sums received.	Description of service.	When placed on the pension roll.	Commencement of pension.	Ages.	Laws under which they were formerly inscribed on the pension roll; and remarks.
Samuel Byland	Private	40 00	120 00	Virginia line	Apr'l 4, 1834	Mar. 4, 1831	68	
Samuel Belville	do	20 00	60 00	Delaware militia	Apr. 14, 1834	do	72	
Samuel Baley	do	36 66	109 98	N. C. State troops	Nov. 25, 1835	do	77	
Stephens Collins	do	50 00	150 00	Connecticut line	Jan. 19, 1833	do	80	
Joseph Casey	do	30 00	90 00	Pennsylvania line	Apr. 11, 1834	do	71	
John Ducker	do	60 00	150 00	Virginia line	May 24, 1833	do	75	
Julius C. Goodwin	do	20 00	50 00	do	Oct. 18, 1833	do	70	
John Hays	do	40 00	80 00	Pennsylvania line	May 30, 1833	do	77	
Jonathan Huling	do	20 00	50 00	Virginia militia	Oct. 18, 1833	do	73	
Josiah Herbert, sr.	do	60 00	180 00	do	Dec. 14, 1833	do	79	
Nicholas Long	Ser. adj. & b. major	193 33	579 99	Virginia line	Sep. 3, 1832	do	80	
Edmond Massey	Private	20 00	60 00	Virginia militia	Feb. 5, 1833	do	87	
Edward Morin	do	80 00	240 00	Virginia line	Feb. 28, 1833	do	89	
Peter Mason	do	40 00	120 00	do	Jan. 13, 1834	do	70	
Robert Marshall	do	80 00	240 00	Maryland line	Mar. 27, 1834	do	71	
Abraham Parker	do	40 00	120 00	Virginia line	Jan. 17, 1834	do	76	
Benjamin Sutton	do	40 00	120 00	N. J. militia	June 6, 1834	do	78	
Samuel Todd	do	26 66	66 65	Virginia militia	Aug. 23, 1833	do	73	

Statement, &c. of Casey county, Kentucky.

NAMES.	Rank.	Annual allowance.	Sums received.	Description of service.	When placed on the pension roll.	Commencement of pension.	Age.	Laws under which they were formerly inscribed on the pension roll; and remarks.
John Cannady	Private	36 66	109 98	Virginia State tr.	May 6, 1833	Mar. 4, 1831	71	
Osbourne Coffey	Pri. & ser.	110 00	330 00	Virginia line	May 11, 1833	do	75	
James Carson	Pri. & lt.	50 00	150 00	Virginia militia	Oct. 18, 1833	do	73	
Julius Glazebrook	Private	26 66	66 65	do	July 10, 1833	do	82	
John Good	do	30 00	90 00	Virginia line	Aug. 17, 1833	do	85	
John M'Whorter	do	80 00	240 00	N. Carolina line	May 6, 1833	do	85	
Absalom Russell	do	23 33	69 99	Virginia militia	May 6, 1833	do	74	
John Royaltree	do	26 66	79 98	Virginia line	do	do	75	
William Sutherland	do	80 00	240 00	Maryland line	Sep. 25, 1833	do	87	

Statement, &c. of Christian county, Kentucky.

NAMES.	Rank.	Annual allowance.	Sums received.	Description of service.	When placed on the pension roll.	Commencement of pension.	Age.	Laws under which they were formerly inscribed on the pension roll; and remarks.
James Anderson	Private	37 00	111 00	N. Carolina militia	May 13, 1833	Mar. 4, 1831	87	
George Barnes	do	80 00	240 00	Virginia line	Feb. 13, 1833	do	78	
Jonathan Clark	Lieut.	320 00	960 00	N. Carolina line	Sep. 26, 1833	do	75	
Thomas Dimkinson	Private	40 00	120 00	Virginia line	Jan. 26, 1833	do	71	
William Dupuy	do	21 66	64 98	Georgia militia	do	do	68	
Henry Davis	do	80 00	200 00	N. Carolina line	Ap'l 1, 1833	do	75	
Absalom Franklin	do	20 00	60 00	Virginia militia	Jan. 11, 1834	do	70	
James Gilmore	Serg't & pr.	51 66	179 15	Virginia line	Aug. 17, 1833	do	89	
William Gray	Private	60 00	120 00	do	June 17, 1833	do	80	
John Harlow	do	20 00	60 00	Virginia militia	Jan. 26, 1833	do	83	

11

Statement, &c. of Christian county—Continued.

NAMES.	Rank.	Annual allowance.	Sums received.	Description of service.	When placed on the pension roll.	Commencement of pension.	Ages.	Laws under which they were formerly inscribed on the pension roll; and remarks.
Dalmath Johnson	Private	20 55	61 65	Virginia militia	Oct. 18, 1833	Mar. 4, 1831	73	
Samuel Jones	do	96 00	175 22	Virginia line	May 18, 1819	May 18, 1818	78	Drop'd under act May 1, 1820. Inscribed on roll act June 7, 1832, March 18, 1818.
Do	do	80 00	160 00	do	Mar. 21, 1833	Mar. 4, 1831		
Night Knight	do	80 00	240 00	S. Carolina line	Nov. 30, 1832	do	84	
Joseph Meacham	Pr. of cav.	25 00	75 00	N. Car. St. troops	Nov. 10, 1832	do	73	
John Philips	Private	29 66	74 15	N. Carolina line	Oct. 29, 1832	do	100	
Matthew Patton	do	25 60	-	Maryland militia	June 24, 1834	do	84	
Isaac Palmer	do	25 77	-	Virginia militia	July 10, 1834	do	87	
Isaac Stroud	Pr. i. & cav. & or. seg't	33 33	99 99	N. Carolina militia	Jan. 26, 1833	do	73	
James Stenart	Private	80 00	240 00	S. Carolina militia	Nov. 9, 1833	do	72	
Charles Thomas	Pr. & ser.	25 66	76 98	N. Carolina line	Jan. 4, 1834	do	-	
Do	do	45 66	-	do	do	do	-	Increased from April 28, 1834.
William Warren	Private	80 00	240 00	Virginia line	Jan. 26, 1833	do		
Thomas Waggoner	Sergeant	30 00	90 00	do	Jan. 8, 1834	do	72	
Samuel Younglove	Ser. & pri.	116 66	339 98	Virginia militia	Ap'l 16, 1833	do	71	

Statement, &c. of Clark county, Kentucky.

NAMES.	Rank.	Annual allowance.	Sums received.	Description of service.	When placed on the pension roll.	Commencement of pension.	Age	Laws under which they were formerly inscribed on the pension roll; and remarks.
James Anderson	Private	80 00	240 00	Virginia line	Apl. 2, 1833	Mar. 4, 1831	74	
John Alexander, sen.	do	23 33	-	Penn. militia	Apl 12, 1833	do	78	
James Adkins	do	20 00	60 00	Virginia militia	Sep. 24, 1833	do	88	
John Arnold	do	80 00	240 00	Va. State troops	Mar. 25, 1834	do	75	
Smallwood Acton	do	30 00	90 00	do	June 6, 1834	do	75	
Limfield Burbridge	do	80 00	240 00	Virginia line	Sep. 17, 1832	do	74	
Thomas Berry	do	50 00	150 00	Virginia militia	May 3, 1833	do	77	
William Berkley, *alias* Bartlett	do	80 00	240 00	Virginia line	May 11, 1833	do	79	
James Bush	do	24 44	48 88	Va. State troops	Sep. 25, 1833	do	75	
John Dyke	do	30 00	75 00	Virginia line	May 11, 1833	do	83	
Matthew Duke	do	20 00	60 00	Virginia militia	Sep. 24, 1833	do	76	
Septimus Davis	Lieutenant	320 00	960 00	Penn. line	Nov. 29, 1833	do	78	
Peter De witt	Private	20 00	60 00	Virginia militia	Jan. 2, 1834	do	82	
James Elkin	do	63 33	189 99	do	Jan. 31, 1833	do	79	
Vachel Fandre	do	55 00	165 00	do	do	do	72	
Reuben Franklin	do	60 00	180 00	do	May 11, 1833	do	78	
John Gordon	do	26 66	79 98	do	Dec. 15, 1832	do	71	
John Gravitt	do	40 00	120 00	do	Apr. 10, 1833	do	77	
James Greening	do	24 44	73 32	do	May 18, 1833	do	81	
James Gay, sen.	do	80 00	240 00	do	Oct. 2, 1833	do	76	
Joel Hickman	do	80 00	240 00	Virginia line	May 7, 1833	do	73	
Benjamin Hally	do	23 33	69 99	Virginia militia	Dec. 7, 1833	do	82	
Stephen Holliday	do	36 66	109 98	Virginia line	Feb. 27, 1834	do	73	
Edward Hall	do	80 00	240 00	do	do	do	76	
Nicholas Jones	do	36 66	109 98	do	Dec. 10, 1832	do	71	
Joshua Jones	do	23 33	69 99	Maryland militia	Apl. 12, 1833	do	75	
Josiah Jackson	do	20 00	60 00	Virginia militia	Nov. 9, 1833	do	72	
Thomas Lowry	do	70 00	210 00	do	Oct. 2, 1833	do	74	
George Miller	do	20 00	60 00	do	Jan. 31, 1833	do	72	
Andrew Merrell	do	80 00	240 00	N. Jersey line	May 20, 1833	do	77	

Statement, &c. of Clark county—Continued.

NAMES.	Rank.	Annual allowance.	Sums received.	Description of service.	When placed on the pension roll.	Commencement of pension.	Ages.	Laws under which they were formerly inscribed on the pension roll; and remarks.
John Martin	Ser. & cap.	127 83	383 49	Virginia line	Aug. 21, 1833	March 4, 1831	85	
William Martin	Private	80 00	240 00	Virginia militia	Ap'l 9, 1833	do	77	
Richard Oliver	do	30 00	90 00	N. C. line	Jan. 11, 1834	do	82	
Joseph Palmer	do	53 33	106 66	Virginia line	Nov. 5, 1832	do	74	
James Spillman	do	36 66	-	Virginia militia	Feb. 22, 1833	do	78	
John Smith	do	33 33	99 99	Maryland militia	May 31, 1833	do	85	
Christopher Snail	Ser. & pri.	50 00	150 00	N. C. militia	Aug. 9, 1833	do	82	
John Stinson	Ensign and private	33 33	99 99	Maryland militia	Oct. 21, 1833	do		
Thomas Smith	Pr. & serg.	40 83	122 49	Virginia militia	Oct. 31, 1833	do	79	
Charles Tracy	Private	76 66	-	Maryland line	Oct. 24, 1832	do	82	Died March 19, 1834.
William Tuggle	do	64 66	161 65	Virginia line	Aug. 17, 1833	do	75	
James Thomas	do	43 33	129 99	N. C. militia	May 10, 1834	do	75	
William Wright	do	40 00	120 00	Virginia militia	Dec. 15, 1832	do	69	

Statement, &c. of Clay county, Kentucky.

NAMES.	Rank.	Annual allowance.	Sums received.	Description of service.	When placed on the roll.	Commencement of pension.	Ages.	Laws under which they were formerly inscribed on the pension roll; and remarks.
William Burns	Private	50 00	125 00	Virginia line	Jan. 30, 1833	Mar. 4, 1831	78	
Bowling Baker	Pr.inf.&cav.	60 83	182 49	North Carolina line	Jan. 26, 1833	do	71	
Jesse Bowling	Private	26 66	53 32	N. Carolina militia	do	do	76	
John Benge	do	56 66	169 98	do	June 18, 1834	do	74	
John Chandler	do	20 00	60 00	Virginia militia	Dec. 2, 1833	do	69	
Messenger Lewis	do	46 66	116 65	Connecticut line		do	72	
Azariah Martin	do	36 66	91 65	Virginia militia	Aug. 21, 1833	do	70	
John Phillips	do	50 00	150 00	S. Carolina militia	Oct. 2, 1833	do	73	
Harper Ratcliffe	do	20 00	60 00	N. Carolina militia	Jan. 9, 1834	do	72	
Thomas Stapleton	do	24 66	73 98	do	April 3, 1834	do	76	

Statement, &c. of Cumberland county, Kentucky.

NAMES.	Rank.	Annual allowance.	Sums received.	Description of service.	When placed on the pension roll.	Commencement of pension.	Ages.	Laws under which they were formerly inscribed on the pension roll; and remarks.
William Baker	Private	21 66	64 98	Virginia militia	Mar. 8, 1833	Mar. 4, 1831	70	
Benjamin Brummal	do	40 00	120 00	do	do	do	75	
Francis Barrett	Ser. & pri.	99 16	-	Virginia line	Mar. 26, 1833	do	72	
John Baker	Sergeant	120 00	360 00	do	April 1, 1833	do	83	
William Burchett	Private	30 00	90 00	Virginia St. troops	Sep. 24, 1833	do	79	
John Burchett	do	20 00	50 00	do	Nov. 15, 1833	do	73	
Charles Carter	do	80 00	240 00	Virginia line	Dec. 18, 1832	do	76	
William Chetham	do	38 34	115 02	Virginia militia	Mar. 8, 1833	do	72	
William Garry	do	44 99	134 97	do	do	do	78	

Statement, &c. of Cumberland county—Continued.

NAMES.	Rank.	Annual allowance.	Sums received.	Description of service.	When placed on the pension roll.	Commencement of pension.	Ages.	Laws under which they were formerly inscribed on the pension roll; and remarks.
John Chapman	Private	29 43	73 59	Virginia militia	May 18, 1833	Mar. 4, 1831	72	
Shadrach Claywell	Pri. of cav. & inf.	70 00	175 00	do	July 9, 1833	do	74	
John Creasey	Private	20 00	60 00	do	June 6, 1834	do	80	
Robert Crockett	do	45 43	136 29	do	Sept. 2, 1833	do	71	
Godfrey Elam	do	40 00	120 00	do	Mar. 8, 1833	do	71	
William Fergason	do	60 00	180 00	Virginia line	Nov. 15, 1833	do	83	
Martin Gryder	do	66 66	199 98	N. Carolina line	June 30, 1833	do	72	
Valentine Gryder	do	60 00	180 00	do	Aug. 17, 1833	do	84	
John Gibson	do	63 33	-	do	July 10, 1834	do	75	
William Goodson	Ensign	240 00	720 00	Virginia militia	Nov. 7, 1833	do	82	
Joseph Jewell	Lieutenant	320 00	960 00	N. York militia	Apr. 12, 1834	do	85	
George King	Private	20 00	60 00	Virginia militia	May 13, 1833	do	73	
Morgan Morgan	do	76 66	229 98	Virginia line	do	do	72	
John Miller	do	20 00	50 00	Maryland militia	May 29, 1833	do	74	
Francis Pierce	do	80 00	240 00	Virginia line	Mar. 18, 1833	do	84	
Solomon Prewitt	do	80 00	240 00	do	Aug. 9, 1833	do	77	
George Richardson	do	80 00	240 00	do	May 6, 1833	do	72	
James Radford	do	50 00	150 00	N. Carolina militia	Oct. 21, 1833	do	79	
Samuel Smith	do	30 00	90 00	S. Carolina St. tr.	Ap'l 10, 1833	do	79	
Joseph Sewell	do	60 00	180 00	Virginia line	June 17, 1833	do	80	
John Scott	do	80 00	240 00	Virginia militia	Aug. 9, 1833	do	73	
John Self	do	30 00	90 00	Virginia militia	do	do	72	
Charles Thurman	do	96 00		Virginia line	Mar. 10, 1832	Feb. 25, 1832	-	Dropped and inscribed on roll under the act June 7, 1832.
Do	do	80 00		do	Aug. 20, 1832	Mar. 4, 1831	76	March 18, 1818.
James Williams, 2d	do	80 00	240 00	Virginia militia	Aug. 29, 1833	do	72	
Richard Wade, sen.	do	80 00	240 00	N. Carolina militia	Sep. 26, 1833	do	82	
Thomas Williams	do	80 00	240 00	Virginia militia	Dec. 27, 1833	do	79	
William Whitaker	do	70 00	240 00	do	July 10, 1834	do	74	

Statement, &c. of Daviess county, Kentucky.

NAMES.	Rank.	Annual allowance.	Sums received.	Description of service.	When placed on the pension roll.	Commencement of pension.	Ages.	Laws under which they were formerly inscribed on the pension roll; and remarks.
Zacbariah Briant	Private	80 00	240 00	Virginia line	June 24, 1833	Mar. 4, 1831	68	
George Calhoon	Lt. ens. & qr: m.	246 66	739 98	Pennsylvania line	June 11, 1833	do	80	
Benjamin Field	Pri. of inf. ens, & cap.	289 32	867 96	Virginia line	Aug. 17, 1833	do	77	
John Hall	Private	30 44	91 32	Virginia militia	Dec. 21, 1833	do	88	
Samuel Johnson, sen.	do	36 66	109 98	do	Feb. 28, 1833	do	90	
James Jones	Pr. of inf y & cav.	49 16	122 90	N. Carolina militia	June 11, 1833	do	74	
James Kelly	Private	40 00	-	Virginia line	Mar. 1, 1833	do	76	
Anthony Thompson	Pri. & sgt.	33 33	99 99	Pennsylvania line	Oct. 21, 1833	do	75	
James Tannehill	Private	26 66	79 98	Maryland line	Mar. 7, 1833	do	73	
Benjamin Taylor	do	54 66	163 98	Pennsylvania line	Jan. 11, 1834	do	78	

Statement, &c. of Estill county, Kentucky.

NAMES.	Rank.	Annual allowance.	Sums received.	Description of service.	When placed on the pension roll.	Commencement of pension.	Ages.	Laws under which they were formerly inscribed on the pension roll; and remarks.
Thomas Brown	Private	40 00	120 00	Virginia militia	Ap'l 20, 1833	Mar. 4, 1831	92	
Mathias Horn	do	80 00	240 00	Virginia line	Dec. 11, 1832	do	72	
William Harris	do	23 33	69 99	Virginia militia	Jan. 16, 1833	do	70	
William Johnson	do	40 00	120 00	do	Feb. 28, 1833	do	77	
James Noland	Pri. & cap.	280 00	700 00	do	Jan. 16, 1833	do	94	
Jesse Noland	Private	20 00	60 00	N. Carolina militia	do	do	73	
Richard Oldham	do	30 00	75 00	do	Ap'l 20, 1833	do	89	
Joseph Proctor	do	80 00	240 00	Virginia line	Dec. 11, 1832	do	78	
Ambrose Powell	do	21 66	64 98	Virginia militia	Mar. 25, 1833	do	73	
Jesse Robertson	do	35 00	105 00	Virginia line	Jan. 16, 1833	do	76	
John Stufflebean	do	80 00	200 00	Penn. line	Mar. 29, 1833	do	82	
David Snowden	do	80 00	240 00	do	do	do	75	
George Sheffield	Ser. & pri.	68 33	204 99	N. C. State troops	Ap'l 1, 1833	do	75	
Henry Winkler	Private	46 66	139 98	do	do	do	76	
John Waters	do	33 33	99 99	Virginia militia	Ap'l 20, 1833	do	82	
Elisha Witt	do	46 66	139 98	do	Jan. 16, 1833	do	83	

Statement, &c. of Fayette county, Kentucky.

NAMES.	Rank,	Annual allowance.	Sums received.	Description of service.	When placed on the pension roll,	Commencement of pension,	Ages.	Laws under which they were formerly inscribed on the pension roll; and remarks.
Thomas Andrews	Private	80 00	240 00	Virginia militia	Jan. 15, 1833	Mar. 4, 1831	76	
Ambrose Armstrong	do	80 00	240 00	Virginia line	Mar. 15, 1833	do	74	
Peter B. F. Adams	do	58 33	147 99	N. Carolina line	Dec. 18, 1833	do	76	
Samuel Blair	Pri. & ser.	23 33	69 99	Pennsylvania mil,	May 4, 1833	do	76	
John G. Boyer	Private	30 00	90 00	Maryland line	May 18, 1833	do	71	
Samuel Boon	do	40 00	120 00	S. Carolina line	Sep. 4, 1833	do	76	
John Barton	do	33 33	83 33	N. J. State troops	Oct. 18, 1833	do	79	
John Christian	do	76 66	229 98	Virginia militia	Jan. 15, 1833	do	82	
Tilman Camper	do	79 23	237 69	do	Feb. 26, 1833	do	75	
Andrew Christian	do	50 00	150 00	Virginia line	Aug. 13, 1833	do	73	
James Davenport	do	80 00	240 00	Virginia militia	Jan. 15, 1833	do	92	
John Darnaby	do	40 00	100 00	do	Feb. 26, 1833	do	74	
Reuben Emmerson	Pri. & ser.	23 10	69 30	do	Aug. 10, 1833	do	88	
Francis Epperson	Private	20 00	60 00	do	May 29, 1834	do	83	
John Fowler	Lieut.	320 00	960 00	Virginia line	Oct. 30, 1832	do	78	
Abram Farguson	Private	80 00	240 00	do	Feb. 26, 1833	do	73	
Joseph Faulconer	do	62 33	186 99	do	Aug. 22, 1833	do	76	
John Graves	do	20 00	60 00	Virginia militia	Jan. 15, 1833	do	77	
Wilson Hunt	do	40 00	120 00	do	Jan. 16, 1833	do	80	
Randall Haley	do	30 00	90 00	Virginia line	May 6, 1833	do	79	
James Hamilton	do	58 00	174 00	Pennsylvania mil.	July 1, 1834	do	71	
John Hunter	do	63 33	189 99	N. Carolina line	Dec. 18, 1833	do	75	
James Laffoon	do	56 66	169 98	Virginia line	May 6, 1833	do	71	
James M'Dowell	Pri. & ens-	61 66	185 98	do	Jan. 19, 1833	do	75	
James Masterson	do	88 33	264 99	N. Carolina militia	Feb. 28, 1833	do	81	
Andrew M'Calla	Sergeant	50 00	150 00	Pennsylvania line	Mar. 1, 1833	do	74	
Isaac M'Issacks	Private	60 00	180 00	do	Sep. 5, 1833	do	83	
Richard Mitchell	do	20 00	50 00	Virginia militia	Sep. 9, 1833	do	70	Died November 27, 1832.
Benjamin Morrell	do	61 66	184 68	N. Carolina militia	Oct. 18, 1833	do	74	
Joseph Mosby	do	35 00	105 00	do	Mar. 3, 1834	do	76	
Radford M'Cargo	do	46 66	139 98	do	Mar. 6, 1834	do	72	

12

Statement, &c. of Fayette county—Continued.

NAMES.	Rank.	Annual allowance.	Sums received.	Description of service.	When placed on the pension roll.	Commencement of pension.	Ages.	Laws under which they were formerly inscribed on the pension roll; and remarks.
John Parker	Pri., wagon master,&c.	290 00	870 00	Pennsylvania mil.	Jan. 15, 1833	Mar. 4, 1831	80	
George Proctor	Private	30 00	90 00	Virginia line	Mar. 6, 1834	do	74	
John Peck	Mariner	20 00	60 00	Ship Queen of France			65	
William Palmateer	Private	26 66	79 98	New York militia	Ap'l 12, 1834	do	73	
Robert S. Russell	Pri. & cor.	53 33	159 99	Virginia militia	Oct. 15, 1833	do	73	
Benjamin Robinson	Private	60 00	150 00	do	Jan. 15, 1833	do	82	
Benjamin Robertson	do	60 00	180 00	N. Carolina line	Feb. 28, 1863	do	78	
James Smith	do	80 00	240 00	Virginia line	Mar. 6, 1833	do	86	
William Stewart	do	80 00	240 00	do	May 17, 1833	do	72	
Cornelius Sullivan	do	46 66	139 98	do	Aug. 17, 1833	do	78	
Elijah Stout	do	80 00	60 00	New Jersey militia	Sep. 5, 1833	do	74	
James True	do	30 00	90 00	Virginia line	May 29, 1834	do	86	
Geo. Vallandigham	do	20 00	60 00	Virginia militia	Aug. 9, 1833	do	73	
Isaac Webb	Lieut.	320 00	920 00	Virginia line	July 15, 1833	do		
Charles Wickliffe	Pri.in.&cav.	22 50	67 50	Virginia militia	May 31, 1833	do	68	
John Young	Private	40 00	120 00	N. Carolina line	Feb. 28, 1833	do		

Statement, &c. of Floyd county, Kentucky.

NAMES.	Rank.	Annual allowance.	Sums received.	Description of service.	When placed on the pension roll.	Commencement of pension.	Ages.	Laws under which they were formerly inscribed on the pension roll; and remarks.
Thomas C. Brown	Cornet	320 00	960 00	Virginia militia	July 19, 1833	Mar. 4, 1831	74	
James Camron	Private	80 00	240 00	Virginia line	May 17, 1833	do	76	
Henry Connelly	Cap. of cav.	150 00	450 00	North Carolina mil.	Feb. 24, 1834	do	82	
Edward Darten	Private	80 00	240 00	Virginia line	Jan 20, 1834	do	83	
Abina Fairchild	do	40 00	120 00	North Carolina line	Mar. 27, 1834	do	72	
James Harris	do	70 00	210 00	Virginia militia	July 19, 1833	do	82	
Joshua Hitchcock	do	20 00	60 00	North Caroline line	Jan. 20, 1834	do	92	
Simeon Justice	Drummer	88 00	264 00	do	Feb. 20, 1833	do	69	
John Moore	Private	33 33	99 99	do	Mar. 27, 1834	do	75	
Jonathan Pytts	do	80 00	240 00	do	June 21, 1833	do	78	
James Patrick	do	80 00	240 00	Virginia militia	Sep. 4, 1833	do	75	
John Porter	do	65 55	196 65	Virginia line	Feb. 7, 1834	do	72	
Benedict Wadkins	do	80 00	240 00	North Carolina line	June 21, 1833	do	74	
Richard Wells	do	63 33	189 99	do	Mar. 29, 1834	do		

Statement, &c. of Fleming county, Kentucky.

NAMES.	Rank.	Annual allowance.	Sums received.	Description of service.	When placed on the roll.	Commencement of pension.	Ages.	Laws under which they were formerly inscribed on the pension roll; and remarks.
James Crawford	Private	20 00	60 00	Virginia militia	Oct. 18, 1833	Mar. 4, 1831	75	
Joseph Davis	do	20 00	60 00	Virginia line	Oct. 24, 1832	do	74	
Jesse Davis	do	80 00	240 00	do	Mar. 18, 1833	do	72	
Joshua Davidson	Pri. of cav.	100 00	300 00	do	May 3, 1833	do	73	
Hugh Dreman	Private	53 33	159 99	Pennsylvania line	May 16, 1834	do	72	
John Fons	do	20 00	60 00	Virginia militia	Feb. 21, 1833	do	67	

Statement, &c. of Fleming county—Continued.

NAMES.	Rank:	Annual allowance.	Sums received.	Description of service.	When placed on the pension roll.	Commencement of pension.	Ages.	Laws under which they were formerly inscribed on the pension roll; and remarks.
John Fraseur	Private	20 00	60 00	Virginia militia	Ap'l 12, 1833	March 4, 1831	69	
Thomas Ferguson	do	37 77	75 54	Pennsylvania militia	Ap'l 16, 1833	do	73	
Archibald Gorman	do	76 66	229 98	Pennsylvania line	Sep. 24, 1833	do	80	
Joseph Goddard	do	80 00	240 00	Virginia line	Mar. 25, 1833	do	73	
John Hammond	Pri. of art.	100 00	300 00	do	Oct. 24, 1832	do	79	
David Howe	Pr.of inf.& cavalry	83·33	208 33	S. Carolina militia	Jan. 10, 1833	do	87	
Samuel Humphrees	Private	80 00	240 00	Virginia line	Mar. 18, 1833	do	85	
David Hopkins	do	80 00	240 00	Pennsylvania line	Ap'l 20, 1833	do	74	
William H. Layton	do	80 00	240 00	do	Mar. 1, 1833	do	79	
George London	do	80 00	-	do	Mar. 16, 1833	do	76	Died November 14, 1832.
John Miller	do	80 00	240 00	Pennsylvania vol.	Sep. 10, 1832	do	69	
William Miller	do	80 00	240 00	Pennsylvania line	Oct. 24, 1832	do	77	
John M'Kee	do	80 00	240 00	do	Jan. 10, 1833	do	70	
Peter Mahzy	do	20 00	60 00	Virginia militia	Mar. 20, 1833	do	83	
Joseph Maddin	Lt. & pri.	126 66	379 98	Maryland State tr.	Jan. 20, 1834	do	77	
William Proctor	Private	80 00	240 00	Pennsylvania line	Jan. 25, 1833	do	75	
Burtis Ringo	Pri.of cav.	100 00	300 00	Virginia line	Oct. 24, 1832	do	72	
James Rigdon	Private	20 00	60 00	Maryland militia	Dec. 28, 1832	do	72	
William Robertson	do	25 66	-	N. Carolina militia	Ap'l 16, 1833	do	80	
Thomas Rhodan	do	20 00	60 00	N. Jersey militia	May 6, 1833	do	83	
John Ross	do	38 44	96 10	Virginia line	Dec. 24, 1833	do	79	
John Summers	do	20 00	60 00	Virginia militia	Oct. 30, 1832	do	70	
Redmond Smith	do	63 33	189 99	do	do	do	74	
Philip Weaver	do	20 00	60 00	Virginia line	Mar. 20, 1833	do	70	
Lawrence Williams	Pri.& serg.	90 00	270 00	Maryland line	Mar. 27, 1833	do	76	Died June 21, 1833.
Gerard Williams	do	91 66	210 48	do	do	do	75	

Statement, &c. of Franklin county, Kentucky.

Names.	Rank.	Annual allowance.	Sums received.	Description of service.	When placed on the pension roll.	Commencment of pension.	Ages.	Laws under which they were formerly inscribed on the pension roll; and remarks.
Abraham Baley	Private	80 00	240 00	Virginia line	Feb. 5, 1833	Mar. 4, 1831	74	
James Biscoe	Seaman	96 00	288 00	Navy of Virginia	Dec. 12, 1832	do	74	
Thomas Bell	Private	80 00	-	Virginia line	May 21, 1833	do	78	
Anthony Crockett	Lieutenant	320 00	960 00	do	Jan. 24, 1833	do	71	
Silas Douthit	Private	20 00	60 00	Virginia militia	Feb. 12, 1833	do	75	
William Fenwick	do	73 33	167 79	Maryland militia	Feb. 11, 1833	do	76	
William Forsee	Pri. & ser.	50 00	125 00	Virginia line	Dec. 27, 1833	do	77	
Daniel Fitzgerald	Private	46 66	139 98	do	Jan. 20, 1834	do	72	
Lawrence Gordon	do	20 00	-	N: Carolina militia	July 21, 1834	do	79	
Elisha Hawkins	do	80 00	217 80	Virginia line	Oct. 29, 1832	do		Died June 18, 1833.
Robert Hedges	Pr. & ser. of cavalry	98 33	-	do	Dec. 26, 1832	do		Died November 24, 1833.
John C. Jackson	Private	79 33	237 99	Virginia militia	Jan. 2, 1834	do	74	
John Keeton	do	30 00	-	do	Feb. 23, 1833	do	77	
Humphrey Marshall	Capt. & lt.	400 00	1,200 00	Virginia State troops	July 25, 1832	do	72	
John Magill	Private	23 33	69 99	Virginia line	Oct. 20, 1832	do	75	
John McDonald	do	20 00	40 00	Vermont militia	May 28, 1833	do	69	
John Oliver	do	80 00	200 00	Virginia line	Dec. 12, 1832	do	78	
John Reading	do	60 00	160 00	Pennsylvania line	Nov. 29, 1832	do	74	
John Stephens, senr.	do	60 00	180 00	Virginia militia	Oct. 19, 1832	do	71	
Richard Sebree	do	23 33	69 99	Virginia line	Dec. 6, 1832	do	82	
Thomas C. Scroggin	do	45 55	136 65	Maryland militia	Feb. 11, 1833	do	70	
Hedgman Triplett	Lieutenant	320 00	960 00	Virginia line	Dec. 12, 1832	do		
James Taylor	Private	60 00	180 00	do	Feb. 12, 1833	do		
Ambrose White	do	80 00	240 00	do	Aug. 1, 1833	do	78	
Philemon Yancey	do	80 00	240 00	do	Sep. 17, 1833	do	78	

Statement, &c. of Gallatin county, Kentucky.

NAMES.	Rank.	Annual allowance.	Sums received.	Description of service.	When placed on the pension roll.	Commencement of pension.	Ages.	Laws under which they were formerly inscribed on the pension roll; and remarks.
Benjamin Barnes	Private	20 00	60 00	Virginia militia	May 6, 1833	Mar. 4, 1831	69	
Shadrach Barnes	do	80 00	240 00	Virginia line	Dec. 14, 1833	do	70	
Samuel D. Davis	do	20 90	52 25	Maryland militia	May 28, 1833	do	74	
Jarret Dement	do	60 00	150 00	Pennsylvania line	Dec. 10, 1833	do	74	
John Dean	do	40 00	120 00	do	do	do	72	
Charles Gowens	do	30 90	90 00	Virginia line	Dec. 14, 1833	do	71	
Thomas Hawes	do	50 00	133 96	North Carolina line	Feb. 25, 1834	do	91	Died October 24, 1833.
Amos V. Mathews	do	80 00	240 00	Virginia line	Sep. 23, 1833	do	75	
William McDowell	do	20 00	40 00	do	Oct. 30, 1833	do	73	
Thomas Noel	do	20 00	60 00	Virginia militia	Dec. 2, 1833	do	72	
Abijah North	do	80 00	240 00	Connecticut line	Jan. 6, 1834	do	75	
Robert Scott	do	30 00	90 00	Virginia line	Dec. 10, 1833	do	70	
William Thompson, sr.	do	80 00	240 00	New Jersey militia	Sep. 16, 1833	do	74	
John Wells	do	20 00	60 00	North Carolina mil.	Dec. 2, 1833	do	70	

Statement, &c. of Garrard county, Kentucky.

NAMES.	Rank.	Annual allowance.	Sums received.	Description of service.	When placed on the pension roll.	Commencement of pension.	Ages.	Laws under which they were formerly inscribed on the pension roll; and remarks.
Robert Braak	Private	63 33	189 99	N. Carolina line	Sep. 3, 1832	Mar. 4, 1831	77	
Joseph Baker	do	60 00	180 00	do	Feb. 27, 1833	do	79	
Arabia Brown	do	26 66	79 98	Virginia militia	Jan. 26, 1833	do	78	
John Bryant	do	50 00	150 00	do	Aug. 22, 1833	do	74	
John Buford	do	30 00	90 00	Virginia line	Nov. 12, 1833	do	95	
Goolsberry Childers	do	80 00	240 00	do	Oct. 18, 1832	do	78	
John Crutchfield	do	20 00	60 00	N. Carolina militia	Nov. 19, 1832	do	80	
Benjamin Egerton	do	30 00	90 00	N. Carolina line	Sep. 1, 1832	do	73	
Thomas Edmeston	do	21 12	63 36	Penn'a militia	July 15, 1833	do	73	
John Floyd	do	33 33	83 33	Virginia militia	Jan. 22, 1833	do	74	
George Floyd	do	36 66	73 32	do	Jan. 26, 1833	do	78	
Joshua Fry	do	23 55	70 65	do	May 6, 1834	do	74	
William Haggard	do	40 00	100 00	N. Carolina line	May 16, 1833	do	78	
William Jefferies	do	25 10	75 30	Virginia militia	Jan. 4, 1833	do	75	
John Jones	de	30 00	60 00	do	July 18, 1834	do	70	
Thomas Kennedy	Captain	420 00	1260 00	N. Carolina line	Sep. 3, 1832	do	78	
David Kennedy	Private	80 00	240 00	Virginia line	Oct. 12, 1833	do	67	
Timothy Noel	do	80 00	200 00	do	Oct. 12, 1833	do	75	
Taylor Noel	do	20 00	60 00	Virginia militia	Sep. 5, 1833	do	83	
William Powe	do	77 33	231 99	do	Jan. 4, 1833	do	76	
William Parks	do	45 00	90 00	do	Jan. 22, 1833	do	79	
James Robertson	do	30 00	90 00	Virginia line	Mar. 30, 1833	do	79	
Jesse Robards	do	56 66	169 98	Virginia militia	Jan. 22, 1833	do	72	
Alexander Reid	do	40 00	120 00	do	Sep. 2, 1833	do	82	
Benjamin Sutton	do	80 00	240 00	Va. State troops	Oct. 18, 1832	do	78	
John Slavins	do	20 00	60 00	N. Carolina militia	Jan. 26, 1833	do	77	
Anthony Street	do	26 66	79 98	Virginia militia	Oct. 21, 1833	do	77	
Elijah Williams	do	20 00	60 00	do	Nov. 9, 1832	do	73	
John Walden	do	46 66	139 98	do	Jan. 26, 1833	do		
Joseph Wood	do	80 00	200 00	New Jersey line	Feb. 27, 1833	do	79	

Statement, &c. of Grant county, Kentucky.

NAMES.	Rank.	Annual allowance.	Sums received.	Description of service.	When placed on the pension roll.	Commencement of pension.	Laws under which they were formerly inscribed on the pension roll; and remarks.
James Bates	Pri. of inf. & cavalry	85 00	255 00	Virginia line	Dec. 27, 1833	Mar. 4, 1831	
Henry Childers	Private	20 00	60 00	Virginia militia	Feb. 28, 1833	do	69
Jeremiah Crook	do	20 00	60 00	do	do	do	70
Joshua Jones	do	60 00	180 00	do	Sep. 25, 1833	do	74
John Jump	do	40 00	120 00	N. Car. St. troops	Dec. 18, 1833	do	86
Jacob New	do	20 00	60 00	Virginia militia	Feb. 7, 1834	do	73
Daniel Seward	do	30 00	90 00	Penn. militia	Jan. 31, 1834	do	73
James Theobald	do	80 00	240 00	Virginia militia	Jan. 9, 1833	do	
John Zinn	do	80 00	240 00	do	June 11, 1834	do	71

Statement, &c. of Graves county, Kentucky.

NAMES.	Rank.	Annual allowance.	Sums received.	Description of service.	When placed on the pension roll.	Commencement of pension.	Laws under which they were formerly inscribed on the pension roll; and remarks.
Walter Adams	Private	43 33	129 99	N. Carolina militia	Aug. 17, 1833	Mar. 4, 1831	79
John Brimmage	do	20 00	60 00	Maryland militia	May 10, 1834	do	73
William Cook	do	80 00	240 00	N. Carolina militia	Jan. 26, 1833	do	71
Charles Gilbert	do	60 00	180 00	Maryland militia	Jan. 11, 1834	do	78
John Hawthorn	do	63 33	189 99	S. Car. St. troops	Jan. 10, 1834	do	87
William Johnson	do	40 00	120 00	Virginia militia	Aug. 27, 1833	do	74

Names	Rank	Annual allowance	Sums received	Description of service	When placed on the pension roll	Commencement of pension	Ages	Laws under which they were formerly inscribed on the pension roll; and remarks.
Vachel Lovelace	do	30 00	90 00	N. Carolina militia	Aug. 17, 1835	do	76	
Willis Odom	Pri. of inf. and cav.							
John Odil	Private	28 16	84 48	S. Carolina militia	Feb. 24, 1834	do	71	
Benjamin Rhodes	Pri. of cav.	67 50	202 50	S. Car. St troops	June 11, 1834	do	75	
George Rowden	Pri. of inf. and cav.	29 16	87 00	N. Carolina militia	Jan. 26, 1833	do	69	Died March 1, 1834.
John Stoakes	Private	84 54	253 62	Maryland militia	Mar. 25, 1834	do	91	
John Stafford	do	66 66	199 98	N. Carolina militia	Oct. 21, 1833	do	71	
		20 00	60 00	Maryland militia	May 13, 1834	do	67	

13

Statement, &c. of Grayson county, Kentucky.

Names.	Rank.	Annual allowance.	Sums received.	Description of service.	When placed on the pension roll.	Commencement of pension.	Ages.	Laws under which they were formerly inscribed on the pension roll; and remarks.
Daniel Ashcroft	Private	30 00	90 00	Virginia line	Sep. 9, 1833	Mar. 4, 1831	65	
Matthew Bowles	do.	36 66	109 98	Virginia militia	April 16, 1833	do	71	
William Cleaver	do.	33 33	99 99	do	Aug. 17, 1833	do	73	
William Decker	do.	22 33	66 99	do	May 6, 1833	do	89	
John Decker	do.	33 33	99 99	do	Aug. 22, 1833	do	82	
John Fulkerson	do.	80 00	240 00	New Jersey line	Mar. 16, 1833	do	79	
Isaac Gore	do.	40 00	120 00	Virginia militia	Oct. 18, 1833	do	73	
Simon Prior	do.	80 00	240 00	New Jersey line	Aug. 17, 1833	do	74	
John Phelps	Sergeant	120 00	360 00	Virginia line	June 6, 1834	do	75	
Henry Skaggs	Private	30 00	90 00	Virginia militia	Aug. 17, 1833	do	75	
Isaac Vaninetler	do	35 96	107 88	Penn. militia	Feb. 23, 1833	do	82	
Isaac Williams	do	30 00	90 00	Virginia militia	Feb. 19, 1834	do	80	
Josiah Zerry	do	70.00	210 00	Virginia line	Aug. 9, 1833	do	79	

Statement, &c. of Greene county, Kentucky.

Names.	Rank.	Annual allowance.	Sums received.	Description of service.	When placed on the pension roll.	Commencement of pension.	Ages.	Laws under which they were formerly inscribed on the pension roll; and remarks.
Elias Barbee	Private	60 00	180 00	Virginia line	Mar. 29, 1833	Mar. 4, 1831	71	
Wyndle Bright	do	80 00	240 00	do	April 9, 1833	do	78	
William Barnet	do	80 00	240 00	S. C. militia	May 30, 1833	do	76	
Andrew Barnet	do	80 00	240 00	do	May 31, 1833	do	73	
James Cowherd	Sergeant	120 00	360 00	Virginia line	Mar. 27, 1833	do	76	
Andrew Chadoin	Private	60 00	180 00	Va. State troops	Apr. 9, 1833	do	73	
Lawrence Campbell	do	20 00	60 00	Virginia militia	Apl 12, 1833	do	71	
James P. Carlile	do	20 00	60 00	do	Nov. 15, 1833	do	73	
Jonathan Cowherd	Pr. & lt.	120 00	360 00	Virginia line	Dec. 7, 1833	do	78	
Peter De Spain	Private	60 00	180 00	Virginia militia	Dec. 1, 1832	do	71	
John Dicken	do	80 00	240 00	do	Aug. 22, 1833	do	75	
Sherrod Griffin	do	75 00	225 00	Virginia line	Mar. 29, 1833	do	76	
Thomas Gaines	Bombard'r	108 00	324 00	do	Aug. 17, 1833	do	75	
William Green	Pri. & cap.	76 66	229 98	do	Apl 25, 1834	do	80	
Henry Hatcher	Private	80 00	240 00	do	Nov. 7, 1832	do	78	
Thomas Harding	do	80 00	240 00	Penn. line	Aug. 9, 1833	do	76	
William Lee	Pri. & ser.	39 16	117 48	Virginia militia	Nov. 7, 1832	do	80	
Joshua Lee	Private	24 88	74 64	Georgia militia	Aug. 9, 1833	do	76	
Moses Meers	do	32 44	97 32	N. C. militia	Aug. 21, 1833	do	71	
Samuel Mc Cockle	do	26 66	79 98	Virginia militia	Aug. 9, 1833	do	77	
Jesse Morris	do	21 13	63 39	S. C. militia	June 17, 1834	do	86	
Thomas Parsons	do	66 54	199 62	Virginia militia	Nov. 7, 1832	do	90	
Richard Pierceall	do	20 00	60 00	do	Apl. 25, 1833	do	79	
William H. Price	do	30 00	90 00	N. C. militia	Sep. 26, 1833	do	72	
Randolph Rice	do	80 00	240 00	Virginia line	Nov. 7, 1832	do	79	
Henry Spoffner	do	50 00	150 00	N. C. militia	do	do	79	
Thomas Smith	do	80 00	240 00	Virginia line	do	do	75	
John Smith	do	80 00	240 00	do	do	do	79	
William W. Steerman	do	80 00	240 00	do	Nov. 8, 1832	do	79	Died August 7, 1833.
James Sherrill	do	63 33	189 99	Va. State troops	April 9, 1833	do	60	

NAMES.	Rank.	Annual allowance.	Sums received.	Description of service.	When placed on the pension roll.	Commencement of pension.	Ages.	Laws under which they were formerly inscribed on the pension roll; and remarks.
John Shoun	do	25 43	76 29	Virginia militia	Aug. 9, 1833	do	74	
William Skaggs	do	36 66	109 98	do	Aug. 21, 1833	do	77	
William Sympson	do	20 00	60 00	Virginia line	Ap'l 9, 1834	do	67	
John Thurman	do	40 00	120 00	Georgia militia	Oct. 21, 1833	do	67	
William Tapscott	do	23 33	69 99	Virginia militia	June 11, 1834	do	70	
George Woodard	do	36 66	109 98	do	Ap'l 12, 1833	do	73	
David Watson	do	80 00	240 00	Virginia line	Aug. 21, 1833	do	75	
Hugh Warren	do	40 00	120 00	N. C. militia	July 18, 1834	do	70	

Statement, &c. of Greenup county, Kentucky.

NAMES.	Rank.	Annual allowance.	Sums received.	Description of service.	When placed on the pension roll.	Commencement of pension.	Ages.	Laws under which they were formerly inscribed on the pension roll; and remarks.
John W. Howe	Private	33 33	83 33	Virginia line	Oct. 18, 1833	Mar. 4, 1831	82	
James Lawson	do	30 00	75 00	Virginia militia	Aug. 21, 1833	do	74	
James Patten	do	21 66	64 98	Penn. line	Nov. 12, 1833	do	83	
Charles Riggs	do	80 00	240 00	Maryland line	June 8, 1833	do	78	
Clayburn Sartin	do	80 00	240 00	Virginia line	Aug. 9, 1833	do	79	

Statement, &c. of Hancock county, Kentucky.

NAMES.	Rank.	Annual allowance.	Sums received.	Description of service.	When placed on the pension roll.	Commencement of pension.	Ages.	Laws under which they were formerly inscribed on the pension roll; and remarks.
Edmund Newman	Sergeant	90 00	225 00	Virginia line	Nov. 3, 1832	Mar. 4, 1831	72	

Statement, &c. of Hardin county, Kentucky.

NAMES.	Rank.	Annual allowance.	Sums received.	Description of service.	When placed on the pension roll.	Commencement of pension.	Ages.	Laws under which they were formerly inscribed on the pension roll; and remarks.
Samuel Awbey	Private	80 00	200 00	Virginia line	Ap'l 12, 1833	Mar. 4, 1831	75	
Anthony Annet	do	20 00	50 00	Pennsylvania militia	Sep. 9, 1833	do	76	
Warren Cash	do	80 00	240 00	Virginia line	Nov. 12, 1832	do	74	
John Cundiff	do	20 00	60 00	Virginia militia	Sep. 2, 1833	do	78	
Forrest Davis	do	20 00	60 00	Maryland militia	Sep. 2, 1833	do	72	
John Green	do	35 32	105 96	New Hamp. militia	Mar. 26, 1833	do	70	
Isaac Goodin	do	43 33	129 99	Pennsylvania line	Oct. 11, 1833	do	79	
Michael Hargan	do	46 66	139 98	Maryland line	Mar. 24, 1833	do	80	
Patrick Murvin	Pri. & ser.	63 33	189 99	Virginia line	Sep. 5, 1833	do	75	
James McWilliams	Private	20 00	60 00	North Carolina mil.	Sep. 24, 1833	do	72	
James McCullum	do	60 00	180 00	Virginia militia	Nov. 9, 1833	do	73	
Alexander McDougal	do	66 66	199 98	South Carolina line	do	do	92	
Samuel Patton	Sergeant	75 00	225 00	Maryland line	Oct. 4, 1832	do	79	
Benjamin Parker	Private	20 00	60 00	Virginia militia	Mar. 26, 1833	do	75	
Henry Rains	do	80 00	240 00	Virginia line	Ap'l 12, 1833	do	75	
Joseph Rider	do	80 00	240 00	Mass. line	Feb. 2, 1833	do	91	
John Scott	do	20 00	60 00	Virg'a State troops	Ap'l 2, 1833	do	79	
John Smoot	do	80 00	200 00	Virginia militia	Sep. 2, 1833	do	79	
Joseph Smith	do	20 00	60 00	Pennsylvania militia	Dec. 23, 1833	do	72	
Jacob Vanmeter	En. & cap.	103 00	315 00	Virginia militia	Mar. 2, 1833	do	73	
Richard Winchester	Private	36 66	91 65	Rhode Island militia	Ap'l 16, 1833	do	79	

Statement, &c. of Harlan county, Kentucky.

NAMES.	Rank	Annual allowance.	Sums received.	Description of service.	When placed on the pension roll.	Commencement of pension.	Ages.	Laws under which they were formerly inscribed on the pension roll; and remarks.
Richard Ballew -	Pri. inf'y & cav'y	34 30	102 90	North Carolina mil.	Feb. 14, 1834	Mar. 4, 1831	71	
Jesse Brook -	Private	30 00	90 00	do	Dec. 17, 1833	do	83	
Berry Cawood -	do	46 66	139 98	do	May 23, 1834	do	76	
Lewis Green -	do	40 00	120 00	Virginia line	Dec. 10, 1833	do	83	
James Hall -	do	46 66	139 98	South Carolina line	Nov. 25 1833	do	83	
Stephen Jones -	do	23 33	69 99	North Carolina mil.	May 23, 1834	do	83	
Henry Shackleford -	do	20 00	60 00	Virginia militia	Nov. 25, 1833	do	70	

Statement, &c. of Harrison county, Kentucky.

NAMES.	Rank.	Annual allowance.	Sums received.	Description of service.	When placed on the pension roll.	Commencement of pension.	Ages.	Laws under which they were formerly inscribed on the pension roll; and remarks.
Claiborne Chandler -	Private	20 00	60 00	Virginia militia	Feb. 11, 1833	Mar. 4, 1831	73	
Samuel Chadd -	do	20 00	60 00	Maryland militia	do	do	80	
John Cleaveland -	do	80 00	113 54	Virginia line	May 9, 1834	do	77	Died August 5, 1832.
Thomas Furnish -	do	20 00	60 00	Virgin'a militia	Jan. 15, 1833	do	74	
James Furnish -	do	20 00	60 00	do	Feb. 1, 1833	do	70	
John Foxworthy -	do	30 00	90 00	do	May 18, 1833	do	81	
James Gomsanlis	do	60 00	180 00	New York line	Feb. 5, 1833	do	79	
Gerard Green -	do	26 66	79 98	Virginia militia	June 22, 1833	do	72	
Wm. Johnson, sen. -	do	36 66	109 98	do	Jan. 10, 1833	do	76	
John Jenkins -	do	63 33	189 99	do	Feb. 11, 1833	do	74	
Philip Kilander -	do	40 00	120 00	New Jersey line	Aug. 25, 1833	do	71	

Statement, &c. of Harrison county—Continued.

NAMES.	Rank.	Annual allowance.	Sums received.	Description of service.	When placed on the pension roll.	Commencement of pension.	Ages.	Laws under which they were formerly inscribed on the pension roll ; and remarks.
William Laney	Private	30 00	68 70	Virginia militia	Dec. 19, 1832	Mar. 4, 1831	74	Died June 18, 1833.
Jacob Lanter	do	20 00	60 00	do	Feb. 5, 1833	do	73	
James Moore	do	80 00	240 00	Virginia line	Jan. 17, 1833	do	84	
John Morrow	do	30 00	90 00	Pennsylvania line	Feb. 26, 1833	do	73	
Francis Mann	do	20 00	60 00	Virginia militia	Feb. 28, 1833	do	76	
Jacob Miller	Pr.in.& cav.	22 50	67 50	Virginia line	Ap'l 1, 1833	do	74	
John Maffett	Private	20 00	50 00	Penn'a militia	Ap'l 16, 1833	do	90	
Nicholas Millner	do	30 00	60 00	do	May 18, 1833	do	71	
Luke Millner, sen.	do	70 00	210 00	Virginia line	Aug. 6, 1833	do	83	
Thomas McCauley	do	40 00	120 00	Virginia militia	Ap'l 16, 1833	do	76	
Joseph Oder	do	26 66	79 98	do	Feb. 11, 1833	do	83	
Edmund Pollard	do	50 00	150 00	do	Feb. 5, 1833	do	75	
John Ralston	do	40 00	120 00	do	Oct. 2, 1832	do	79	
Francis Robinson	do	26 66	79 98	do	Feb. 11, 1833	do	69	
Zela Reno	Pri. & scr.	83 33	249 99	do	July 11, 1833	do	77	
Philip Roberts	Private	80 00	240 00	S. Carolina line	Dec. 10, 1833	do	71	
William Sutton	do	46 66	139 98	Virginia line	Dec. 19, 1832	do	69	
Michael Smith	do	80 00	240 00	Massachusetts line	Jan. 25, 1833	do	82	
John Trimble	do	46 66	139 98	Penn'a militia	Jan. 25, 1833	do		
William Venard	do	23 33	69 99	Virginia militia	Jan. 15, 1833	do	78	
John Watkins	do	37 10	74 20	do	May 13, 1833	do	88	
Wm. Woods, sen.	do	43 33	129 99	Penn'a militia	Aug. 6, 1833	do		

Statement, &c. of Hart county, Kentucky.

NAMES.	Rank.	Annual allowance.	Sums received.	Description of service.	When placed on the pension roll.	Commencement of pension.	Ages.	Laws under which they were formerly inscribed on the pension roll; and remarks.
John Boman, sr.	Private	25 16	75 48	Virginia militia	Oct. 18, 1833	Mar. 4, 1831	76	
Joshua Crump	do	23 33	69 99	do	Aug. 22, 1833	do	69	
Benjamin D. Corder	do	20 00	60 00	do	June 15, 1834	do	69	
John Edgar	do	80 00	200 00	Pennsylvania line	Aug. 17, 1833	do	77	
James V. Logsden	do	36 66	109 98	N. Carolina line	Aug. 21, 1833	do	68	
Daniel Morris	do	26 66	79 98	N. C. militia	Oct. 18, 1833	do	70	
Nathaniel Roundtree	Pri. & ser.	40 22	120 66	Virginia militia	May 30, 1833	do	74	
John Row	Private	40 00	120 00	Penn. militia	Aug. 17, 1833	do	84	
John Wright	do	40 00	120 00	N. Carolina line	Dec. 2, 1833	do	73	
Richard Whitman	do	23 33	69 99	Virginia militia	June 6, 1834	do	78	

Statement, &c. of Henderson county, Kentucky.

NAMES.	Rank.	Annual allowance.	Sums received.	Description of service.	When placed on the pension roll.	Commencement of pension.	Ages.	Laws under which they were formerly inscribed on the pension roll; and remarks.
Thomas Baker	Private	80 00	240 00	Virginia militia	Feb. 12, 1834	Mar. 4, 1831	74	
Furna Carmon	do	26 66	79 98	North Carolinia line	Nov. 10, 1832	do	72	
John Mo:s	do	25 00	75 00	North Carolinia mil.	do	do	75	
John Ramsey	do	35 00	105 00	South Carolina mil.	May 30, 1833	do	76	
Lewis Rouse	do	30 00	90 00	Virginia militia	Jan. 9, 1834	do	80	
Isham Sellers	do	68 22	136 44	N. C. State troops	Apl. 20, 1833	do	80	

Statement, &c. of Henry county, Kentucky.

Names.	Rank.	Annual allowance.	Sums received.	Description of service.	When placed on the pension roll.	Commencement of pension.	Ages.	Laws under which they were formerly inscribed on the pension roll; and remarks.
William Adams	Private	40 00	120 00	Pennsylvania line	Nov. 6, 1832	Mar. 4, 1831	86	
David Adams	do	20 00	60 00	Virginia militia	Feb. 25, 1834	do	71	
John Blackburn	Lieutenant	320 00	960 00	Pennsylvania line	Mar. 21, 1833	do	82	
Charles Bush	Private	23 33	69 99	Virginia militia	Feb. 7, 1834	do	80	
Adam Beetom	do	80 00	240 00	Pennsylvania line	Oct. 30, 1833	do	75	
Thomas Bryant	do	66 66	199 98	Virginia line	Nov. 4, 1833	do	73	
Dennis Bice	Lieutenant	320 00	960 00	do	Dec. 14, 1833	do	89	
Elijah Bishop	Private	80 00	240 00	do	Jan. 4, 1834	do	74	
William Brewer	do	26 66	79 98	do	July 30, 1834	do	90	
Andrew Conine	do	40 00	120 00	Virginia militia	May 11, 1833	do	73	
Jonathan Cooper	do	80 00	240 00	Pennsylvania militia	Sep. 23, 1833	do	76	
David Criswell	do	26 66	79 98	do	Jan. 3, 1834	do	73	
Isaac Collett	do	20 00	60 00	Virginia militia	do	do	74	
William Conn	Pri. cav'y & inf'y	20 00	60 00	Virginia militia	Feb. 7, 1834	do	74	
Samuel Dunaway	Pri. & ser.	88 33	264 99	Virginia State troops	Oct. 1, 1833	do	70	
John Downey	Private	45 00	135 00	Virginia militia	Oct. 18, 1833	do	78	
Jeremiah J. Degan	do	40 00	120 00	Pennsylvania militia	Dec. 14, 1833	do	70	
Alexander Dunn	Drummer	88 00	264 00	Virginia line		do	72	
Joseph Davis, 3d	Private	80 00	170 00	Pennsylvania line	Ap'l 11, 1834	-		Died April 19, 1833.
Simon Davis	do	30 00	90 00	North Carolina mil.	May 27, 1834	do	68	
Leonard Ellis	do	80 00	240 00	Virginia militia	Dec. 10, 1833	do	80	
Peter Force	do	73 33	180 90	Virginia line	Jan. 31, 1834	do	90	Died August 22, 1833.
John Geygedann	do	80 00	240 00	North Carolina line	Oct. 1, 1833	do	78	
Benjamin Hardin	do	50 00	125 00	Virginia line	Sep. 25, 1832	do	81	
James Haskins	Pri. & ser.	40 00	100 00	do	June 3, 1833	do	77	
Benjamin Hayden	Private	25 00	50 00	Virginia militia	June 12, 1834	do	74	
Charles Hugeley	do	33 33	99 99	do	Dec. 2, 1833	do	73	
Samuel Hisle	do	20 00	60 00	do	Dec. 14, 1833	do	70	
Henry Houseworth	do	23 33	69 99	New York militia	Mar. 4, 1834	do	70	

Name	Rank			Description of service	Date		Age
Achilles Haskins	do	68 33	204 99	Virginia line	June 3, 1833	do	72
John Johnson, sen.	do	60 00	180 00	do	Oct. 19, 1832	do	75
James Johnston	do	30 00	90 00	Virginia militia	Sep 23, 1833	do	70
George Jones	do	50 00	150 00	do	Oct. 30, 1833	do	77
Jonathan Kidwell	do	50 00	150 00	N. Carolina line	Oct. 1, 1833	do	84
Henry Kiphart	do	20 00	60 00	Virginia militia	Jan. 20, 1834	do	73
William Knight	do	40 00	120 00	N. Carolina militia	June 15, 1834	do	75
John Lindsey	do	60 00	180 00	Penns. militia	Oct. 30, 1833	do	75
James Logan	do	80 00	240 00	Virginia line	Dec 2, 1833	do	77
John Logan	do	80 00	240 00	do	do	da	74
Jacob List	do	30 00	90 00	N. York line	Jan. 20, 1834	do	84
Richard Maynard	do	43 33	129 99	Virginia militia	Mar. 29, 1833	do	82
Joseph McGuire	do	60 00	180 00	do	do	do	71
George Mitchell	do	60 00	180 00	do	do	do	73
John Minton	do	20 00	60 00	do	do	do	93
Basil Meek	do	40 00	120 00	do	Mar. 4, 1834	do	74
Lewis Neill	do	20 00	40 00	do	Apr. 17, 1834	do	81
Benjamin Perry	do	63 33	189 99	Virginia line	Nov. 3, 1832	do	69
William Peake	do	40 00	120 00	Virginia militia	Oct. 30, 1833	do	69
Joshua Prewitt	do	80 00	240 00	do	Mar. 14, 1834	do	81
Cornelius Ringo	Pr. & ser.	28 33	84 99	do	June 11, 1834	do	73
John Riddle	Private	30 00	90 00	New Jersey militia	Dec. 2, 1833	do	74
Matthew Shuck	do	40 00	40 00	Virginia militia	Ap'l 11, 1834	do	75
Nicholas Smith	do	21 66	43 32	do	Mar. 29, 1833	do	81
Thomas Scott	do	40 00	100 00	N. Carolina militia	do	do	87
Wilson Shelton	do*	30 00	90 00	Virginia militia	Aug. 9, 1833	do	82
William Simmons	do	30 00	90 00	do	June 6, 1834	do	89
Traverse Sutherland	do	30 00	90 00	do	Nov. 25, 1833	do	85
Walter E Sutherland	do	20 00	60 00	Maryland militia	Feb. 4, 1834	do	81
Samuel Vanhorne	do	60 00	180 00	Virginia line	do	do	71
Littlebury Wells	do	46 66	139 98	Virginia militia	Dec. 10, 1833	do	78
Thomas Wooldridge	do	30 00	90 00	do	Aug. 9, 1833	do	73
Joshua Waller	do	66 66	199 98	S. Car. St. troops	Jan. 4, 1834	do	74
Kanard Younger	do	20 00	60 00	Virginia militia	Jan 20, 1834	do	

14

Statement, &c. of Hickman county, Kentucky.

NAMES.	Rank.	Annual allowance.	Sums received.	Description of service.	When placed on the pension roll.	Commencement of pension.	Ages.	Laws under which they were formerly inscribed on the pension roll; and remarks.
Tapley Bynam -	Pri. of cav.	25 00	75 00	S. Carolina militia	May 11, 1833	Mar. 4, 1831	74	
John Bone, 2d -	Private	80 00	240 00	S. Carolina line	do	do	77	
Morrell Cunningham -	do	30 00	90 00	Virginia militia	June 23, 1834	do	74	
William Cockrum -	Drummer	88 00	264 00	do	Jan. 11, 1834	do	71	
Notley Gore -	Private	33 33	99 99	Virginia line	Jan. 13, 1834	do	81	
Lewis Huey -	do	41 55	124 65	N. Carolina line	do	do	72	
William Jones -	do	40 00	80 00	Virginia militia	May 11, 1833	do	75	
Benjamin Jones -	do	66 66	199 98	S. Carolina line	Jan. 11, 1834	do	71	
Jesse Messhew -	do	80 00	240 00	do	Ap'l 9, 1834	do	78	
Henry Pickett -	do	20 00	60 00	N. Carolina militia	Jan. 13, 1834	do	76	
Charles Tharp -	do	44 66	111 65	Virginia State tr.	Jan. 31, 1833	do		

Statement, &c. of Hopkins county, Kentucky.

NAMES.	Rank.	Annual allow-ance.	Sums re-ceived.	Description of ser-vice.	When placed on the pen-sion roll.	Commencement of pension.	Ages.	Laws under which they were for-merly inscribed on the pension roll; and remarks.
Peter Ashley - -	Private	20 00	60 00	Virginia militia	Nov. 16, 1832	Mar. 4, 1831	84	
Daniel Ashby, sr. -	Pr.ser.& en.	110 00	330 00	do	do	do	75	
Edward Bauldwin -	Private	40 00	120 00	N. Carolina line	July 15, 1833	do	67	
William M'Castleberry	do	31 31	93 93	Georgia militia	Feb. 6, 1833	do	79	
John Carter - -	do	23 33	69 99	S. Carolina militia	do	do	86	
David Clark - -	Pr.in.& cav.	53 33	159 99	N. Carolina do	Aug. 6, 1833	do	75	
Samuel Downey -	Private	22 20	66 60	Virginia militia	Nov. 16, 1832	do	68	
William Davis -	Pri. & ser.	100 67	302 01	N. Carolina militia	Feb. 6, 1833	do	73	
Thomas Dossett -	Private	20 00	60 00	S. Carolina line	May 29, 1834	do	76	
John Herrin - -	do	54 44	163 32	do	Nov. 16, 1832	do	88	
Johf Hill - -	do	76 66	229 98	N. Carolina line	do	do	75	
James Logan - -	do	80 00	240 00	Virginia line	Feb. 6, 1833	do	74	
Alexander Major -	Pr. & wagon master	110 00	330 00	New Jersey line	Nov. 16, 1832	do	79	
Peter H. Matthews	Private	23 33	58 33	Maryland militia	May 13, 1833	do	77	
Robert Newton -	Fifer & pri.	33 33	99 99	Pennsylvania line	Ap'l 25, 1834	do	70	
John Phipps - -	Private	38 88	116 64	N. Carolina line	Aug. 21, 1833	do	87	
George Timmons -	Sergeant	120 00	360 00	Georgia line	May 9, 1833	do	79	
David Weeks - -	do	40 00	120 00	Virginia line	Nov. 16, 1832	do	74	
Maudley Winstead -	do	28 55	57 10	N. Carolina militia	May 13, 1833	do	83	
George Wright -	do	30 00	90 00	do	Nov. 16, 1832	do		
Josiah Wilson - -	do	47 97	143 91	Virginia militia	Feb. 6, 1833	do		
	do	46 45	116 13	N. Carolina militia	Nov. 16, 1832	do		

Statement, &c. of Jefferson county, Kentucky.

Names.	Rank.	Annual allowance.	Sums received.	Description of service.	When placed on the pension roll.	Commencement of pension.	Ages.	Laws under which they were formerly inscribed on the pension roll; and remarks.
Henry Briscoe	Private	20 00	60 00	Maryland line	Feb. 27, 1833	Mar. 4, 1831	72	
Samuel Conn	do	30 00	90 00	Virginia militia	Ap'l 17, 1834	do	74	
Amos Goodwin	do	80 00	200 00	Virginia line	Nov. 6, 1832	do	68	
Vachel Harding	do	30 00	90 00	Maryland line	June 12, 1834	do	73	
John Humfres	do	96 00	133 37	Virginia line	Feb. 10, 1819	Oct. 14, 1818	72	Dropped under act May 1, 1820.
Same	do	60 00	120 00	do	Sep. 23, 1832	Mar. 4, 1831		Inscribed on roll under act June 7, 1832.
William Merewether	Sergeant of cavelry	177 25	531 75	do	Feb. 12, 1833	do	76	
John Murphy	Private of cavelry	100 00	300 00	N. Carolina militia	May 6, 1833	do	71	
Fredorick Miller	Private	46 66	139 98	Virginia militia	May 29, 1833	do	78	
Robert Maloney	do	24 16	72 48	New Jersey militia	June 20, 1834	do	68	
Hezekiah Pounds	do	33 33	99 99	Virginia militia	Ap'l 16, 1833	do	72	
Larkin Pilkinton	do	40 00	100 00	do	Aug. 21, 1833	do	72	
Thomas Parker	Sergeant	120 00	360 00	do	Sep. 25, 1833	do	78	
James Pennington	Private	44 77	134 31	Virginia line	Dec. 14, 1833	do	82	
William Tyler	do	80 00	240 00	Virginia militia	Ap'l 16, 1833	do	78	
James Urton	do	20 00	60 00		Ap'l 17, 1834	do	82	
Robert Wilson	Captain, adj. and major	480 00	1440 00	Penn. line	Nov. 2, 1832	do	82	
James Welsh	Pri., sergeant & lieut.	87 21	261 63	Penn. State troops	Mar. 27, 1833	do		
Philip Weinnand	Private	26 66	66 65	Maryland militia	May 30, 1833	do	79	
David White	do	42 44	127 32	Virginia line	Sep. 23, 1833	do	80	
Elisha Ycager	do	20 00	60 00	Virginia militia	Feb. 2, 1833	do	81	

Statement, &c. of Jessamine county, Kentucky.

NAMES.	Rank.	Annual allowance.	Sums received.	Description of service.	When placed on the pension roll.	Commencement of pension.	Ages.	Laws under which they were formerly inscribed on the pension roll; and remarks.
Samuel Burk	Private	60 00	180 00	Virginia militia	Aug. 6, 1833	Mar. 4, 1831	75	
Robert Campbell	do	36 66	109 98	do	Jan. 15, 1833	do	73	
James Carothers	do	80 00	240 00	N. Carolina militia	Mar. 21, 1833	do	79	
Abraham Cassel	do	20 00	60 00	Maryland militia	Aug. 16, 1833	do	79	
John Carrol	do	43 33	129 99	do	May 24, 1833	do	80	
Sterling Crowder	do	96 00	176 51	Virginia militia	Feb. 11, 1819	May 3, 1818	-	Dropped under act May 1820. Admitted on roll under act June 7, 1832. Died January 18, 1834.
Do	do	80 00	229 94	do	Jan. 17, 1833	Mar. 4, 1831	77	March 18, 1818.
James Graves	do	23 33	69 99	do	Jan. 15, 1833	do	74	
Jacob Grindstaff	do	20 00	60 00	N. Carolina militia	May 29, 1833	do	68	
Giles Hawkins	do	20 33	60 99	Virginia militia	Sep. 24, 1833	do	78	
James Martin	do	80 00	160 00	Virginia line	May 18, 1833	do	75	
John M'Gee	do	20 00	60 00	N. Jersey militia	Sep. 2, 1833	do	74	
Francis Miller	do	20 00	60 00	Virginia militia	Ap'l 13, 1834	do	86	
Benj. Nertherland, sen.	Lieut.	320 00	960 00	Georgia line	Oct. 25, 1832	do	79	
George O'Neal	Private	80 00	240 00	Virginia militia	Sept. 3, 1832	do	79	
Henry Overstreet	do	28 33	70 83	Virginia line	Apr. 25, 1833	do	71	
Samuel Rice	do	30 00	90 00	Virginia militia	Feb. 28, 1833	do	73	
Robert Simpson	Pr. of inf. & cav.	81 04	243 12	N. Carolina line	Dec. 7, 1833	do	77	
Jeremiah Veatch	Private	33 33	99 99	Maryland line	Dec. 2, 1833	do	75	
Alexander Willoughby	do	40 00	120 00	Virginia militia	Jan. 4, 1834	do	73	

Statement, &c. of Knox county, Kentucky.

NAMES.	Rank.	Annual allowance.	Sums received.	Description of service.	When placed on the pension roll.	Commencement of pension.	Ages.	Laws under which they were formerly inscribed on the pension roll; and remarks.
Job Broughton	Private	60 00	180 00	Georgia militia	Sep. 9, 1833	Mar. 4, 1831	79	
James Chick	Pri. inf. & cav. & cor.	25 96	77 88	Virginia militia	Jan. 19, 1833	do	74	
Pierce Dant Hamblin	Private	80 00	240 00	North Carolina line	Sep. 26, 1833	do	79	
Obadiah Hammon	Pri. of inf. & cavalry	62 50	187 50	do	Oct. 12, 1833	do	78	
John Payton Horton	Private	80 00	240 00	Virginia line	do	do	76	
John Hubbs	do	20 00	60 00	South Carolina mil.	Ap'l 11, 1834	do	70	
William McHargue	do	40 00	100 00	North Carolina mil.	Nov. 7, 1833	do	89	
Wade M. Woodson	do	24 44	73 32	North Carolina line	Sep. 27, 1833	do	71	

Statement, &c. of Laurel county, Kentucky.

NAMES.	Rank.	Annual allowance.	Sums received.	Description of service.	When placed on the pension roll.	Commencement of pension.	Ages.	Laws under which they were formerly inscribed on the pension roll; and remarks.
Elijah Clark	Private	20 00	60 00	Maryland militia	April 25, 1834	Mar. 4, 1831	81	
John Evans	do	25 66	79 98	Virginia militia	June 20, 1834	do	79	
James French	do	80 00	240 00	New York line	Sep. 5, 1833	do	94	
John Forbes	Pri. & sgt.	91 66	274 00	N. Carolina line	Dec. 2, 1833	do	75	
John Freeman	Private	20 00	60 00	Virginia militia	Feb. 25, 1834	do	70	
Solomon Stansbury	do	36 66	91 65	N. Carolina line	Feb. 19, 1833	do	79	
John Simpson	do	30 00	90 00	N. Carolina militia	June 1, 1833	do	72	

Statement, &c. of Lawrence county, Kentucky.

NAMES.	Rank.	Sums received.	Annual allowance.	Ages.	When placed on the pension roll.	Commencement of pension.	Description of service.	Laws under which they were formerly inscribed on the pension roll; and remarks.
William Brown	Private	240 00	80 00	87	Oct. 18, 1833	Mar. 4, 1831	Virginia line	
Gilbert Blumer	do	240 00	80 00	82	Feb. 14, 1834	do	New York militia	
William Cox	do	180 00	60 00	73	June 26, 1834	do	Virginia militia	
Bazle Castle	do	150 00	50 00	73	Feb. 28, 1834	do	Virginia line	
Adam Crum	do	150 00	50 00	77	Apr. 4, 1834	do	N. Carolina line	
Joseph Davis	do	120 00	40 00	70	Jan. 28, 1834	do	Virginia line	
George Hardwick	do	240 00	80 00	75	June 6, 1834	do	do	
William Lyon	do	120 00	40 00	82	Apr. 4, 1834	do	N. Carolina line	
Samuel Lee	do	90 00	30 00	71	June 12, 1834	do	Virginia militia	
John Lasty	do	180 00	60 00	-	Nov. 9, 1833	do	Virginia line	
Josiah Marcum	do	180 00	60 00	75	Feb. 14, 1834	do	Virginia militia	
John Marshall	do	240 00	80 00	73	Apr. 18, 1834	do	Virginia line	
James Norton	do	120 00	40 00	74	June 6, 1834	do	Virginia militia	
James Pratt	do	79 98	26 66	70	Jan. 20, 1834	do	Virginia line	
George Parkins	do	207 30	69 10	80	June 17, 1834	do	N. Carolina militia	
John Sexton	do	150 00	50 00	75	Apr. 4, 1834	do	S. Carolina line	
James Ward	do	240 00	80 00	75	Apr. 16, 1834	do	Virginia line	

Statement, &c. of Lewis county, Kentucky.

NAMES.	Rank.	Sums received.	Annual allowance.	Ages.	When placed on the pension roll.	Commencement of pension.	Description of service.	Laws under which they were formerly inscribed on the pension roll; and remarks.
Richard Bean	Private	-	63 33	82	May 6, 1833	Mar. 4, 1831	Virginia line	
Richard Bean	do	-	63 33	81	July 14, 1834	do	Virginia militia	
John Dyal	Pri. cor. & sergeant	124 98	41 66	72	Oct. 18, 1833	do	Penn. State troops	
David Fink	Private	69 99	23 33	78	Jan. 8, 1834	do	Indian spy	
Jonathan M. Grover	Pri. in. & cav.	259 62	86 54	75	Ap'l 12, 1833	do	Virginia line	
William Lucas	Private	139 98	46 66	70	Ap'l 2, 1833	do	New York line	
John Swingle, sen.	do	84 99	28 33	77	Oct. 11, 1833	do	Maryland militia	
Thomas Williams	do	-	20 56	78	Oct. 12, 1833	do	Virginia militia	

Statement, &c. of Lincoln county, Kentucky.

NAMES.	Rank.	Annual allowance.	Sums received.	Description of service.	When placed on the pension roll.	Commencement of pension.	Ages.	Laws under which they were formerly inscribed on the pension roll; and remarks.
John S. Alverson	Private	40 00	120 00	Virginia militia	May 30, 1833	Mar. 4, 1831	79	
James P. Barnett	do	40 00	120 00	N. Carolina militia	Jan. 19, 1833	do	72	
Benjamin Briggs	do	80 00	240 00	Virginia militia	May 30, 1833	do	69	Died March 31, 1834.
William Bruce	do	30 00	90 00	N. Carolina militia	Aug. 22, 1833	do	74	
Samuel Duncan	do	60 00	180 00	Virginia line	Jan. 19, 1833	do	74	
James Divin	Ensign	120 00	360 00	do	Jan. 30, 1833	do	86	
William Dougherty	Private	20 55	61 65	Virginia militia	Feb. 28, 1833	do	87	
George Edwards	do	80 00	160 00	Virginia line	Jan. 22, 1833	do	74	
Robert Elder	do	20 00	60 60	Virginia militia	May 11, 1833	do	74	
Abraham Estes	do	26 66	53 32	do	Jan. 22, 1833	do	70	
Isaac Garven	do	60 00	-	Virginia line	Jan. 16, 1833	do	73	
Robert Givens, 1st	do	20 00	52 79	North Carolina line	Jan. 22, 1833	do	76	Died October 25, 1833.
Robert Givens, 2d	do	80 00	210 00	Virginia line	do	do	77	
Joseph Hall	do	46 66	139 98	Virginia militia	Jan. 19, 1833	do	82	
William Hughs	do	40 00	120 00	do	Jan. 22, 1833	do	73	
Drury Ham	Pri., ser. & captain	405 00	1,215 00	do	do	do	84	
Richard Hunt	Pri. & ser. Pri. of inf. & cav.	200 00	-	do	June 16, 1834	do	74	
Rodham Lunsford	Private	90 00	270 00	do	Feb. 18, 1834	do	76	
Ezra Morrison	do	80 00	240 00	Virginia line	Jan. 26, 1833	do	72	
Benjamin O'Banner	do	80 00	240 00	Georgia line	May 6, 1835	do	78	
John Pemberton	do	46 66	139 98	Virginia line	Oct. 17, 1833	do	75	
James Renich	do	80 00	240 00	Virginia militia	Jan. 22, 1833	do	74	
Abraham Sublett	do	20 00	60 00	S. Carolina line	May 11, 1833	do	82	
William Sampson	do	80 00	200 00	do	Nov. 2, 1832	do	78	
Joseph Skidmore	do	20 00	60 00	N. Carolina militia	Feb. 16, 1833	do	69	
John Taylor	do	80 00	240 00	Virginia line	Ap'l 9, 1834	do	73	
Caldwell Woods	do	20 00	60 00	Virginia militia	Nov. 2, 1832	do	80	

Statement, &c. of Livingston county, Kentucky.

NAMES.	Rank.	Annual allowance.	Sums received.	Description of service.	When placed on the pension roll.	Commencement of pension.	Ages.	Laws under which they were formerly inscribed on the pension roll; and remarks.
Caleb Cox	Private	20 00	60 00	N. Carolina militia	May 30, 1833	Mar. 4, 1831	80	
Patrick Cain	do	63 33	189 99	S. Carolina militia	May 31, 1833	do	92	
William Clark	Ser. & pri.	65 33	-	S. Carolina line	Jan. 13, 1834	do	76	Died April 16, 1834.
Snead Davis	Pr.in.& cav.	92 50	277 50	N. Carolina line	Ap'l 18, 1834	do	81	
Jesse Ford	Private	26 66	79 98	Va. State troops	Jan. 8, 1834	do	77	
William Fiers	do	20 00	60 00	Virginia line	Nov. 9, 1833	do	74	
James Glass	do	20 00	60 00	Pennsylvania line	May 23, 1834	do	72	
Solomon Hicks	do	80 00	240 00	S. Carolina line	June 17, 1833	do	76	
Nathaniel Mattock	do	60 00	180 00	Virginia line	July 15, 1833	do	91	
William G. Pikins	do	80 00	240 00	S. C. militia	May 31, 1833	do	73	
David Robertson	do	23 33	69 99	N. Carolina line	Jan. 17, 1834	do	82	
William Stewart	do	30 00	90 00	N. C. State troops	May 11, 1833	do	71	
James Sullinger	do	50 00	150 00	do	Ap'l 25, 1834	do	69	
Arthur Travis	do	26 66	79 98	S. C. militia	May 31, 1833	do	71	
James Walker	do	26 66	79 98	N. C. militia	May 30, 1833	do	71	
William Wells	do	80 00	240 00	N. Carolina line	June 17, 1833	do	74	
John Wheeler	do	80 00	240 00	do	Sep. 24, 1833	do	77	

15

Statement, &c. of Logan county, Kentucky.

NAMES.	Rank.	Annual allowance.	Sums received.	Description of service.	When placed on the pension roll.	Commencement of pension.	Ages.	Laws under which they were formerly inscribed on the pension roll; and remarks.
William Addison	Private	80 00	240 00	South Carolina line	June 3, 1833	Mar. 4, 1831	68	
Leonard Anderson	Pri. of cav.	100 00	300 00	North Carolina line	Sep. 4, 1833	do	79	
George Blakey	Private	80 00	240 00	Virginia line	May 21, 1833	do	83	
David Briggs	do	23 33	-	Virginia militia	June 13, 1833	do	75	
John Danks	do	20 00	40 00	do	May 13, 1833	do	73	
John Ewing	do	30 00	-	do	May 30, 1833	do	73	
Charles Eads	do	80 00	191 41	Virginia line	Nov. 9, 1833	do	80	Died July 27, 1833.
John Gilliam	do	43 33	108 33	Virginia militia	May 20, 1833	do	74	
George Herndon	do	36 66	109 98	North Carolina line	Dec. 10, 1832	do	72	
Moses Hendricks	do	50 00	150 00	Virginia militia	Mar. 21, 1833	do	68	
John Hamm	do	80 00	240 00	North Carolina mil.	June 13, 1833	do	84	
Phil p Jones	do	80 00	240 00	Virginia line	Jan. 28, 1833	do	72	
Rodham Kenner	Gunner of artillery	160 00	250 00	Virginia navy	May 30, 1833	do	71	
Joshua Murrah	Private	63 33	189 99	North Carolina mil.	Feb. 23, 1833	do	70	
Daniel McGoodwin	do	80 00	240 00	North Carolina line	Sep. 2, 1833	do	70	
Benjamin Neal	do	40 00	120 00	Virginia line	Jan. 9, 1834	do	74	
Leonard Page	do	80 00	240 00	do	Nov. 12, 1832	do	71	
William Patullo	do	60 00	180 00	do	Nov. 7, 1833	do	74	
John Peake	Pri. of inf. & cavalry	35 00	105 00	Virginia militia	Jan. 28, 1834	do	78	
Nathaniel Powell	Private	70 00	175 00	North Carolina mil.	Mar. 21, 1834	do	77	
James Stephenson	do	36 66	109 96	do	Nov. 6, 1832	do	70	
David Saunders	do	40 00	120 00	Virg'a S'ate troops	Ap'l 10, 1833	do	72	
James Slaughter	Pri. & lt.	180 00	450 00	Virginia militia	July 15, 1833	do	80	
Ambrose Smith	Private	80 00	240 00	Virginia line	Aug. 9, 1833	do	78	
Richardson Taylor	do	30 00	99 00	do	Mar. 3, 1834	do	73	
Samuel Wilson	do	22 41	44 82	Virginia militia	Mar. 16, 1833	do	73	

Statement, &c. of McCracken county, Kentucky.

NAMES.	Rank.	Annual allowance.	Sums received.	Description of service.	When placed on the pension roll.	Commencement of pension.	Ages.	Laws under which they were formerly inscribed on the pension roll; and remarks.
Joshua Gamblin	Private	70 00	210.00	Virginia line	Oct. 18, 1833	Mar. 4, 1831	72	
Elias Lovelace	do	43 33	129 99	N. C. line	Aug. 17, 1833	do	79	
William T. Lynn	do	51 66	154 98	do	Oct. 18, 1833	do	72	

Statement, &c. of Madison county, Kentucky.

NAMES.	Rank.	Annual allowance.	Sums received.	Description of service.	When placed on the pension roll.	Commencement of pension.	Ages.	Laws under which they were formerly inscribed on the pension roll; and remarks.
Ellis Alkisson	Private	20 00	60 00	Virginia militia	Ap'l 20, 1833	Mar. 4, 1831	71	
Thomas Backnel	do	23 33	-	N. C. militia	May 6, 1833	do	71	
Thomas Butler	do	20 00	60 00	Virginia militia	May 11, 1833	do	76	
Michael Burk	do	60 00	180 00	Virginia line	June 3, 1833	do	96	
Robert Burnside	do	50 00	150 00	N. C. line	Jan. 4, 1834	do	75	
John Crook	do	20 00	60 00	Virginia militia	Nov. 5, 1832	do	68	
Conrad Cornelison	do	24 63	73 89	N. C. militia	Nov. 13, 1825	do	71	
James Cooley	do	49 20	123 00	S. C. State troops	Ap'l 1, 1833	do	74	
Wm. Cradlebaugh	do	80 00	200 00	N. C. line	Aug. 17, 1833	do	90	
James Carver	do	23 33	69 99	Virginia line	Oct. 18, 1833	do	81	
Gabriel Duncan	do	46 66	139 98	do	Dec. 26, 1832	do	76	
Thomas Dunbar	do	20 00	60 00	do	Ap'l 12, 1833	do	74	

Statement, &c. of Madison county—Continued.

NAMES.	Rank.	Annual allowance.	Sums received.	Description of service.	When placed on the pension roll.	Commencement of pension.	Ages.	Laws under which they were formerly inscribed on the pension roll; and remarks.
James Dowden	Private	80 00	240 00	Virginia line	June 8, 1833	Mar. 4, 1831	77	
Samuel Estill	do	80 00	240 00	do	Oct. 11, 1833	do	79	
Anthony Fullilove	do	30 00	90 00	do	June 17, 1833	do	74	
Thomas Faris	do	30 00	90 00	do	Aug. 17, 1833	do	77	
James Flick, 2d	do	50 00	150 00	N. C. line	Apl. 17, 1834	do	88	
Nathaniel Guthrie	do	23 33	69 99	Virginia line	Mar. 27, 1833	do	71	
Richard Gentry	do	26 66	79 98	do	do	do	71	
Henry Harris	do	50 00	150 00	N. C. line	Mar. 1, 1833	do	92	
Benjamin Howard	Pr. of cav.	100 00	300 00	Virginia line	June 7, 1833	do	78	
Jesse Hodges	Private	80 00	240 00	do	June 22, 1833	do	74	
Evan Haines	do	40 00	100 00	Georgia militia	Dec. 23, 1833	do	78	
John Hunter	do	80 00	240 00	Virginia line	Jan. 3, 1834	do	73	
Anthony Harrington	do	80 00	240 00	Maryland line	Jan. 28, 1834	do	72	
Joseph Kennedy	Ensign	240 00	720 00	Virginia line	Dec. 28, 1832	do	74	
William Kindred	Private	80 00	160 00	do	Apr. 20, 1833	do	90	
John Kidwell	do	30 00	90 00	N. C. State troops	May 11, 1833	do	81	
Isham Lane	Sergeant	120 00	360 00	Virginia line	Mar. 27, 1833	do	77	
Thomas Lanter	Private	70 00	210 00	Virginia militia	Aug. 6, 1833	do	77	
Isaac Lainhart	do	40 00	120 00	do	Aug. 21, 1833	do	79	
Thomas Lamb	do	80 00	240 00	Virginia line	do	do	83	
Matthias Lambert	do	30 00	-	Virginia militia	July 23, 1834	do	79	
Ralph Mc Gee	Sergeant	45 00	135 00	do	Mar. 27, 1833	do	79	
Matthew Mullins	Private	40 00	120 00	do	Apr. 1, 1833	do	70	
Daniel Mauppin	Sergeant	60 00	93 75	Virginia militia	Apr. 12, 1833	do	-	Died Aug. 29, 1832.
Thomas Maupin	Private	30 00	90 00	Virginia line	Apr. 16, 1833	do	70	
Thomas Morris	do	45 00	135 00	S. C. line	Dec. 17, 1833	do	74	
Samuel Morton	do	50 00	150 00	Virginia militia	June 19, 1834	do	88	
Richard Oldham	do	80 00	240 00	N. C. line	Jan. 26, 1833	do	72	
Jesse Oglesby	do	22 22	66 66	Virginia militia	Oct. 18, 1833	do	72	
Wyatt Parker	do	80 00	240 00	Virginia line	Nov. 10, 1832	do	77	

NAMES.	Rank.	Annual allowance.	Sums received.	Description of service.	When placed on the pension roll.	Commencement of pension.	Ages.	Laws under which they were formerly inscribed on the pension roll; and remarks.
Anthony Perkins	do	46 66	139 98	do	Nov. 12, 1832	do	77	
Samuel Perkins	do	46 66	139 98	do	do	do	72	
Thomas Parham	do	26 66		S. C. militia	Apr. 1, 1833	do	70	
John Pace	do	20 00	60 00	Virginia militia	May 6, 1833	do	70	
Loftus Pullins	do	20 00	60 00	do	May 11, 1833	do	70	
Josiah Phelps	do	45 00	135 00	V. State troops	Apr. 16, 1833	do	79	
Yelverton Payton	do	80 00	240 00	Virginia line	Dec. 14, 1833	do	79	
John Ross	do	60 00	180 00	S. C. line	Apr. 1, 1833	do	73	
Norman Roberts	do	20 00	-	Virginia militia	June 18, 1834	do	69	
George Tomlinson	do	80 00	240 00	Virginia line	Nov. 2, 1832	do	80	
Lawrence Thompson	Lt. & cap.	429 36	1,288 08	do	do	do	81	
Peter Todd	Private	26 66	79 98	N. C. line	Nov. 5, 1832	do	79	
John Tudor	do	30 00	90 00	N. C. militia	Nov. 10, 1832	do	80	
Joseph Todd	do	30 00	90 00	do	Nov. 13, 1832	dº	76	
Thomas Todd	Pri. of inf. and cav.			do	Mar. 9, 1833	do	74	
Oswald Townsend	Private	35 00	105 00	Virginia militia	May 30, 1833	do	76	
Galen White	do	80 00	240 00	Virginia line	Nov. 2, 1832	do	75	
Joseph Watson	do	80 00	200 00	do	Nov. 5, 1832	do	77	
William Watson	do	26 66	72 68	do	Apr. 10, 1833	do	92	
Archibald Woods	Lieuten't	160 00	1,440 00	Virginia militia	Jan. 26, 1833	do	76	
Samuel Walkup	Captain	480 00	240 00	N. C. line	Aug. 21, 1833	do	76	

Statement, &c. of Marion county, Kentucky.

NAMES.	Rank.	Annual allowance.	Sums received.	Description of service.	When placed on the pension roll.	Commencement of pension.	Ages.	Laws under which they were formerly inscribed on the pension roll; and remarks.
Bennet Dailey	Pri. artly.	100 00	300 00	Pennsylvania line	Dec. 21, 1833	Mar. 4, 1831	77	
William Peck	Private	20 00	60 00	Virginia militia	Ap'l 16, 1833	do	70	
James Ramsey	do	50 00	150 00	Armand's legion	Oct. 20, 1832	do	73	
Henry Sparrow	do	20 00	60 00	Virginia militia	Jan. 4, 1834	dc	69	
Richard F. Sutton	do	80 00	240 00	Virginia line	do	do	78	
Philip Walker	do	80 00	240 00	Pennsylvania line	May 23, 1834	do	76	

Statement, &c. of Mason county, Kentucky.

NAMES.	Rank.	Annual allowance.	Sums received.	Description of service.	When placed on the pension roll.	Commencement of pension.	Ages.	Laws under which they were formerly inscribed on the pension roll; and remarks.
William Allen	Private	40 00	120 00	Virginia line	Mar. 14, 1834	Mar. 4, 1831	76	
George Brierly	do	20 00	60 00	Maryland militia	Ap'l 12, 1833	do	77	
John Baldwin	do	20 00	60 00	North Carolina mil.	May 1, 1834	do	71	
Benjamin Berry	do	40 00	120 00	Virginia militia	Dec. 20, 1833	do	78	
William Bickly	do	80 00	240 00	Virginia line	Feb. 4, 1834	do	78	
William Devine	do	80 00	240 00	Maryland line	May 13, 1833	do	68	
Michael David	do	26 00	-	Virginia militia	do	do	71	
Moses Fritter	do	30 00	90 00	do	Sep. 24, 1833	do	79	
Peter Hargate	do	30 00	90 00	North Carolina mil.	May 16, 1833	do	79	
Thomas Kirk	do	20 00	60 00	Maryland militia	do	do	75	
John Kercheval	do	80 00	240 00	Virginia line	Apl. 29, 1834	do	71	
Thomas Morris	do	40 00	120 00	New Jersey militia	Aug. 21, 1833	do	84	
William Rankin	do	80 00	240 00	Virginia line	Dec. 10, 1833	do	75	
John Rust	Pri. & ens.	155 44	-	North Carolina line	Mar. 8, 1834	do	79	
Same	do	-	-	do	do	do	-	Increased from June 25, 1834.
George Shepherd	Private	80 00	200 00	Virginia line	Nov. 13, 1832	do	74	
John Salmon	Pri.of cav.	100 00	300 00	North Carolina line	Aug. 21, 1833	do	80	
Abraham Williams	Lieutenant	120 00	360 00	Maryland line	Oct. 21, 1833	do	87	
William Williams	Private	35 00	105 00	New Jersey militia	Feb. 4, 1834	do	75	
Thomas Young	Captain	480 00	1,440 00	Virginia line	Dec. 26, 1832	do	75	

Statement, &c. of Mead county, Kentucky.

NAMES.	Rank.	Annual allowance.	Sums received.	Description of service.	When placed on the pension roll.	Commencement of pension.	Ages.	Laws under which they were formerly inscribed on the pension roll; and remarks.
Leven Sprigg	Private	80 00	240 00	Virginia line	Dec. 28, 1832	Mar. 4, 1831	77	
Joseph Stilth	do	20 00	50 00	Virginia militia	do	do	75	

Statement, &c. of Mercer county, Kentucky.

NAMES.	Rank.	Annual allowance.	Sums received.	Description of service.	When placed on the pension roll:	Commencement of pension.	Ages	Laws under which they were formerly inscribed on the pension roll; with remarks.
John Adair	Major	600 00	1800 00	S. Carolina line	July 14, 1832	Mar. 4, 1832	71	
Charles Asher	Private	80 00	240 00	Virginia line	Oct. 13, 1832	Mar. 4, 1831	83	
Francis Adams	Trump'tr	120 00	360 00	do	Oct. 16, 1832	do	77	
Thomas Allin	Pr. & q. m.	186 66	466 65	N. Carolina line	Jan. 15, 1833	do	77	
James Alsop	Private	30 00	90 00	Virginia militia	Feb. 28, 1833	do	71	
Isaac Alexander	do	20 00	60 00	N. Carolina line	June 3, 1833	do	71	
Claiborne Bradshaw	do	80 00	240 00	Virginia line	July 27, 1832	do	75	
Samuel Brewer	do	46 66	139 98	Penn. line	Feb. 1, 1833	do	77	
Thomas Bereman	do	26 66	79 98	New Jersey line	do	do	73	
Joshua Barber	Ser. & cor.	112 00	336 00	Virginia line	Dec. 5, 1832	do	73	
Philip Board	Private	80 00	200 00	N. Jersey militia	Feb. 28, 1833	do	74	
John Bohon	do	80 00	240 00	Virginia line	Mar. 26, 1833	do	78	
Nathaniel Burris	do	40 00	120 00	Virginia militia	Mar. 30, 1833	do	73	
Philip Burnes	do	53 33	159 99	N. Carolina line	July 15, 1833	do	75	
Daniel Barbee	Sergeant	120 00	360 00	Virginia militia	Dec. 5, 1832	do	77	
John Bridges	Private	80 00	240 00	do	Feb. 1, 1833	do	92	
James Bruster	Pr. inf'y & cav.	22 50	67 50	do	May 23, 1834	do	71	
Martin Carter	Private	23 33	69 99	do	Sept. 11, 1832	do	72	
Daniel Coovert	do	80 00	240 00	New Jersey line	Nov. 10, 1832	do	77	
Thomas Crain	do	70 00	210 00	Virginia St. troops	Feb. 1, 1833	do	79	Died June 20, 1833.
Thomas Crawford	do	65 00	148 96	Penn. State troops	Mar. 30, 1833	do	79	
Ebenezer P. Carey	do	63 33	189 99	Vt. State troops	do	do	73	Died January 9, 1834.
Robert Coleman	do	40 00	113 88	Virginia line	do	do	86	
John Corningore	do	20 00	60 00	Penn. militia	June 3, 1833	do	85	
Henry Corningore	do	40 00	120 00	do	do	do	85	
Matthew Coulter	Pr. inf'y & cav.	50 94	152 82	S. Caroline lina	Nov. 15, 1833	do	75	
Patrick Clark	Private	20 00	60 00	Virginia militia	Dec. 2, 1833	do	77	
James Clark	do	20 00	50 00	do	Dec. 21, 1833	do	75	

Statement, &c. of Mercer county—Continued.

NAMES.	Rank.	Annual allowance.	Sums received.	Description of service.	When placed on the pension roll.	Commencement of pension.	Ages.	Laws under which they were formerly inscribed on the pension roll; and remarks.
Robert Dickey	Private	26 66	79 98	Penn. militia	Sep. 11, 1832	Mar. 4, 1831	84	
Peter Demott	do	80 00	240 00	N. Jersey line	Nov. 10, 1832	do	76	
John Demaree	do	70 00	210 00	Virginia line	do	do	73	
Henry Deshazure	do	80 00	240 00	do	Feb. 1, 1833	do	74	
Elias Fisher	Ser. & pri.	41 66	124 98	do	Dec. 2, 1833	do	74	
Michael Gabbert	Private	20 00	60 00	Virginia militia	Feb. 28, 1833	do	69	
James Galloway	do	80 00	240 00	Penn. line	Mar. 26, 1833	do	76	
John Gritton	do	73 33	219 99	do	do	do	78	
Thomas Graham	Pri. & ser.	85 73	257 19	Virginia militia	May 30, 1833	do	75	
John Grant	Private	53 33	133 33	New Jersey militia	Aug. 3, 1833	do	78	
George Gabbert	do	24 21	-	N. Carolina militia	Jan. 4, 1834	do	73	
John George	do	96 00	1231 96	New Jersey line	Feb. 16, 1819	June 5, 1818	76	Relinquished for benefits of act June 7, 1832.
Do	Sergeant	120 00	360 00	Virginia line	June 17, 1833	Mar. 4, 1831	76	Act March 18, 1818.
Richard Holman	Private	33 33	99 99	do	Oct. 3, 1832	do	78	
Peter Huff	do	80 00	240 00	New Jersey line	Nov. 10, 1832	do	78	
George Harlan	do	33 33	99 99	Virginia militia	Jan. 19, 1833	do	73	
Edward Houchins	do	80 00	240 00	Virginia militia	Feb. 1, 1833	do	75	
Charles Hart	do	80 00	240 00	N. Carolina line	do	do	73	
Samuel Harris	do	63 33	189 99	Pennsylvania line	Mar. 30, 1833	do	70	
James Hutton	Pr. & ens.	110 00	-	Virginia line	do	do	72	
Nathan Hawkins	Private	28 65	85 95	Virginia militia	Nov. 15, 1833	do	71	
Thomas Hedger	do	20 00	60 00	do	do	do	88	
Anthony Jenkins	do	70 00	210 00	Virginia line	Feb. 1, 1833	do	75	
William Kelly	do	30 00	90 00	Virginia militia	Feb. 28, 1833	do	72	
John Kirkland	Pr. of cav.	100 00	300 00	Virginia line	Mar. 30, 1833	do	80	
Thomas Kyle	Private	40 00	80 00	Mass. line	Oct. 18, 1833	do	76	
Thomas Moore	Pr. & capt.	130 00	390 00	Virginia militia	Nov. 10, 1832	do	80	
John Moore	Private	80 00	240 00	Penn. line	Mar. 26, 1833	do	77	
Humphrey May	Sergeant	120 00	360 00	Virginia line	Sep. 6, 1833	do	76	

Name	Rank			Corps	Date		Age	Remarks
William Nourse	Midshipm'n	144 00	360 00	Frigates Confederacy & S. Carolina	Sep. 27, 1832	do	71	Died July 13, 1833.
Benjamin Newton	Private	30 00	60 00	N. Carolina militia	Feb. 1, 1833	do	82	
William Pearson	do	37 88	113 64	Maryland militia	Feb. 1, 1833	do	96	
John Poller	do	30 00	90 00	Virginia militia	Mar. 26, 1833	do	73	
George Philips	Pr. of cav.	100 00	300 00	do	Oct. 16, 1832	do	77	
Richard Rosser	Private	23 33	69 99	Va. State troops	Sep. 1, 1832	do	78	
James Ray	Capt. & lt.	340 00	1020 00	Virginia line	Mar. 30, 1833	do	74	
George Roberts	Ser. & lt.	160 00	364 19	do	Oct. 20, 1832	do	68	
John Rice	Private	40 00	120 00	Virginia militia	Feb. 1, 1833	do	74	
Malachi Randolph	do	80 00	240 00	New Jersey militia	Feb. 28, 1833	do	76	
Thomas Rule	do	40 00	120 00	N. Carolina line	Dec. 2, 1833	do	73	
David Richardson	do	30 00	90 00	Maryland line	Jan. 28, 1834	do	78	
Benjamin B. Rose	do	32 44		N. Carolina militia	Apr. 23, 1834	do	74	
Thomas Smithey	do	60 00	120 00	Virginia line	Feb. 1, 1833	do	80	
Jesse Sky	do	60 00	180 00	do	June 7, 1833	do	74	
James Sleet	Ser. & pri.	80 00	240.00	do	Sep. 25, 1833	do	82	
Samuel Shelton	Private	60 00	-	Virginia militia	July 10, 1834	do	75	Dead.
William Taylor	do	70 00	210 00	Virginia line	Sep. 11, 1832	do	72	
Solomon Trower	do	40 00	120 00	Virginia militia	do	do	101	
John Thompson	Lieut.	98 21	196 42	Virginia line	Oct. 16, 1832	do	78	
Elisha Thomas	Private	26 66	79 98	do	Mar. 30, 1833	do	71	
George Thompson	Major, &c.	436 66	1309 98	Virginia militia	do	do	85	Died March 22, 1834.
John Teumey	Private	80 00	240 00	New Jersey militia	Feb. 1, 1833	do		
William Tolley	Pr. & ser.	35 00	105 00	N. Carolina militia	Dec. 21, 1833	do	79	
Leonard Taylor	Private	73 33	219 99	Virginia militia	do	do	76	
Lawrence Vanarsdall	do	50 00	150 00	New Jersey line	Nov. 10, 1832	do		
John Voris	Pr. & ser.	81 66	244 98	Pennsylvania line	Mar. 30, 1833	do	75	
Cornelius C. Vanardall	Private	51 66	-	New Jersey militia	June 17, 1834	do	86	
Cornelius Vanardall	Lieut.	320 00	960 00	Virginia line	Nov. 26, 1833	do	86	
Tobias Wilhite	Private	22 33	66 99	Va. State troops	Mar. 30, 1833	do	84	
James Whitecotton	do	70 00	210 80	Virginia militia	Oct. 21, 1833	do	83	

16

Statement, &c. of Monroe county, Kentucky.

NAMES.	Rank.	Annual allowance.	Sums received.	Description of service.	When placed on the pension roll.	Commencement of pension	Ages.	Laws under which they were formerly inscribed on the pension roll; and remarks.
Fielding U. Curtiss -	Pri. & ser.	75 00	225 00	S. Carolina line	Aug. 17, 1833	Mar. 4, 1831	77	
James Campbell -	Private	33 00	99 99	N. Carolina line	Sep. 2, 1833	do	81	
Solomon Dickerson -	do	20 00	60 00	Maryland line	Ap'l 12, 1833	do	80	
Ephraim Dicken -	do	20 00	60 00	Virginia militia	Ap'l 16, 1833	do	72	
Joseph Gist	do	80 00	240 00	Virginia line	Apl. 12, 1833	do	83	
Jacob Goodman	do	38 33	114 99	N. Carolina line	Sep. 5, 1833	do	72	
John Giles	do	80 00	240 00	do	May 16, 1834	do	74	
Pleasant Haley	do	40 00	120 00	Virginia militia	May 13, 1833	do	74	
Matthew Kidwell	do	23 33	69 99	Maryland militia	Aug. 17, 1833	do	72	
John Morehead	do	40 00	120 00	Virginia militia	Aug. 21, 1833	do	84	
Fleming Smith	do	25 00	75 00	S. Carolina militia	Oct. 21, 1833	do	88	
Thomas White	do	40 00	120 00	Maryland militia	Apl. 12, 1833	do	76	
James Welch -	do	80 00	240 00	N. Carolina line	Jan. 11, 1834	do	72	

Statement, &c. of Montgomery county, Kentucky.

NAMES.	Rank.	Annual allowance.	Sums received.	Description of service.	When placed on the pension roll.	Commencement of pension.	Ages.	Laws under which they were formerly inscribed on the pension roll; and remarks.
William Anderson -	Private	80 00	240 00	Virginia line	Apl. 2, 1833	Mar. 4, 1831	69	
Daniel Beaty -	do	80 00	240 00	North Carolina line	Dec. 28, 1833	do	76	
James Bourn -	do	20 00	60 00	Virginia militia	do	do	75	
John Beaty -	do	96 00	382 14	do	Nov. 6, 1819	Sep. 11, 1819	-	Suspended under act May 1, 1820. Inscribed on act June 7, 1832.

Name	Rank	Amount	Amount	Service	Date	Mar. 4, 1831	Age	Remarks
Do	do	40 00	120 00	do	Dec. 7, 1833	Mar. 4, 1831	77	March 18, 1818.
William Cave	do	30 00	90 00	N. Carolina line	March 6, 1833	do	85	
Roger Clement	do	50 00	150 00	do	Dec. 28, 1833	do	72	
Joseph Clark	do	30 00	90 00	Virginia militia	do	do	76	
William Conner	do	80 00	240 00	N. Carolina militia	Feb. 24, 1834	do	70	
Beverly Daniel	do	30 00	90 00	Virginia militia	Mar. 10, 1834	do	74	
Nathaniel Foster	do	21 55	64 65	do	Dec. 28, 1833	do	73	
William Gray	do	33 33	99 99	Pennsylvania line	Mar. 6, 1833	do	79	
Robert Garrott	do	55 00	165 00	Virginia line	Dec. 25, 1833	do	84	
Shadrach Hiatt	do	66 66	199 98	Maryland line	Mar. 6, 1833	do	85	
Samuel Hatcher	do	52 09	156 27	Virginia line	do	do	74	
Thomas Hall	do	80 00	240 00	do	Mar. 20, 1833	do	74	
John Hamlin	do	20 00	60 00	N. Carolina militia	Mar. 10, 1834	do	74	
John Lockridge	do	20 00	60 00	Virginia militia	Apr. 2, 1833	do	72	
John Lee	do	30 00	-	do	do	do	79	
John Moss	do	20 00	50 00	do	Feb. 20, 1833	do	72	
James McCulloch	Pri. & P't	200 00	600 00	N. Carolina line	Aug. 21, 1833	do	74	
John Montgomery	Private	25 32	75 96	Virginia militia	Nov. 15, 1833	do	72	
Daniel McCarty	do	66 66	199 98	do	Nov. 20, 1833	do	71	
Thomas Mosley	do	31 55	94 65	do	Mar. 27, 1834	do	75	
John O'Rear	Pri. & ser.	46 66	139 98	Virginia line	Dec. 28, 1833	do	85	
James Raney	Private	33 33	99 99	Virginia militia	do	do	72	
Ezekiel Stewart	do	20 00	60 00	do	do	do	93	
Hezekiah Spencer	do	26 66		do	Mar. 6, 1833	do		
William Tipton, sen.	do	54 98	164 94	Virg'a St. troops	Dec. 28, 1835	do		
Thomas Terry, 2d	do	60 00	180 00	Virginia line		do		
Joseph Wilkinson	do	96 00	167 43	do	Jan. 27, 1819	July 8, 1818	77	Suspended under act May 1, 1820. Inscribed under act June 7, 1832.
Do	do	80 00	240 00	do	Mar. 21, 1833	Mar. 4, 1831	77	Act March 18, 1818.
William Wills	do	60 00	180 00	Virginia militia	April 2, 1833	do	69	
Henry Wilson	Ser. & pri.	93 33	279 99	Virginia line	Aug. 21, 1835	do	74	

Statement, &c. of Morgan county, Kentucky.

NAMES.	Rank.	Annual allow- ance.	Sums re- ceived.	Description of ser- vice.	When placed on the pen- sion roll.	Commencement of pension.	Ages.	Laws under which they were for- merly inscribed on the pension- roll ; and remarks.
John Butler	Private	66 66	198 98	Virginia line	Aug. 22, 1833	Mar. 4, 1831	73	
James Blevin	do	53 33	159 99	do	Mar. 22, 1834	do	83	
George Barker	do	50 00	150 00	do	May 12, 1834	do	76	
John Cooper	do	55 00	165 00	Penn'a militia	July 10, 1834	do	75	
William Cooke	do	30 00	90 00	S. Carolina line	Apr. 29, 1834	do	70	
John Day	do	76 66	219 98	Virginia line	Dec. 2, 1833	do	74	
David Ellington	do	41 12	123 36	Virginia militia	Ap'l 29, 1834	do	71	
Thomas Hamilton	do	80 00	240 00	Virginia line	Ap'l 12, 1833	do	76	
William Howerton	do	60 00	180 00	do	Feb. 7, 1834	do	75	
Benjamin Hamilton	do	43 33	129 99	do	Feb. 25, 1834	do	73	
Jacob Johnson	do	80 00	240 00	South Carolina line	May 11, 1833	do	76	
Isaac Keeton	do	60 00	180 00	North Carolina line	Ap'l 29, 1834	do	70	
Samuel Kelly	do	31 66	-	N. Carolina militia	May 1, 1834	do	78	
Thomas Lewis	do	41 33	123 99	Virginia line	Sep. 25, 1833	do	76	
Isaac McKinzee	do	25 00	75 00	Virginia militia	Oct. 31, 1833	do	71	
John McGuire	do	20 00	60 00	Virginia line	Jan. 4, 1834	do	78	
Reuben Ratliff	do	43 33	129 99	Virginia militia	July 10, 1834	do	72	
John Smethers	do	80 00	160 00	Virginia line	Mar. 20, 1833	do	71	
Gilbert Stevens	do	60 79	182 31	Virginia militia	May 1, 1834	do	74	
Levi Swanson	do	25 00	75 00	do	May 2, 1834	do	77	
Philip Williams	do	80 00	240 00	Virginia line	Sep. 24, 1833	do	77	
William Walsh	do	20 00	60 00	N. Carolina militia	Sep. 25, 1833	do	74	

Statement, &c. of Muhlenberg county, Kentucky.

NAMES.	Rank.	Annual allowance.	Sums received.	Description of service.	When placed on the pension roll.	Commencement of pension.	Ages.	Laws under which they were formerly inscribed on the pension roll; and remarks.
Elisha Atkinson	Private	30 00	90 00	N. Carolina militia	Dec. 21, 1833	Mar. 4, 1381	89	
John Bone, 1st	Ser. & pri.	68 33	-	N. Carolina line	Mar. 27, 1833	do	71	
Joshua Elkin	Private	20 00	60 00	S. Carolina militia	Mar. 14, 1833	do	72	
David Edwards	do	80 00	240 00	Virginia line	Sep. 3, 1833	do	76	
Andrew Glenn	do	80 00	240 00	Penn. line	Aug. 21, 1833	do	80	
Sikes Garris	do	96 00	32 76	N. Carolina line	Mar. 28, 1830	Nov. 2, 1820	72	Dropped under act May 1, 1820. Increased on roll under act June 7, 1832.
Same	do	80 00	240 00	do	Feb. 27, 1833	Mar. 4, 1831	-	
Nathan Harper	do	40 00	120 00	do	June 7, 1833	do	70	
Isaiah Hancock	do	20 00	50 00	do	Aug. 21, 1833	do	67	
Michael Hill	do	60 00	180 00	do	do	do	80	March 18, 1818.
John Hunt	do	20 00	60 00	N. Carolina militia	May 1, 1834	do	84	
Edward Jarvis	do	70 00	210 00	N. Carolina line	Oct. 18, 1833	do	71	
Joseph Pitt	do	66 66	199 98	N. Carolina militia	Feb. 19, 1834	do	70	
Richard D. Reynolds	do	40 00	120 00	Virginia militia	Feb. 27, 1833	do	77	
Michael Roll	do	50 00	-	Pennsylvania line	June 6, 1834	do	71	
William Worthington	do	56 21	168 63	do	Sep. 25, 1833	do	73	
Britton Willis	do	80 00	240 00	S. Carolina militia	Oct. 21, 1833	do	76	
William Young	Sergeant	120 00	360 00	Virginia militia	Feb. 27, 1833	do	76	

Statement, &c. of Nelson county, Kentucky.

NAMES.	Rank.	Annual allowance.	Sums received.	Description of service.	When placed on the pension roll.	Commencement of pension.	Ages.	Laws under which they were formerly inscribed on the pension roll; and remarks.
William Ashlock	Private	20 00	60 00	Virginia militia	Sep. 20, 1833	Mar. 4, 1831	72	
Solomon Bishop	do	80 00	240 00	Virginia line	Nov. 2, 1832	do	79	
Richard Blandford	do	20 00	60 00	Maryland militia	Nov. 8, 1832	do	78	
John Bell	Ensign	340 00	-	Pennsylvania militia	Nov. 1, 1832	do	84	
William Dodson	Private	80 00	240 00	Virginia militia	Dec. 21, 1833	do	75	
Charles Hansford	do	43 33	108 33	do	Mar. 2, 1833	do	75	
Abraham Johnson	do	80 00	240 00	Virginia line	Mar. 3, 1834	do	77	
Robert Johnson	do	30 00	90 00	S. Carolina line	Ap'l 18, 1834	do	84	
William Lent	do	80 00	200 00	Virginia line	Nov. 14, 1832	do	76	
Alexander M'Conn	do	36 66	109 98	Pennsylvania militia	Dec. 28, 1832	do	79	
John Martenson	do	20 00	60 00	do	Feb. 23, 1833	do	75	
Joseph Miligan	do	26 66	66 65	Pennsylvania line	Mar. 2, 1833	do	79	
Thomas Mont'gomery	do	80 00	200 00	do	Ap'l 2, 1833	do	84	
Walter M'Atee	do	23 33	-	Pennsylvania militia	Ap'l 16, 1833	do	77	
William Thompson	do	30 00	90 00	Maryland line	Nov. 12, 1833	do	86	
Samuel Vititon	do	20 00	60 00	Pennsylvania militia	Feb. 23, 1833	do		
Jonathan Wood	do	40 00	120 00	Maryland militia	Dec. 18, 1832	do		

Statement, &c. of Nicholas county, Kentucky.

NAMES.	Rank	Annual allowance.	Sums received.	Description of service.	When placed on the pension roll.	Commencement of pension.	Ages.	Laws under which they were formerly inscribed on the pension roll; and remarks.
John Allison	Private	26 66	79 98	N. Carolina militia	Mar. 6, 1833	Mar. 4, 1831	75	
George Bryant	do	30 00	90 00	do	Mar. 21, 1834	do	85	Dropped under act May, 1820. Admitted on act June 7, 1832.
Ambrose Barnett	do	96 00	110 94	Virginia militia	Jan. 8, 1819	Sep. 30, 1818	71	Died December 18, 1832.
Same	do	80 00	143 03	do	Feb. 28, 1833	Mar. 4, 1831	-	March 18, 1818.
John Conway	do	80 00	240 00	Virginia line	May 12, 1834	do	75	
Jacob Fifer	do	30 00	75 00	Maryland militia	Aug. 17, 1833	do	80	
Henry Foster	do	80 00	240 00	Virginia line	Dec. 20, 1833	do	72	
John Henry	do	50 00	150 00	do	Dec. 26, 1832	do	75	
John Kersey	do	80 00	240 00	Virginia militia	May 30, 1833	do	70	
William Logan	do	80 00	240 00	Virginia line	Apl 16, 1833	do	75	
Hugh M'Clintock	do	60 00	240 00	Pennsylvania militia	Feb. 26, 1833	do	76	
Hammon Uterback	do	23 33	69 99	N. Carolina line	Dec. 7, 1833	do	79	
James Wilson	do	80 00	240 00	Virginia line	Nov. 12, 1853	do	78	

Statement, &c. of Ohio county, Kentucky.

NAMES.	Rank.	Annual allowance.	Sums received.	Description of service.	When placed on the pension roll.	Commencement of pension.	Ages.	Laws under which they were formerly inscribed on the pension roll ; and remarks.
William L. Barnard	Private	20 00	60 00	Maryland militia	Feb. 28, 1833	March 4, 1831	75	
Seley Burton	do	40 00	120 00	N. Carolina militia	Jan. 19, 1833	do	78	
Chesley Calloway	do	80 00	240 00	Massachusetts line	June 11, 1833	do	74	
William Carter	do	33 33	99 99	Virginia militia.	May 23, 1834	do	74	
John Monroe	Pr. ser & lt.	68 33	204 99	do	Jan. 10, 1834	do	84	
John Sorrels	Pr, & ser.	92 33	276 99	N. Carolina line	Oct. 11, 1833	do	78	
Matthias Shults	Private.	29 76	79 28	Virginia militia	Nov. 7, 1833	do	76	Died May 19, 1834.

Statement, &c. of Oldham county, Kentucky.

NAMES.	Rank.	Annual allowance.	Sums received.	Description of service.	When placed on the pension roll.	Commencement of pension.	Ages.	Laws under which they were formerly inscribed on the pension roll; and remarks.
John Austin	Private	80 00	240 00	Virginia line	Nov. 6, 1832	Mar. 4, 1831	98	
Edmund Archer	do	23 33	69 99	Virginia militia	Mar. 16, 1833	do	75	
Fielding Ashby	do	28 33	84 99	Virginia line	Nov. 7, 1833	do	71	
Jesse Force	do	26 66	53 32	Virginia militia	Ap'l 12, 1833	do	72	
Thomas George	do	36 66	91 65	do	Ap'l 9, 1833	do	74	
John Himdley	do	60 00	180 00	N. Carolina line	Jan. 13, 1834	do	71	
Merrit Humphrey	do	30 00	90 00	do	Jan. 25, 1834	do	74	
Michael Lingenfelter	do	40 00	120 00	Maryland line	Oct. 10, 1833	do	72	
Jesse Law	do	73 33	219 99	Virginia line	Nov. 7, 1833	do	77	
John Morgan	do	30 00	75 00	Maryland militia	Sep. 9, 1833	do	73	
Thomas Morgan	do	46 66	139 98	Maryland line	Oct. 18, 1833	do	73	
John Netherton	Capt. & maj.	135 00	405 00	Virginia militia	May 30, 1833	do	87	
John Reed	Private	80 00	240 00	Virginia line	Dec. 18, 1832	do	77	
George Singer	do	20 00	50 00	Virginia militia	Feb. 27, 1833	do	72	
John True	do	30 00	90 00	do	Oct. 21, 1833	do	81	
George Wright	do	30 00	90 00	do	Feb. 4, 1834	do	71	

Statement, &c. of Owen county, Kentucky.

NAMES.	Rank.	Annual allowance.	Sums received.	Description of service.	When placed on the pension roll.	Commencement of pension.	Ages.	Laws under which they were formerly inscribed on the pension roll; and remarks.
John Berry	Private	23 33	58 33	Virginia militia	Feb. 11, 1833	Mar. 4, 1831	74	
Robert Burke	Pr. & ser.	70 00	210 00	do	June 26, 1833	do	73	
John Bonds	Private	80 00	240 00	do	Feb. 12, 1833	do	71	
James Chandler	Ser. & pri.	115 00	230 00	North Carolina line	Ap'l 16, 1833	do	78	
Hugh Conway	Private	73 33	219 99	Penn'a militia	June 26, 1833	do	71	
Isaac Ellis	Pri. ser. lt. & capt.	256 66	-	do	do	do	81	
John Garnett	Private	30 00	90 00	Virginia line	Feb. 25, 1834	do	84	
Lawrence Hoover	do	80 00	240 00	do	Ap'l 25, 1833	do	74	
Benjamin Holliday	Pri. & ser.	65 00	195 00	S. Carolina militia	June 26, 1833	do	83	
Jacob Hunter	Private	80 00	200 00	Virginia line	Sep. 23, 1833	do	71	
Joseph Jones	do	80 00	240 00	do	Feb. 5, 1833	do	83	
John Jamison	do	80 00	240 00	New Jersey line	Ap'l 16, 1833	do	83	
John Kugel	do	40 00	120 00	Connecticut line	Ap'l 25, 1833	do	76	
William Ligon	Pr in.& art	42 50	127 50	Virginia line	Dec. 3, 1832	do	72	
William Lorance	Private	73 33	219 99	N. Carolina militia	June 26, 1833	do	71	
Sherwood Maddox	do	26 66	79 98	Virginia line	Feb. 12, 1833	do	73	
Joseph Minor	do	68 33	204 99	do	Ap'l 25, 1833	do	73	
Minus Radcliff	Fifer	88 00	264 00	Delaware line	Dec. 2, 1833	do	71	
Jacob Stamper	Private	60 00	180 00	N. Carolina line	Feb. 5, 1833	do	71	
John Sanders	do	23 33	69 99	Virginia militia	Feb. 11, 1833	do	83	
Henry Sparks	do	30 00	90 00	do	Ap'l 25, 1833	do	80	
Robert Stewart	Cap. lt. ser. & private	283 33	849 99	Virginia line	Sep. 23, 1833	do	79	Died June 27, 1833
John Searcy	Private	38 43	115 29	N. Carolina line	Jan. 6, 1834	do	72	
Henry Toon	do	30 00	75 00	Maryland militia	May 7, 1833	do	78	
John Thomas	do	60 00	138 91	Virginia line	Feb. 25, 1834	do	71	
Lewis Vallendingham	do	80 00	240 00	Virginia St. troops	Feb. 12, 1833	do		
John Wade	do	80 00	200 00	Virginia line	Ap'l 16, 1833	do		
John Wilhite	do	36 66	109 98	Virginia militia	Jan. 15, 1833	do	80	

17

Statement, &c. of Pendleton county, Kentucky.

Names.	Rank.	Annual allowance.	Sums received.	Description of service.	When placed on the pension roll.	Commencement of pension.	Ages.	Laws under which they were formerly inscribed on the pension roll; and remarks.
Joel Berry	Private	80 00	240 00	Virginia militia	Aug. 26, 1833	Mar. 4, 1831	81	
Henry Colvin	do	80 00	240 00	Virginia line	Nov. 21, 1832	do	78	
Isaac Conner	do	80 00	240 00	N. Carolina mil.	Jan. 9, 1833	do	77	
William Cleaveland	do	40 00	120 00	Virginia militia	Aug. 22, 1833	do	77	
Michael Cookendorfer	Fifer	88 00	264 00	Maryland militia	do	do	84	
Peter Demoss	Private	96 00	147 86	Virginia line	Dec. 21, 1818	Oct. 21, 1818	-	Dropped under act May, 1820. Inscribed on roll June 7, 1832.
Do	do	80 00	240 00	do	Oct. 14, 1832	Mar. 4, 1831	82	March 18, 1818.
John Glinn	do	40 00	120 00	do	Jan. 17, 1833	do	75	
Alexander Gibson	do	80 00	240 00	do	Mar. 20, 1834	do	78	
James Hammerly	do	23 33	69 99	Penn. line	Dec. 28, 1833	do	73	
John Hand	Sergeant	120 00	240 00	Virginia line	Jan. 13, 1834	do	83	
William Latimer	Private	36 66	109 98	Virginia mil.	Jan. 10, 1833	do	72	Died March 8, 1833.
Gabriel Mullins	do	88 00	240 00	do	Aug. 26, 1833	do	76	
Braxton Pollard	Cor.of art.	108 00	324 00	Virginia line	Mar. 29, 1833	do	76	
James Pribble	Pri.& serg.	80 33	264 99	Penn. militia	May 7, 1833	do	72	
John Regrdon	Private	80 00	240 00	Virginia line	Oct. 10, 1833	do	82	
John Ridinbour	do	80 00	240 00	N. Carolina line	Apl 25, 1834	do	77	
Adam Taylor	do	80 00	240 00	Penn. line	Mar. 7, 1834	do	70	
Robert Taylor	do	36 66	-	Virginia mil.	June 16, 1834	do	76	
James Yelton	do	80 00	240 00	do	Aug. 26, 1833	do	86	

Statement, &c. of Perry county, Kentucky.

NAMES.	Rank.	Annual allowance.	Sums received.	Description of service.	When placed on the pension roll.	Commencement of pension.	Ages.	Laws under which they were formerly inscribed on the pension roll; and remarks.
Andrew Burns	Private	25 88	77 64	Virg'a State troops	Nov. 15, 1833	Mar. 4, 1831	76	
Drury Bush	Pr. of cav.	100 00	300 00	Virginia line	July 10, 1834	do	76	
Stephen Cordill	Private	30 00	75 00	North Carolina line	Nov. 7, 1833	do	71	
William Cornett	do	40 00	100 00	Virginia line	do	do	72	
James Cordill	do	20 00	50 00	North Carolina line	do	do	81	
Achilles Craft	do	46 66	139 98	do	Nov. 15, 1833	do	76	
Peter Hammond	do	36 66	109 98	North Carolina line	do	do	75	
William Hagins	do	50 00	150 00	do	do	do	75	
Henry Hurst	do	36 66	109 98	Virginia militia	Nov. 25, 1833	do	72	
James Howard	do	80 00	240 00	Virginia line	Jan. 20, 1834	do	82	
Thomas Howard	do	80 00	240 00	do	do	do	84	
Andrew Harwell	do	33 33	99 99	do	do	do		
Samuel Stidham	do	30 00	90 00	North Carolina mil.	Jan. 19, 1833	do	87	
Roger Turner	do	53 33	159 99	do	do	do		
Thomas Watkins	do	60 00	180 00	North Carolina line	May 29, 1834	do	83	

Statement, &c. of Pike county, Kentucky.

NAMES.	Rank.	Annual allowance.	Sums received.	Description of service.	When placed on the pension roll.	Commencement of pension.	Ages.	Laws under which they were formerly inscribed on the pension roll; and remarks.
James Adkinson	Private	40 00	120 00	Virginia line	March 21, 1834	March 4, 1831	86	
Joseph Ford	do	79 63	238 39	N. Carolina line	March 27, 1834	do	77	
James Jackson	do	80 00	-	do	May 21, 1834	do	77	
Moses Stipp	do	63 10	189 30	S. Carolina line	March 6, 1834	do	77	

Statement, &c. of Pulaski county, Kentucky.

Names.	Rank.	Annual allowance.	Sums received.	Description of service.	When placed on the pension roll.	Commencement of pension.	Ages.	Laws under which they were formerly inscribed on the pension roll; and remarks.
Robert Anderson	Private	49 76	124 40	Virginia line	Sept. 5, 1833	March 4, 1831	71	
Samuel Allen, sen.	do	50 00	150 00	Virginia militia	Sept. 24, 1833	do	78	
Michael Burter	Pr. cav. & infantry	83 57	261 71	Va. State troops	do	do	76	
William Barron	Private	33 33	99 99	N. C. State troops	Oct. 11, 1833	do	72	
Henry Baugh	do	21 55	64 65	N. C. militia	Oct. 18, 1833	do	72	
John Barker	do	80 00	240 00	Virginia line	do	do	72	
John Barron	do	26 66	79 98	Virginia militia	July 18, 1834	do	84	
Lovel H. Dogan	do	20 00	60 00	Va. State troops	Oct. 18, 1833	do	70	
John Evans	Sergeant	120 00	300 00	N. Jersey line	May 13, 1833	do	77	
Josiah Farp	Private	20 00	60 00	Virginia militia	Dec. 21, 1833	do	73	
Richard Goggin	do	40 00	120 00	do	Dec. 3, 1832	do	72	
James Hamilton	do	40 00	120 00	Virginia line	Sept. 5, 1833	do	77	
William Hays	do	31 66	79 15	Virginia militia	Sept. 24, 1833	do	79	
James Horrell	do	37 66	112 98	do	Oct. 11, 1833	do	75	
Moses Martin	Drummer	31 77	95 31	N. Carolina militia	Aug. 17, 1833	do	79	
Barnabas Murray	Private	40 00	120 00	do	do	do	77	
Joseph McAlister	do	80 00	190 67	Penn. militia	July 18, 1834	do	79	
Samuel Newell, sen.	Serg't and lieutenant	231 93	579 83	Virginia militia	Sept. 11, 1833	do	79	Died July 22, 1833.
John Newby	Pr. of art.	100 00	300 00	Virginia line	Dec. 2, 1833	do	75	
William Owens	Pr. & ser.	100 00	300 00	Virginia militia	Feb. 14, 1834	do	83	
David Roper	Private	40 00	100 00	Virginia line	Oct. 31, 1833	do	78	
William Swinney	do	26 66	66 65	N. Carolina militia	do	do	73	
Martin Turpin	do	30 00	90 00	Virginia militia	Oct. 21, 1833	do	74	
William Trimble	Pr. of inf. and cav'y	39 77	98 31	Virginia line	Dec. 2, 1833	do	72	
Nathaniel Tomlinson	Private	20 00	60 00	Virginia militia	Dec. 21, 1833	do	86	
Peter Tarter	do	20 00	60 00	N. Carolina line	May 6, 1884	do	76	
John Willson	Pr. of inf. and cav'y	33 15	99 45	Virginia liné	Sept. 5, 1833	do	78	

Statement, &c. of Rock Castle county, Kentucky.

NAMES.	Rank.	Annual allowance.	Sums received.	Description of service.	When placed on the pension roll.	Commencement of pension.	Ages.	Laws under which they were formerly inscribed on the pension roll; and remarks.
James Anderson	Private	80 00	240 00	Pennsylvania line	March 1, 1833	March 4, 1831	72	
Humphrey Bates	do	20 00	60 00	N. Carolina militia	Aug. 6, 1833	do	69	
William Craig	do	20 00	50 00	Virginia militia	do	do	72	
William Cash	do	40 00	120 00	do	May 23, 1834	do	81	
Elijah Denney	do	60 00	180 00	N. Carolina line	Aug. 22, 1833	do	72	
Micajah Frost	do	33 33	99 99	do militia	Aug. 6, 1833	do	72	
Moses Faris	do	40 00	120 00	Virginia militia	July 16, 1834	do	75	
Richard Gentry	do	43 33	108 33	S. Carolina line	Jan. 19, 1833	do	79	
Thomas Gadd	do	20 00	60 00	Maryland militia	May 30, 1833	do	74	
Henry Haggard	do	40 00	100 00	Virginia militia	May 11, 1833	do	76	
Nicholas Houk	do	20 00	60 00	N. Carolina militia	Nov. 12, 1833	do	70	
George Harlew	do	50 00	150 00	Virginia line	Dec. 31, 1833	do	78	
Thomas Johnson	dc	20 00	60 00	Virginia militia	July 10, 1834	do	70	
William Lawrence	do	58 76	176 00	do	June 11, 1834	do	70	
George Proctor	do	20 00	60 00	do	Oct. 31, 1833	do	92	
Reuben Pew	do	80 00	240 00	New Jersey line	Dec. 31, 1833	do	77	
Henry Pumphrey	do	80 00	240 00	Virginia State troops	Jan. 8, 1834	do	80	
Mourning Roberts	do	33 33	99 99	Virginia militia	Aug. 9, 1833	do	76	
Jesse Scott	do	40 00	120 00	N. Carolina militia	May 30, 1833	do	72	
William Taylor	do	20 00	40 00	Virginia militia	Jan. 16, 1833	do		
Charles Woodall	do	40 00	120 00	do	Jan. 5, 1833	do		
Jesse Woodall	Ser. & pri.	21 26	53 15	Maryland line	Aug. 17, 1833	do	84	

Statement, &c. of Russell county, Kentucky.

NAMES.	Rank.	Annual allowance.	Sums received.	Description of service.	When placed on the pension roll.	Commencement of pension.	Ages.	Laws under which they were formerly inscribed on the pension roll; and remarks.
John Cape	Lieut.	320 00	360 00	Virginia line	June 8, 1834	Mar. 4, 1831	89	
James Conn	Private	80 00	240 00	North Carolina line	Mar. 14, 1834	do	83	
Ansel Goodman	do	70 00	210 00	Virginia line	Jan. 5, 1833	do	82	
Thomas Graves	do	30 00	90 00	Virginia militia	Aug. 17, 1833	do	71	
Jorden George	do	69 33	207 99	do	Oct. 18, 1833	do	70	
John Hall	do	33 33	83 33	North Carolina line	Sep. 24, 1833	do	75	
James Haynes, sr.	do	80 00	240 00	Viaginia line	Oct. 18, 1833	do	82	
Henry Law	do	23 33	69 99	Virginia militia	Dec. 2, 1833	do	75	
William Perryman	Pri. of inf. & cavalry	22 50	67 50	do	Ap'l 12, 1833	do	75	
Ledford Payne	Private	80 00	240 00	Virginia line	Sep. 9, 1833	do	72	
John Polly	do	30 00	90 00	Virginia militia	Jan. 23, 1834	do	73	
Matthew Robertson	do	80 00	240 00	North Carolina line	June 5, 1833	do	73	
William Smith	do	30 00	90 00	Virginia militia	Oct. 21, 1833	do	78	
Isham Sharp	do	40 00	120 00	North Carolina mil.	June 17, 1834	do	79	
Stephen Underdoun	do	33 33	99 99	North Carolina line	Oct. 21, 1833	do	78	

Statement, &c. of Scott county, Kentucky.

NAMES.	Rank.	Annual allowance.	Sums received.	Description of service.	When placed on the pension roll.	Commencement of pension.	Ages.	Laws under which they were formerly inscribed on the pension roll; and remarks.
George Burbridge	Private	20 00	60 00	Virginia militia	Sep. 18, 1832	Mar. 4, 1831	72	
Joseph Burch	do	26 66	79 98	do	Oct. 5, 1832	do	71	
Thomas Brown	Pri. & lieut.	54 98	54 98	Virg. State troops	Nov. 2, 1832	do	89	
John Berkley	Private	20 00	60 00	Virginia militia	Jan. 25, 1833	do	72	
Samuel Barnhill	do	43 33	108 33	Penn. militia	Jan. 9, 1833	do	74	

Name	Rank			Service			Age	Remarks
William Beaty	do	30 00	90 00	Virginia militia	Dec. 19, 1832	do	72	
Daniel Bryan	do	59 76	-	N. Carolina militia	Sep. 25, 1832	do	76	
James Chisham	do	23 33	69 99	Virginia militia	Oct. 5, 1832	do	66	
John Campbell	do	23 33	69 99	Maryland line	June 10, 1833	do	73	
Francis Downing	do	20 00	60 00	Maryland militia	Sep. 17, 1832	do	88	
John O. Dabney	do	30 00	60 00	Virginia militia	Jan. 9, 1833	do	71	
Randall F. Fugate	do	80 00	240 00	do		do	72	
John Gibson	do	20 00	50 00	Virginia volunteers	Sep. 17, 1832	do	73	
Julius Gibbs	do	60 00	180 00	Virginia line	Oct. 5, 1832	do	81	
John Garth	do	33 33	83 33	Virginia militia	do	do	72	
John Gatewood	do	20 00	60 00	do	Jan. 9, 1833	do	69	
Bennett Greenwell	do	40 00	120 00	Maryland militia	Feb. 28, 1833	do	72	
Daniel Gano	Cap. & l't	240 00	2151 23	New York line	Feb. 9, 1819	Apr. 18, 1818	76	Relinquished for benefit of act June 7, 1832. Act March 18, 1818.
Same	do	400 00	1200 00	do	July 25, 1832	Mar. 4, 1831	76	
John Hiles	Private	20 00	40 00	Virginia militia	Oct. 5, 1832	do	72	
Henry Hurst	do	30 00	90 00	Virginia line	June 5, 1833	do	79	
John Jacobs	Pri. & cav.	100 00	300 00	do	June 10, 1833	do	71	
James Jones	Private	40 00	100 00	Penn. line	Dec. 10, 1833	do	68	
David Kerr	do	80 00	240 00	S. Carolina line	Oct. 5, 1832	do	77	
Thomas Landrum	do	80 00	-	Virginia line	Sep. 29, 1832	do	82	Dead.
John Lackland	do		60 00	Virginia militia	Jan. 9, 1833	do	79	
Paul Leathers	Sergeant	120 00	360 00	Virginia line	Feb. 11, 1833	do	88	
James McCrosky	Pri. of cad.	60 00	180 00	Virginia militia	Jan. 9, 1833	do	74	
John Miller	Private	80 00	160 00	Penn. line	May 16, 1833	do	88	
Jeremiah Minor	do	30 00	90 00	Penn. militia	Oct. 14, 1833	do	75	
James Officer	do	26 65	79 98	do	Oct. 5, 1832	do	70	
Bennet Osborn	Pri. & lieut.	62 66	187 98	S. Carolina line	do	do	80	
Jeremiah Powers	Private	80 00	240 00	Virginia militia	Jan. 9, 1833	do	80	
Isaac Price	do	80 00	240 00	N. Jersey line	Ap'l 9, 1833	do	74	
Jonathan Robinson	Captain	480 00	1440 00	Penn. line	Dec. 5, 1832	do	82	
Achilles Slap	Private	80 00	240 00	Virginia line	Oct. 5, 1832	do	79	
William Scruggs	do	20 00	40 00	do		do		
John Suggett	do	40 00	120 00	Virginia militia	Dec. 3, 1832	do	83	
John Sharp	do	20 00	60 00	do	Nov. 25, 1833	do	71	
Charles Stewart	Ser. of art.	96 00	1411 43	Maryland line	Ap'l 15, 1820	Aug. 21, 1818	81	Relinquished for the benefits of act June 7, 1832. March 18, 1818. Died February 22, 1834.
Same	do	120 00	360 00	do	Mar. 13, 1834	Mar. 4, 1831	-	
James Twyman	Private	23 33	69 99	Virginia militia	Jan. 9, 1833	do	-	
John Vinzant	do	80 00	240 00	Penn. line	Jan. 25, 1833	do	70	

Statement, &c. of Shelby county, Kentucky.

NAMES.	Rank.	Annual allowance.	Sums received.	Description of service.	When placed on the pension roll.	Commencement of pension.	Ages.	Laws under which they were formerly inscribed on the pension roll; and remarks.
Niclas Blomkenbaker	Private	63 33	189 99	Virginia line	Oct. 24, 1832	Mar. 4, 1831	75	
John Blackmore	do	23 33	69 99	Virginia militia	Nov. 3, 1832	do	72	
William Brown	do	31 66	94 98	Virginia line	Dec. 26, 1832	do	75	
Martin Baskett	do	23 33	–	Virginia militia	Sep. 23, 1832	do	73	Dead.
Benjamin Brevard	do	20 00	60 00	North Carolina mil.	Nov. 29, 1833	do	73	
John Blackwell	do	46 66	139 98	Virginia militia	Jan. 16, 1834	do	76	
Peter Bryant	do	60 00	165 78	Virginia line	Nov. 29, 1833	do	73	Died December 9, 1832.
Peter Brumback	do	96 00	1,385 06	do	Feb. 5, 1819	Sep. 30, 1818	80	Relinquished for benefit of act June 7, 1832.
Same	Pri. of cav.	100 00	–	do	June 10, 1832	Mar. 4, 1831	80	Act March 18, 1818.
James Christie	Private	56 00	168 00	Virginia militia	Feb. 11, 1833	do	76	
Peter Carnine	Sergeant	120 00	360 00	New Jersey line	Sept. 24, 1833	do	82	
Charles Casey	Private	20 00	60 00	Virginia militia	Feb. 7, 1834	do	85	
Benjamin Conyers	do	40 00	120 00	do	May 23, 1834	do	74	
Obadiah Clark	Pri. & cor.	40 00	120 00	North Carolina mil.	May 27, 1834	do	78	
Samuel Parra	Private	20 00	50 00	Pennsylvania militia	May 16, 1833	do	85	
Elisha Ford	do	80 00	240 00	South Carolinia line	Sep. 23, 1833	do	76	
William French	do	40 00	120 00	Virginia militia	June 6, 1834	do	73	
James M. Franklin	do	80 00	240 00	North Carolina line	Jan. 9, 1834	do	71	
Joseph Force	do	28 33	84 99	Virginia militia	May 23, 1834	do	92	
Robert F. Gale	do	60 00	180 00	Pennsylvania militia	Aug. 3, 1833	do	68	
Benjamin Gridsby	do	23 33	69 99	Virginia militia	Sep. 23, 1833	do	85	
Elisha Gibson	do	20 00	60 00	North Carolina line	July 10, 1834	do	86	
Edmund Graves	do	40 00	120 00	Virginia line	May 27, 1834	do	72	
George Hawkins	do	80 00	240 00	Virginia militia	Oct. 26, 1832	do	84	
James M. Holland	Pri. & ser.	38 33	114 99	do	Jan. 21, 1833	do	78	
Thomas Higgason	Ser. & pri.	55 33	165 99	New Jersey militia	Mar. 29, 1833	do	78	
William Heppard	Private	40 00	120 00	Virginia militia	Apr. 25, 1833	do	73	
George Herring	do	20 00	60 00	do	Sep. 2, 1833	do	73	
James Hickman	do	20 00	40 00	do	April 1, 1832	do	73	

Pensioned increased 1833.

Name	Rank			Service	Commenced		Age
Archibald Johnton	do	20 00	60 00	do	May 23, 1834	do	83
Thomas Kelso	do	30 00	90 00	Maryland militia	Jan. 21, 1833	do	70
William Kendricks	Ser. & pri.	35 00	105 00	Virginia militia	July 15, 1833	do	87
John Knox	Private	20 00	-	Delaware militia	Feb. 11, 1832	do	75
Same	do	100 00	300 00	do	do	do	75
Hugh Lemaster	do	30 00	90 00	Virginia line	Feb. 7, 1834	do	83
Wilson Maddox	do	80 00	240 00	Virginia militia	Feb. 11, 1833	do	79
Daniel M'Calister	do	36 66	109 98	do	May 29, 1833	do	74
Daniel M'Cleland	Captain	480 00	-	North Carolina line	July 15, 1833	do	82
Abraham Moore	Private	51 33	128 33	Virginia militia	Sep. 28, 1833	do	77
Charles Mitchell	do	23 33	69 99	do	Jan. 20, 1834	do	75
Alexander Morse	do	30 22	90 66	do	Ap'l 25, 1834	do	
Micajah Neal	do	80 00	240 00	Virginia line	Jan. 24, 1834	do	81
Robert Paris	do	80 00	240 00	do	Jan. 4, 1834	do	84
James Rowe	Pri, of art,	100 00	300 00	do	Oct. 24, 1832	do	75
John Riley	Pri. lieut. & ensign	26 66	169 98	do	Oct. 26, 1832	do	
Benjamin Roberts	Captain	480 00	1,440 00	do	Nov. 3, 1832	do	78
Godfrey Ragsdale	Ser. of cav.	180 00	540 00	do	Jan. 22, 1833	do	84
Joshua Richards	Private	25 00	75 00	do	Dec. 2, 1833	do	72
Paul Rayzor	do	20 00	60 00	Virginia militia	Feb. 7, 1834	do	71
Reuben Stout	do	60 00	120 00	Va. State troops	Mar. 18, 1833	do	83
Reuben Sanders	do	30 00	75 00	Virginia line	Sep. 23, 1833	do	73
Henry Smith	do	20 00	60 00	Virginia militia	July 21, 1834	do	71
Evan Thompson	Ser. & pri.	45 00	135 00	Maryland militia	Apl. 25, 1833	do	75
William Tinsley	Private	20 00	50 00	South Carolina line	Oct. 21, 1833	do	71
Joseph Thompsom	do	20 00	60 00	Virginia militia	Jan. 4, 1834	do	71
John Thompson	Pri. of inf. & cav.	52 50	157 50	do	Jan. 7, 1834	do	
James Travis	Private	80 00	240 00	North Carolina mil.	June 18, 1834	do	79
Van Swearingen	Pri. & lieut.	80 00	200 00	Virginia militia	Oct 26, 1832	do	
Peter Watts	Private	40 00	120 00	Pennsylvania line	Aug. 21, 1833	do	80
Benjamin Washburn	do	80 00	240 00	North Carolina line	Jan. 21, 1833	do	78
Robert Woolfolk	do	60 00	180 00	Virginia line	Jan. 19, 1833	do	
Daniel Wilcoxen	Pri. & lieut.	120 00	360 00	North Carolina line	Mar. 2, 1833	do	
Henry Wiley	Private	40 00	120 00	North Carolina mil.	May 26, 1834	do	80

Statement, &c. of Simpson county, Kentucky.

NAMES.	Rank.	Sums received.	Annual allowance.	Description of service.	When placed on the pension roll.	Commencement of pension.	Ages.	Laws under which they were formerly inscribed on the pension roll; and remarks.
William Breedlove	Private	210 00	70 00	Virginia line	Sep. 26, 1833	Mar. 4, 1831	72	
Solomon Cox	do	120 00	40 00	N. Carolina militia	Feb. 14, 1834	do	82	
Ebenezer Dickey	do	50 00	20 00	N. Carolina St. tr.	Jan. 28, 1833	do	72	
Robert Hall	do	139 98	46 66	S. Carolina line	Oct. 1, 1833	do	71	
Thomas Hay	do	60 00	20 00	Virginia militia	July 18, 1834	do	71	
John Hickman	do	120 00	40 00	N. Carolina line	Dec. 30, 1833	do	72	
John Kelly	do	240 00	80 00	Virginia line	Aug. 30, 1832	do	72	
William Lowe	do	79 98	26 66	N. Carolina militia	Mar. 27, 1833	do	79	
Thomas M'Clanahan	do	240 00	80 00	Virginia line	April 25, 1833	do	82	
James Roper	do	166 65	66 66	N. Carolina line	May 29, 1833	do	89	
James Williams	do	79 98	26 66	Virginia militia	July 10, 1833	do	78	
John Williams	do	199 02	80 00	N. Carolina line	Jan. 28, 1834	do	75	

Statement, &c. of Spencer county, Kentucky.

NAMES.	Rank.	Sums received.	Annual allowance.	Description of service.	When placed on the pension roll.	Commencement of pension.	Ages.	Laws under which they were formerly inscribed on the pension roll; and remarks.
John Anderson	Private	90 00	30 00	Virginia militia	Mar. 2, 1833	Mar. 4, 1831	77	
Simon Bridwell	do	120 00	40 00	Virginia line	Jan. 26, 1833	do	78	
John Barr	do	240 00	80 00	Pennsylvania line	Sep. 26, 1833	do	78	
Joseph Brown	do	69 99	23 33	Pennsylvania St. tr.	Jan. 8, 1834	do	79	
Anthony Crafton	do	60 00	20 00	Virginia militia	Feb. 16, 1833	do	87	
John Davis	do	159 99	53 33	Pennsylvania militia	Mar. 2, 1833	do	81	
Spittaby Gregorry	Sergeant	360 00	120 00	Virginia line	Dec. 8, 1832	do	77	
Joseph Gray	Fri. & ser.	270 00	90 00	Virginia militia	Feb. 11, 1833	do	80	
Jacob Heady	Private	90 00	30 00	N. Carolina line	Oct. 18, 1833	do	84	
Moses Hugh	do	60 00	20 00	N. Jersey militia	Feb. 19, 1834	do	75	
Leander Murphey	do	240 00	80 00	Virginia line	Dec. 19, 1832	do	72	
Edward Miller	do	120 00	40 00	Virginia militia	Feb. 22, 1833	do	83	

NAMES.	Rank.	Annual allowance.	Sums received.	Description of service.	When placed on the pension roll.	Commencement of pension.	Ages.	Laws under which they were formerly inscribed on the pension roll; and remarks.
Abraham Pittinger	do	30 00	90 00	Virginia line	May 25, 1834	do	72	
Abner Roberts	do	23 33	69 99	Virginia militia	Jan. 15, 1833	do	92	
John Ringo	do	80 00	240 00	Virginia line	Jan. 26, 1833	do	73	
Michael Reasor	do	60 00	180 00	Virginia militia	Mar. 2, 1833	do	74	
Briant Stone	do	80 00	240 00	Virginia line	Dec. 19, 1832	do		
John Strange	do	30 00	90 00	Virginia militia	Mar. 1, 1833	do	75	
Elijah Stout	do	26 66	79 98	do	Feb. 7, 1834	do	91	
Philip W. Taylor	do	20 00	40 00	Virginia State tr.	Feb. 23, 1833	do		
James Walden	do	80 00	240 00	Virginia line	July 15, 1833	do	72	
Joseph Watson	do	73 33	219 99	do	Jan. 26, 1833	do		
Massenello Womack	Sergeant	120 00	360 00	Virginia State tr.	Feb. 21, 1833	do	83	
James Weeks	Private	20 00	60 00	Virginia militia	Dec. 7, 1833	do	85	
Joseph Young	do	62 78	188 34	Pennsylvania line	Dec. 30, 1833	do	72	

Statement, &c. of Todd county, Kentucky.

NAMES.	Rank.	Annual allowance.	Sums received.	Description of service.	When placed on the pension roll.	Commencement of pension.	Ages.	Laws under which they were formerly inscribed on the pension roll; and remarks.
Henry Boyd	Private	80 00	240 00	Virginia militia	Jan. 13, 1834	Mar. 4, 1831	75	
James Flack, 1st	do	36 66	109 98	N. C. State troops	Aug. 22, 1833	do	72	
John Gillaspie	do	66 96	199 98	S. Carolina line	Apr. 10, 1833	do	71	
George Gibson	do	26 66	66 65	Virginia line	Aug. 21, 1833	do	69	
Samuel Gordon	Ser. & pri.	115 00	345 00	S. Carolina line	Nov. 15, 1833	do	72	
Overton Harris	Private	26 66	79 98	Virginia militia	Dec. 20, 1833	do	73	
Conrad Lear	Private & trumpet.	100 00	300 00	Virginia line	Jan. 31, 1834	do	95	
Ambrose Madison	Pri. of cav.	75 00	225 00	do	Oct. 22, 1832	do	77	
Henry Maben	Private	80 00	240 00	S. Carolina line	May 6, 1833	do	77	
Peter Petree, sen.	do	40 00	120 00	N. Carolina militia	Dec. 10, 1832	do	70	
Benjamin Parmel	do	51 88	155 64	Virginia militia	Oct. 18, 1833	do	79	
Ephraim Porter	do	33 33	99 99	Maryland St.troops	Feb. 7, 1834	do	73	
Ephraim Shuffield	do	30 00	90 00	N. Carolina militia	Oct. 31, 1833	do	79	
Robert Sherrod	do	20 00	60 00	do	Dec. 2, 1833	do	74	
Gideon Thompson	do	33 55	100 65	N. Carolina line	Jan. 31, 1833	do		
Josiah Wooldridge	do	40 00	100 00	Virginia line	Aug. 21, 1833	do	79	

Statement, &c. of Trigg county, Kentucky.

NAMES.	Rank.	Annual allowance.	Sums received.	Description of service.	When placed on the pension roll.	Commencement of pension.	Ages.	Laws under which they were formerly inscribed on the pension roll; and remarks.
Russel Curtis	Pri. & cor.	45 00	112 50	N. Carolina militia	May 11, 1833	Mar. 4, 1831	77	
Joel Cohoon	Private	20 00	60 00	do	Dec. 24, 1833	do	71	
Balaam Ezell	do	23 33	69 99	Virginia militia	Ap'l 2, 1833	do	78	
John Grasty	do	80 00	216 22	N. Carolina line	May 6, 1833	do	72	
Miles Hollowell	do	30 00	90 00	do	Oct. 18, 1833	do	73	Died November 17, 1833.
Absalom Humphreys	do	60 00	180 00	S. Carolina line		do	74	
William Johnson	do	22 50	45 00	N. Carolina militia	May 13, 1835	do	79	
Charles Kennedy	do	30 00	90 00	New Jersey line	Jan. 26, 1833	do	71	
John Mabry	do	80 00	240 00	N. Carolina line	Dec. 11, 1832	do	70	
Philip Smith	do	43 33	129 99	New Jersey militia	Dec. 9, 1833	do	74	

Statement, &c. of Union county, Kentucky.

NAMES.	Rank.	Annual allowance.	Sums received.	Description of service.	When placed on the pension roll.	Commencement of pension.	Ages.	Laws under which they were formerly inscribed on the pension roll; and remarks.
Armstead Anderson	Private	30 00	90 00	Virginia line	May 16, 1833	Mar. 4, 1831	78	
Nicholas Binger	do	80 00	200 00	do	Oct. 30, 1832	do	73	
William Baylis	Lieut.	320 00	960 00	do	Dec. 18, 1832	do	76	
Edward Curry	Private	50 00	150 00	South Carolina line	Mar. 27, 1834	do	84	
Henry Floyd	do	20 00	60 00	Virginia militia	July 21, 1834	do	73	
William Givens	do	20 00	60 00	North Carolina line	Jan. 11, 1834	do	72	
William Hammock	do	30 00	90 00	do	Ap'l 14, 1834	do	74	
James Morrison	Ser. & pri.	51 66	129 15	Virginia line	May 21, 1833	do	79	
James Neil	Private	20 00	60 00	North Carolina mil.	Ap'l 21, 1834	do	80	
John Pierson	do	50 00	150 00	Connecticut militia	Dec. 9, 1833	do	71	
Lewis Richards	Sergeant	120 00	360 00	Virginia line	Oct. 30, 1832	do	70	
John Ray	Private	43 33	129 99	Maryland militia	Ap'l 20, 1833	do	77	
Richard Woodyard	do	30 00	90 00	Virginia line	Dec. 9, 1833	do	80	

Statement, &c. of Warren county, Kentucky.

NAMES.	Rank.	Annual allowance.	Sums received.	Description of service.	When placed on the pension roll.	Commencement of pension.	Ages.	Laws under which they were formerly inscribed on the pension roll; and remarks.
Isaiah Alley	Private	40 00	120 00	Virginia militia	Mar. 27, 1833	March 4, 1831	84	
Benjamin Bryant	do	20 00	60 00	do	Oct. 22, 1832	do	85	
John Byrom	do	20 00	60 00	S. Carolina militia	Jan. 28, 1834	do	67	
John Billingsby	do	40 00	120 00	N. Carolina militia	Jan. 28, 1834	do	81	
Augustine Clayton	Pri. cav. & inf.	90 00	270 00	Vir. State troops	April 20, 1833	do	79	
John Claspy	Private	40 00	120 00	Virginia line	Aug. 9, 1833	do	74	
William Carson	do	20 00	60 00	S. Carolina militia	Aug. 17, 1833	do	73	
Phineas Cox	do	53 33	159 99	Vir. State troops	Jan. 28, 1834	do	70	
Micajah Clark	Pri. & cap.	313 33	939 99	N. Carolina militia	do	do	84	
Samuel Garrison	Private	30 00	90 00	N. Carolina line	Nov. 6, 1832	do	71	
Henry Grider	Sergeant	51 16	153 48	Virginia line	Oct. 19, 1832	do	79	
William Hays	Private	40 00	120 00	N. Carolina militia	June 20, 1834	do	74	
Christopher Heavener	do	20 00	60 00	Penn. militia	Jan. 28, 1834	do	83	
George Hillen	do	80 00	240 00	N. Carolina line	May 6, 1834	do	72	
James Isbell	do	40 00	120 00	N. Carolina militia	Aug. 21, 1833	do	74	
Leonard T. Kerby	do	36 66	109 98	Virginia line	Oct. 22, 1832	do	74	
Jesse Kerby	do	32 22	96 66	do	do	do	77	
Beal Kelly	do	20 00	60 00	do	April 18, 1834	do	76	
Gideon Martin	do	20 00	60 00	Virginia militia	Oct. 22, 1832	do	102	
James Millican	do	23 33	69 99	N. Carolina line	April 12, 1833	do	74	
Hugh Moore	Lieutenant	320 00	844 43	Virginia line	Mar. 25, 1833	do	84	Died Oct. 24, 1833.
Benjamin Pendleton	Private	40 00	120 00	Virginia militia	May 6, 1833	do	83	
Moses Sweeney	do	26 66	79 98	Virginia line	Oct. 22, 1832	do	81	
Hugh Simpson	do	80 00	240 00	do	April 12, 1833	do	73	
James Stephens	do	80 00	120 00	Virginia militia	Nov. 23, 1833	do	75	Died Sept. 3, 1832.
Thomas Tallott	do	20 00	60 00	do	June 28, 1834	do	72	
Evan T. Watson	do	23 33	69 99	Virginia line	Oct. 31, 1833	do	75	
Ralph Young	do	20 00	60 00	Virginia militia	Jan. 28, 1834	do	74	

Statement, &c. of Washington county, Kentucky.

Names.	Rank.	Annual allowance.	Sums received.	Description of service.	When placed on the pension roll.	Commencement of pension.	Ages.	Laws under which they were formerly inscribed on the pension roll; and remarks.
John Adams	Private	20 00	60 00	Maryland militia	July 23, 1834	Mar. 4, 1831	74	
Richard Bunch	do	20 00	50 00	Virginia line	Feb. 1, 1833	do	75	
Conrad Bean	do	80 00	240 00	Maryland militia	Dec. 21, 1833	do	81	
Joseph Carter	do	80 00	240 00	Virginia militia	Nov. 25, 1833	do	74	
John Ceasy	do	80 00	240 00	Virginia line	Dec. 21, 1833	do	74	
Thomas Crump	Pr. of cav.	100 00	258 63	do	Apr. 11, 1834	do	75	Died January 5, 1833.
Elijah Faris	Private	80 00	240 00	Virginia militia	Aug. 10, 1833	do	72	
Amos Graham	do	40 00	120 00	do	Feb. 28, 1833	do	74	
Jeremiah Herbert	do	23 33	69 99	Maryland militia	Feb. 23, 1833	do	72	
Mark Hardin	Captain	600 00	1200 00	Penn. militia	Mar. 2, 1833	do	84	
Do	do	480 00	480 00	do	do	do	-	Pension reduced from $600 to $480, March 4, 1833.
John Lambert	Private	20 00	60 00	S. Carolina line	Feb. 1, 1833	do	74	
Nathan Lawson	do	50 00	150 00	Virginia line	Mar. 30, 1833	do	79	
John McKitrick, sen.	Pr. ser. & capt.						75	
Frederick Nance	Sergeant	95 00	255 00	Virginia militia	Feb. 28, 1833	do		
Samuel Overton	Commissary	120 00	360 00	Virginia line	Dec. 2, 1833	do	74	
Jacob Seay	Private	320 00	960 00	Virginia St. troops	Feb. 2, 1833	do	76	
James Scherlin	do	20 88	62 64	Virginia militia	Aug. 10, 1833	do	77	
Joseph Sweeney	do	30 00	90 00	Penn. militia	July 10, 1834	do	75	
William Webster	do	26 66	79 98	Virginia militia	Mar. 10, 1834	do	70	
Jonathan Wright	do	25 77	77 31	do	Oct. 1, 1833	do	71	
Thomas Wright	do	26 66	79 98	N. Carolina line	Ap'l 3, 1834	do	83	
	do	44 44	133 32	Virginia line	May 23, 1834	do		
Lewis Webb	Captain	240 00	965 43	do	Apr. 1, 1829	Feb. 25, 1829	84	Relinquished for the benefit of act June 7, 1832.
Do	do	480 00	1440 00	do	Ap'l 26, 1834	March 4, 1831		
Andrew Young	Pr. of cav.	41 66	104 15	do	Nov. 7, 1833	do	74	March 18, 1818.

Statement, &c. of Wayne county, Kentucky.

Names.	Rank.	Annual allowance.	Sums received.	Description of service.	When placed on the pension roll.	Commencement of pension.	Ages.	Laws under which they were formerly inscribed on the pension roll; and remarks.
William Acre	Private	40 00	80 00	N. Carolina line	Sep. 5, 1833	March 4, 1831	82	Died March 3, 1833.
John Adair	do	40 00	120 00	do	do	do	79	
Robert Bleakley	do	52 77	158 31	do	do	do	76	
William Butram	do	23 33	69 99	N. C. militia	Mar. 4, 1834	do	84	
James Brown	do	20 00	60 00	N. Carolina line	Apl 14, 1834	do	79	
George Bruton	do	50 00	150 00	S. C. militia	Dec. 21, 1833	do	72	
Robert Covington	do	80 00	240 00	Virginia militia	Ap'l 10, 1833	do	72	
Frederick Cooper	do	80 00	240 00	Penn. militia	Sept. 5, 1833	do	75	
William Carpenter	do	26 66	79 98	Virginia militia	Oct. 31, 1833	do	73	
Reuben Coffey	do	40 00	120 00	N. C. State troops	do	do	74	
Patrick Coyle	do	40 00	120 00	Virginia line	Feb. 7, 1834	do	71	
Peter Catron	do	40 00	120 00	Virginia militia	Feb. 12, 1834	do	80	
John Davis	do	63 33	189 99	Virginia line	Sept. 2, 1833	do	76	
George Decker	do	56 66	169 93	do	do	do	92	
Mastin Durham	do	20 00	60 00	N. C. militia	do	do	79	
George Dabney	do	40 00	120 00	Virginia militia	Oct. 18, 1833	do	74	
Rody Daffron	Pr. in &cav.	22 50	67 50	N. C. militia	Nov. 7, 1833	do	77	
Abraham Hunt	Private	26 21	78 63	Virginia line	Apl 14, 1834	do	72	
Conrad Henegan	do	20 00	60 00	N. Carolina line	May 29, 1834	do	80	
William Johnson, 2d	Sergeant	120 00	360 00	Virginia line	Sept. 2, 1833	do	77	
James Jones	Private	80 00	240 00	do	Oct. 18, 1833	do	74	
William Keath	do	23 33	69 99	do	Oct. 31, 1833	do	73	
Thomas Merritt	do	60 00	180 00	N. Carolina line	Sept. 2, 1833	do	73	
Frederick Miller	do	60 00	60 00	Virginia militia	Oct. 31, 1833	do	82	
Dudley Moreland	do	60 00	180 00	do	Oct. 31, 1833	do	73	
John Majors	do	80 00	240 00	N. Carolina line	Jan. 3, 1834	do	77	
James McHenry	Pr. cav & in	51 33	153 99	N. C. State troops	Jan. 21, 1834	do	73	
James C. McGee	Private	80 00	240 00	Penn. line	Feb. 25, 1834	do	72	
Stephen Pratt	do	30 00	90 00	Virginia militia	Oct. 18, 1833	do	70	
James Pierce	do	26 66	79 98	do	Oct. 31, 1833	do	72	

Statement, &c. of *Wayne county*—Continued.

NAMES.	Rank.	Annual allowance.	Sums received.	Description of service.	When placed on the pension roll.	Commencement of pension.	Ages.	Laws under which they were formerly inscribed on the pension roll; and remarks.
Jesse Powers	Private	30 00	90 00	Virginia line	Nov. 9, 1833	Mar. 4, 1831	75	
George Rogers	do	30 00	75 00	Virginia militia	Sept. 2, 1833	do	70	
Isaac Stephens	do	66 66	199 98	Virginia line	Dec. 5, 1832	do	74	
Zachariah Sanders	do	80 00	240 00	Virginia militia	Sept. 5, 1833	do	75	
Elisha Thomas	do	80 00	240 00	Virginia line	Sep. 2, 1833	do	75	
James Turner	do	40 00	120 00	do	Oct. 21, 1833	do	72	
John Walters	do	20 00	60 00	N. Carolina line	Oct. 31, 1833	do	72	
Charles Warham	Pr. in &cav.	36 94	110 82	Virginia line	Nov. 7, 1833	do	78	
James Woody	Private	23 33	69 99	N. Carolina militia	July 10, 1834	do	70	

Statement, &c. of *Whitely county, Kentucky.*

NAMES.	Rank.	Annual allowance.	Sums received.	Description of service.	When placed on the pension roll.	Commencement of pension.	Ages.	Laws under which they were formerly inscribed on the pension roll; and remarks.
John Anderson	Ser. & pri.	51 66	154 98	N. Carolina line	Nov. 15, 1833	Mar. 4, 1831	76	
Charles Gatliff	Private	51 66	154 98	Virginia militia	do	do	86	
John Hood	do	36 66	109 98	N. Carolina line	Feb. 18, 1834	do	72	
Thomas Laughlin	do	36 66	109 98	do	Nov. 15, 1833	do	71	
Joshua Moses	do	53 33	159 99	N. Carolina militia	do	do	81	
James Mahan	do	80 00	240 00	Virginia militia	do	do	79	
Henry Porch	do	60 00	180 00	N. Carolina militia	Dec. 2, 1833	do	76	
William Rose	Ensign	160 00	480 00	N. Carolina line	Dec. 7, 1833	do	77	

Statement, &c. of Woodford county, Kentucky.

NAMES.	Rank.	Annual allowance.	Sums received.	Description of service.	When placed on the pension roll.	Commencement of pension.	Ages.	Laws under which they were formerly inscribed on the pension roll; and remarks.
James Arnold -	Private	80 00	240 00	Virginia line	Oct. 20, 1832	Mar. 4, 1831	79	Dropped under act May 1820.
John Allen -	do	96 00	70 67	do	Aug. 7, 1819	June 9, 1819	82	Admitted under act June 7, 1832.
Do -	do	80 00	160 00	do	Sep. 3, 1832	Mar. 4, 1831	-	March 18, 1818.
James Booth -	Ord'ly ser.	120 00	360 00	do	Oct. 19, 1832	do	77	
Edmund Ball -	Private	20 00	60 00	N. C. & Va. militia	May 13, 1833	do	79	
Robert Black -	do	20 00	60 00	Virginia militia	Sep. 23, 1833	do	84	
Marcus Calmes -	Captain	480 00	1430 82	Virginia line	Dec. 1, 1832	do	80	Died February 27, 1834.
John B. Carter -	Private	80 00	240 00	do	Feb. 11, 1833	do	84	
George Chelton -	do	20 00	60 00	do	June 3, 1833	do	86	
Stephen Chelton -	do	80 00	240 00	do	do	do	73	
Thomas Davis, 1st -	do	95 00	151 22	Virginia militia	Feb. 12, 1819	Aug. 8, 1818	72	Dropped under act May, 1820. Inscribed on roll under act June 7, 1832.
Do -	Private	80 00	240 00	do	July 30, 1832	Mar. 4, 1831	-	March 18, 1818,
Joseph Eaton -	do	20 00	60 00	Pennsylvania line	Dec. 2, 1833	do	88	
Paul Green -	do	80 00	160 00	Maryland line	Dec. 12, 1832	do	81	
Robert Gaines -	do	28 88	72 20	Virginia militia	Aug. 26, 1833	do	69	
John Gregory -	do	36 66	109 98	do	Sep. 18, 1832	do	76	
Robert Humble -	do	80 00	240 00	Pennsylvania line	Jan. 10, 1833	do	80	
Nathaniel Harris -	do	20 00	60 00	North Carolina line	May 23, 1834	do	74	
Francis Jackson -	do	60 00	180 00	Virginia line	Dec. 10, 1832	do	77	
Michael Kirkham -	Pri. & ens.	39 66	118 98	Virginia militia	May 17, 1833	do	87	
Samuel P. Minzies -	Pr. lt. & cpt.	235 83	-	Virginia line	Jan. 19, 1833	do	76	
John Mitchell -	Private	80 00	240 00	do	Feb. 12, 1833	do	72	
John M'Kinney -	Lieut. &c.	186 66	559 98	South Carolina line	do	do	76	
William Martin -	Private	80 00	240 00	Virginia militia	June 5, 1833	do	72	
Samuel M'Gee -	do	80 00	240 00	Virginia militia	July 11, 1833	do	85	
Elijah Milton -	Pri. of cav.	25 00	75 00	do	Aug. 26, 1833	do	78	
John M'Quady -	Private	40 00	100 00	Virginia line	Oct. 26, 1833	do	74	

19

Statement, &c. of *Woodford county*—Continued.

Names.	Rank.	Annual allowance.	Sums received.	Description of service.	When placed on the pension roll.	Commencement of pension.	Ages.	Laws under which they were formerly inscribed on the pension roll; and remarks.
John Smith - -	Private	43 33	129 99	Pennsylvania line	Aug. 17, 1833	Mar. 4, 1831	82	
William Smithy -	do	80 00	240 00	Virginia militia	Sep. 6, 1833	do	85	
Reuben Smithey -	do	30 00	90 00	do	Oct. 2, 1833	do	75	
Henry Smith -	do	33 33	99 99	do	May 23, 1834	do	80	
Zachariah Taylor -	do	96 00	1134 19	Virginia line	Mar. 17, 1819	May 12, 1818	78	
Do -	do	80 00	160 00	do	Aug. 7, 1832	Mar. 4, 1831	78	Dropped : not continental. Inscribed under act June 7, 1832.
Reuben Twyman -	do	26 66	79 98	Virginia militia	Oct. 23, 1832	do	75	Act March 18, 1818.
James Tinder -	do	53 33	159 99	do	Mar. 25, 1833	do	72	
Jeremiah Wilson -	do	46 66	139 98	Virginia line	Oct. 19, 1832	do	76	
Enoch Wingfield -	do	40 00	120 00	Virginia militia	Feb. 11, 1833	do		

Statement showing the Names, Rank, &c. of persons residing in the State of Kentucky, who have received the benefits of the act of Congress passed May 15, 1828.

NAMES AND COUNTIES.	Rank.	Annual allowance.	Sums received.	Description of service.	When placed on the roll.	Names of agents or representatives.	Remarks.
					Commencement of pay, March 3, 1826.		
ADAIR.							
John Biggs	Matross	100 00	900 00	Harrison's artillery	Feb. 28, 1829	Hon. R. A. Bucknor, agent,	
John Hamilton	Sergeant	120 00	1,080 00	3d reg. Maryl'd line	Feb. 24, 1829	do	
ANDERSON.							
William B. Wallace	Lieutenant	400 00	2,800 00	1st reg't artillery	July 16, 1828		
BARREN.							
Thomas Goodman	Matross	100 00	—	Harrison's artillery	Nov. 29, 1828	Tho's Underwood, ag't	Transferred from Henrico co., Virginia, since the last semi-annual payment.
BATH.							
Thomas Triplett, sen.	Captain	480 00	3,354 66	— reg't Va. line	Oct. 31, 1831	Thomas Triplett, jr. W. T. Barry, Hon Richard M. Johnson. Hon. H. Daniel and M. Harrison, agents, Betsy H. Triplett, widow	
BOURBON.							
James Pritchard	Dragoon	100 00	700 00	Col. Washn's cav.	Jan. 8, 1829		
Robert Wilmott	Lieutenant	400 00	3,600 00	Harrison's artillery	do		Died February 28, 1833.
BRACKEN.							
Nicholas Kimmer	Corporal	88 00	572 00	4th reg't Penn. line	Oct. 6, 1829		Transferred to Fayette county, Indiana.
William Robinson	Sergeant	120 00	1,074 33	Bull's Penn. reg't	Sep. 10, 1828		Died February 15, 1835.

Statement, &c.—Continued.

NAMES AND COUNTIES.	Rank.	Annual allowance.	Sums received.	Description of service.	When placed on the pension roll.	Name of agents or representatives.	Remarks.
BRACKENRIDGE.							
John Goatly	Dragoon	100 00	900 00	Washn's cavalry	Sep. 11, 1828		
BUTLER.							
William Porter	Lieutenant	320 00	752 00	— reg't Va. line	Nov. 29, 1828	F. D. and Tho's Porter, administrator	
CAMPBELL.							
John McKinney	do	320 00	2,473 77	5th reg't Penn. line	July 23, 1828	Mary T. McKinney, widow	Died July 8, 1828.
Massa Ara Smith	Private	80 00	560 00	-- reg't Vs. line	Mar. 29, 1830	Hon. R. M. Johnson, agent	Died November 25, 1833.
George Turner	Captain	480 00	1,160 00	1st reg't S. C. line	July 14, 1828		Transferred from Hamilton co, Ohio.
CUMBERLAND.							
John Emerson	Lieutenant	320 00	2,400 00	13th reg't Va. line	Feb. 12, 1829		
FAYETTE.							
Abraham Bowman	Colonel	600 00	5,100 00	— reg't Va. line	Oct. 30, 1829	George H. Bowman, agent	
John McDowell	Lieutenant	320 00	2,880 00	Wood's Va. reg't	May 16, 1831	J. T. Johnson, agent	
John Nelson	Captain	480 00	3,840 00	5th reg't Va. line	Sep. 17, 1828	J. P. Robinson, agent	
Richard Pindall	Surgeon	480 00	3,360 00	1st reg. Maryl'd line	Aug. 2, 1828	A. Ogden and J. R. Nourse, attornies	
William Schooler	Sergeant	120 00	840 00	3d reg't Va. line	Feb. 7, 1829	D. McC. Payne agent	
FLEMMING.							
Moses Clack	Dragoon	100 00	900 00	Virginia dragoons	Nov. 20, 1828		
William Davis	do	100 00	900 00	do	Oct. 22, 1828	J. Evans, agent	
John Finley	Captain	460 00	3,907 34	8th reg't Pa. line	Aug. 22, 1828	A. Ogden and J. R. Nourse, attornies	

Commencement of pay, March 3, 1826.

Commencement of pay, March 3, 1826.

Name	Rank			Regiment	Date	Agent	Died
FRANKLIN.							
Joshua McQueen	Sergeant	120 00	1,080 00	9th reg't Va. line	May 8, 1832	Joseph Watson, agent	
Rannel Reading	Major	600 00	5,400 00	2d reg't N. J. line	July 29, 1828		
GARRARD.							
James Bailey	Private	80 00	680 00	— reg't Va. line	Jan. 5, 1833	Hon. R. P. Letcher, agent	
Absalom Pollard	do	80 00	720 00	do	Mar. 5, 1832	do	
Michael Salter	Musician	88 00	750 00	Hazen's regiment	Aug. 19, 1828		
GALLATIN.							
William Thompson	Dragoon	100 00	900 00	Armand's corps	May 23, 1829	Daniel Breck, agent	
GREENUP.							
Godfrey Smith	do	100 00	900 00	Lee's legion	Nov. 29, 1828		
HENDERSON.							
Wynne Dixon	Lieutenant	320 00	1,192 28	1st reg't N. C. line	Aug. 22, 1828	Archibald Dixon, adm.	Died November 24, 1829.
HENRY.							
William Jeffers	Dragoon	100 00	900 00	Virginia dragoons	Dec. 22, 1829	W. P. Thompson, ag't	
JEFFERSON.							
Robert Breckenridge	Lieutenant	320 00	2,408 00	— reg't Va. line	Aug. 2, 1828	Jas. D. Breckenridge, executor	Died September 11, 1835.
Abraham Hite	Captain	480 00	2,880 00	8th reg't Va. line	do		
John Nelson	Musician	104 00	936 00	Lamb's artill'ery	Sep. 9, 1828		
Richard Taylor	Major	600 00	5,400 00	1th reg't Va. line	July 29, 1818		
JESSAMINE.							
Joseph Crockett	do	600 00	2,208 33	7th reg't Va. line	Feb. 7, 1829	Hon. Joel Yancey, ag't	Died November 7, 1829.
LINCOLN-							
Mark McPherson	Lieutenant	320 00	2,424 00	1st reg't Va. line	Aug. 8, 1828		
LIVINGSTON.							
Robert Kirk	do	400 00	994 44	White's dragoons	Sep. 1, 1828	Dickson Given, att'y; Robert Kirk, adm'r	Died August 28, 1828.
LOGAN.							
Charles Morehead	Sergeant	180 00	360 00	Lee's legion	Feb. 19, 1829	F. R. Johnson, agent	

Statement, &c.—Continued.

NAMES AND COUNTIES.	Rank.	Annual allowance.	Sums received.	Description of service.	When placed on the pension roll.	Names of agents or representatives.	Remarks.
MARION.							
Edmund Compton -	Lieutenant	320 00	2,720 00	1st reg't Md. line	Aug. 19, 1828		
Perry Tharp -	Private	80 00	720 00	8th reg't Penn. line	Oct. 6, 1828		
MASON.							
Joshua Burgess -	Lieutenant	320 00	1,730 00	4th reg't Md. line	July 29, 1828	John Pelham, adm'r	Died August 29, 1829.
Charles Pelham -	Major	600 00	2,095 00	2d reg't Va. line	July 17, 1828	John Chambers, agent	
John Ward -	Dragoon	100 00	900 00	Virginia cavalry	Aug. 13, 1829		
MERCER.							
William Basey -	Sergeant	180 00	1,421 50	Washn's cavalry	Dec. 9, 1828	Hon. T. P. Moore, ag't Jane Basey, widow	
Isaac Falls -	Private	80 00	720 00	5th reg't Penn. line	May 14, 1832	Rob't B. McAfee, ag't R B. McAfee, agent,	Died January 25, 1834.
David Williams -	Lieutenant	320 00	1,818 66	8th reg't Va. line	Mar. 29, 1830	Jos. W. Thompson, exec'tor	
M'CRACKEN.							
Charles Ewell -	Captain	480 00	1,958 67	— reg't Va. line	Oct. 29, 1831	Maria D. Ewell, Henry Northup and A. M. Green, agents	Died November 8, 1831.
Bazzel Lewis -	Private	30 00	629 33	-- reg't Conn. line	Nov. 28, 1833	J. B. Husbands, agent and administrator	Died April 1, 1830.
MADISON.							
James Barnett -	Lieutenant	320 00	2,720 00	-- reg't Va. line	Dec. 18, 1828	Daniel Breck, agent	Died Janury 14, 1834.
NELSON.							
Nicholas Carter -	Private	80 00	720 00	Putnam's Mass. reg.	Dec. 16, 1830	Hon. C. A. Wickliffe, agent	
Benjamin Smith -	do	80 00	720 00	6th reg't Md. line	Jan. 15, 1829	do	

Commencement of pay, March 3, 1826.

Name	Rank			Regiment/Line	Date	Agent / Representative	Remarks
OHIO. Benjamin Burch	Sergeant	120 00	575 00	3d reg't Md. line	May 8, 1829	H. T. Taylor, agent, George M. Addison, and Hendly Burch, administrators	Died December 17, 1830.
John Howell	Captain	480 00	1,699 04	1st reg't N. J. line	Aug. 19, 1828	Richard Elliott, agent, Seely J. Howell, executor	Died September 18, 1830.
OLDHAM. David Love	Sergeant	120 00	571 33	1st reg't Md. line	Aug. 13, 1828	David Love, executor	Died December 6, 1830.
Peter Outhouse	Private	80 00	200 00	do	Aug. 12, 1828		Transferred to Clinton county, Illinois.
William Taylor	Major	600 00	1,990 00	9th reg't Va. line	July 29, 1828	R. H. C. Taylor and Jonathan Barry, administrators	Died April 14, 1830.
Henry Wirble	Private	80 00	560 00	Hazen's regiment	Aug. 13, 1828		
PULASKI. John Edwards	Musician	88 00	484 00	10th reg. Penn. line	Oct. 21, 1829		Transferred to Jackson county, Indiana.
ROCK CASTLE. Francis Ramsay	Dragoon	100 00	900 00	Lee's legion	Dec. 24, 1830	Hon. R. P. Letcher, agent	
SCOTT. Abraham Buford	Colonel	600 00	4,395 00	-- reg't Va. line	Sep. 8, 1828	Martha Burford, wid'w	Died June 29, 1833.
SHELBY. Tho's Fitzsimmons	Private	80 00	720 00	do	Jan. 10, 1829		
Samuel Holley	do	80 00	400 00	2d reg't N. Y. line	Sept. 1, 1828		
Thomas Jones	Dragoon	100 00	750 00	White's dragoons	Sep. 5, 1828		
John Knight	Surgeon	480 00	4,320 00	2d reg't Va. line	Dec. 18, 1828		
William Long	Corporal	88 00	792 00	10th reg't N. C. line	Aug. 8, 1828		
William Morgan	Private	80 00	680 00	1st reg't Va. line	Dec. 18, 1828		
Elliot Rucker	Lieutenant	320 00	1,915 10	Gibson's Va. reg't	Dec. 11, 1830	Samuel Tevis, Hon. R. M. Johnson and Jas. Bradshard, ag'ts Nancy Rucker wid.	Transferred to Johnson county, Indiana.
Seth Stratton	Dragoon	100 00	900 00	Washn's cavalry	Sep. 1, 1828		
Joseph Winlock	Lieutenant	320 00	1,600 00	Gibson's Va. reg't	July 25, 1828		Died March 19, 1832

Commencement of pay, March 3, 1826.

Statement, &c.—Continued.

Commencement of pay, March 3, 1826.

NAMES AND COUNTIES.	Rank.	Annual allowance.	Sums received.	Description of service.	When placed on the pension roll.	Names of agents or representatives.	Remarks.
SPENCER.							
Jeremiah Brittain	Sergeant	120 00	866 00	1st reg't N. J. line	Dec. 10, 1828	R. Lancaster, ag't and Jacob Jewell, adm'r	
Benjamin Carter	do	120 00	1,020 00	3d reg't N. J. line	Dec. 30, 1830	R. Lancaster and Hon. C. A. Wickliffe, ag'ts	Died May 20, 1833.
Benjamin H. Kerrick	Musician	88 00	792 00	6th reg't Md. line	Nov. 29, 1828	R. Lancaster, agent	
George Tripplett	Lieutenant	320 00	2,411 00	Gibson's Va. reg't	Sep. 20, 1831	Thomas Tripplett and Hon. R. M. Johnson, ag'ts Sarah Tripplett, widow	Died September 15, 1833.
TODD.							
Nathaniel Terry	Captain	480 00	4,320 00	10th reg't Va. line	Dec. 13, 1828		
UNION.							
Thomas Blackwell	do	480 00	1,954 66	do	Feb. 19, 1829	Hon. Chittenden Lyon, agent, Judith Blackwell, administratrix	Died April 28, 1831.
WARREN.							
Robert Craddock	Lieutenant	320 00	2,880 00	4th reg't Va line	Feb. 7, 1829	A. Ogden, and J. R. Nourse, attorneys, William L. Meredith, representative	
William Meredith	Captain	600 00	4,180 00	-- reg't Va. artillery	Aug. 19, 1828		Died February 20, 1833.
WASHINGTON.							
John Fleece	Dragoon	100 00	800 00	Lee's legion	Mar. 11, 1829		
Clammaus Gilliham	Private	80 00	352 88	7th reg't Va. line	Oct. 6, 1828	Mark H. Gilliham, ex'r	Died July 30, 1830.
John Lawson	do	80 00	720 00	1st reg't Va. line	Dec. 18, 1828		
Barnard Thompson	Dragoon	100 00	900 00	Armand's corps	Aug. 19, 1828	William McElroy, ag't	

www.ingramcontent.com/pod-product-compliance
Lightning Source LLC
Chambersburg PA
CBHW050528270326
41926CB00015B/3128